Cha
Dictiona

Chambers
Dictionary of Dates

G. L. Hough

Chambers

ISBN 0 550 11827 6

Printed in Great Britain

Preface

The **Dictionary of Dates** is a reference book that everyone will find at once informative and enjoyable. It provides a fascinating summary of events for each and every day of the year throughout history—from early times to the present day.

The book is much more than the traditional list of historical dates. It contains information related to a wide diversity of fields such as sport, entertainment, transport and politics, as well as history and literature.

It is essentially a book of interesting snippets—when and what was the first British TV commercial; when was the Great Fire of Chicago; when was the last of the Blaydon races; when did the Paris Métro open; when and where was insulin isolated; when was the Cullinan diamond discovered; when did the first Marks and Spencer's store open; when did Amundsen reach the South Pole; when and where did the Australian gold rush begin; when does the oyster season open. All of this information—and much more —you will find easily in this compact reference book.

The comprehensive index adds another dimension to the book's usefulness. Browsing through it will stimulate your curiosity about topic after topic that you would not otherwise have thought of. The index will also direct you with ease to the point in the book where your curiosity will be satisfied.

People of all ages will find the **Dictionary of Dates** useful. Everyone has occasion, from time to time, to check upon a date, whether for purposes of work or leisure. The book will be invaluable to all quiz enthusiasts and to after-dinner speakers searching desperately for a suitable topic.

National day of Cuba, Sudan and Haiti.

1660 Samuel Pepys began his famous diary—written in Shelton's system of shorthand—was discontinued on 31st May 1669.

1735 Paul Revere, American patriot famous for his ride from Charlestown to Lexington to warn of the British advance on Concord, born at Boston in Massachusetts.

1766 James Stuart, the 'Old Pretender' and father of Bonnie Prince Charlie, died in Rome.

1863 Pierre de Coubertin, responsible for the revival of the Olympic Games in 1896, born.

1879 (Edward Morgan) E. M. Forster, English novelist, born in London.
William Fox, film impresario and founder of 20th Century Fox, born in Hungary as William Friedman.

1881 Postal orders were first issued in Britain.

1894 The 35-mile Manchester Ship Canal, linking Manchester with the Mersey estuary and the Irish Sea, was opened to traffic—was officially opened by Queen Victoria on 21st May.

1895 J. Edgar Hoover, American criminologist and founder and head of the FBI, born at Washington, DC.

1901 The six states and two territories federated to form the Commonwealth of Australia.

1904 The first motor vehicle registration plate in Britain, A1, was secured by Earl Russell for his 'Napier'.

1913 Film censorship in Britain came into operation.

1921 The Navy, Army and Air Force Institute, more commonly called 'NAAFI', was founded in Britain.

1944 Sir Edwin Lutyens, English architect, designer of the Cenotaph in London and planner of New Delhi, died in London.

1947 The British coal industry became nationalised.

1948 British railways became nationalised.

1951 The steel industry in Britain became nationalised.

1956 Sudan became an independent Republic after joint Anglo-Egyptian administration.

1959 Fidel Castro seized power in Cuba, overthrowing the government of Fulgencio Batista.

1970 The British half-crown coin ceased to be legal tender.

1972 Maurice Chevalier, French singer and musical comedy star in films, died aged 83.

2 JANUARY (2)

1727 James Wolfe, British Army general and commander at the capture of Quebec from the French, born at Westerham vicarage in Kent, the son of a general.

1788 Georgia, the Peach or Empire State of the South, became the 4th state of the Union.

1839 Frenchman Louis Daguerre took the first photograph of the moon.

1892 Sir George Airy, English Astronomer Royal who modernised the Greenwich Observatory, died at Alnwick in Northumberland.

1896 The Jameson raid into the Boer colony of Transvaal to support the British settlers ended in failure.

1905 Sir Michael Tippett, English composer, born in London, the son of a lawyer.

1946 King Zog of Albania was deposed *in absentia*—the country declared a Republic on 11th.

1959 Lunik I, Russia's first solar satellite, was launched as a moon rocket at Tyuratam.

1971 Ibrox Park football ground at Glasgow in Scotland was the scene of an ugly accident, when a barrier collapsed and 66 were crushed to death.

1974 Tex Ritter, American singing cowboy of stage and screen, died.

3 JANUARY (3)

1777 The Battle of Princeton took place in the War of American Independence, in which Washington defeated the British forces under Lord Cornwallis.

1795 Josiah Wedgwood, English potter and creator of blue jasper ware, died.

1823 Robert Whitehead, English engineer and inventor of the naval torpedo, born at Bolton-le-Moors in Lancashire.

1840 Father Damien, Belgian priest and RC missionary, born as Joseph de Veuster.

1883 Clement Attlee, British statesman, Labour Party leader and Prime Minister, born at Putney in Greater London.

1888 Herbert Morrison, British Labour politician and statesman, born at Lambeth in London.

1892 J. R. R. Tolkien, British author, born at Bloemfontein in the Orange Free State in South Africa.

1908 Ray Milland, American film actor and Oscar winner in 1945, born at Neath in Wales as Reginald Truscott-Jones.

1909 Victor Borge, American comedian and pianist, born in Copenhagen, Denmark, as Borge Rosenbaum.

1915 Tear gas was used for the first time in warfare—by the Germans against the Russians in Poland.

1931 Joseph Joffre, French marshal and commander-in-chief of the French armies on the western front, died.

1946 William Joyce, British Nazi propagandist, known as 'Lord Haw Haw', was hanged in London for treason.

1959 Alaska became the 49th state of America—and the largest.

4 JANUARY (4)

National day of Burma.

1785 Jacob Grimm, the elder of the two German brothers famous for fairy tales, born at Hanau.

1809 Louis Braille, French benefactor of the blind, born at Coupvray, near Paris.

1813 Isaac Pitman, English pioneer of phonetic shorthand, born at Trowbridge in Wiltshire.

1878 Augustus John, Welsh portrait painter, born at Tenby.

1896 Utah, the Beehive State, became the 45th state of the Union.

1914 Jane Wyman, American film actress and Oscar winner in 1948, born at St Joseph in Missouri as Sarah Jane Faulks.

1935 Floyd Patterson, American boxer and youngest holder of the world heavyweight title, born at Waco in North Carolina.

1948 Burma became an independent Republic outside the Commonwealth.

1965 (Thomas Stearns) T. S. Eliot, American-born English poet, playwright and Nobel Prize winner in 1948, died in London.

1967 Donald Campbell was killed on Coniston Water in 'Bluebird K 7' attempting to break his own world water speed record.

5 JANUARY (5)

1855 King Camp Gillette, American inventor of the safety razor about 1900, born at Fond du Lac in Wisconsin.

1858 Joseph Radetsky, Austrian field marshal, commander and national hero, died at Milan aged 91.

1876 Konrad Adenauer, West German statesman and Chancellor, born at Cologne.

1922 Sir Ernest Shackleton, British Antarctic explorer, died on the island of South Georgia in the South Atlantic, on his expedition to Enderby Land.

1933 Calvin Coolidge, American Republican statesman and 30th President from 1923 to 1929, died of a heart attack in Northampton in Massachusetts.

1938 King Juan Carlos I, Head of State of Spain in succession to General Franco, born in Rome.

1941 Amy Johnson, English aviator and first woman to fly solo from England to Australia in 1930, was mysteriously lost in a crash in the Thames estuary on a routine flight.

1964 The first automatic ticket barrier on the London Underground Railway was installed at Stamford Brook.

The Christian festival of Epiphany.

1367 King Richard II was born at Bordeaux in France, the son of Edward the Black Prince and grandson of King Edward III.

1840 Fanny Burney, English novelist and diarist, died aged 87.

1852 Louis Braille, French inventor in 1829 of the raised-dot system of writing used by the blind, died.

1880 Tom Mix, American film actor in Westerns, born at El Paso in Texas.

1884 Gregor Mendel, Augustine monk and botanist who pioneered the study of biological heredity, died at Brunn in Bavaria.

1912 New Mexico, the Sunshine State, became the 47th state of the Union.

1919 Theodore Roosevelt, American Republican statesman and 26th President from 1901 to 1909 and Nobel Prize winner in 1906, died at Sagamore Hill, Oyster Bay in the State of New York.

1931 The New Sadler's Wells Theatre in London was opened.

1964 Pope Paul VI finished his 3-day tour of the Holy Land, the first Pope to visit there since Christianity began, and the first to leave Italy in over 150 years.

1981 (Archibald Joseph) A. J. Cronin, Scottish novelist, author of 'Hatter's Castle' and 'The Citadel', died in Switzerland aged 84.

7 JANUARY (7)

1536 Catharine of Aragon, the first of Henry VIII's six wives and mother of Queen Mary I, died at Kimbolton Palace in Huntingdonshire.

1558 Calais, the last English possession on the mainland of France, was regained by the French.

1768 Joseph Bonaparte, eldest brother of Napoleon, born on the Mediterranean island of Corsica.

1785 Jean Pierre Blanchard and his sponsor American doctor John Jeffries made the first aerial crossing of the English Channel, from Dover to Calais, in a hydrogen-filled balloon.

1789 The first national election took place in America.

1800 Millard Fillmore, American Whig statesman and 13th President, born at Summerhill in the State of New York, the son of a farmer.

1830 The first railway station was opened, at Mount Clare, Baltimore.

1904 The 'CQD' distress call signal was introduced— 'CQ' meant 'seek you', with 'D' for danger added. Was replaced by 'SOS' in 1906.

1927 The famous American basketball team, the 'Harlem Globetrotters', was founded at Hinckley in Illinois by Abraham Saperstein of Chicago.
The transatlantic telephone service between London and New York opened, charging £15 for 3 minutes.

1937 Juliana, Queen of the Netherlands from 1948, married Prince Bernhard.

8 JANUARY (8)

1642 Galileo, Italian mathematician, physicist and astronomer, died.

1815 The Battle of New Orleans took place—the last battle between England and America—in which Andrew Jackson defeated General Sir Edward Pakenham's British forces.

1824 Wilkie Collins, English detective story writer, born in London.

1825 Eli Whitney, American inventor of the cotton gin facilitating separation of fibre and seed, died at New Haven in Connecticut.

1897 Dennis Wheatley, English novelist, born.

1899 Solomon Bandaranaike, Prime Minister of Sri Lanka, born at Colombo the capital.

1902 Georgi Malenkov, Soviet politician, born at Orenburg.

1916 The final withdrawal of Allied troops from Gallipoli took place, after an unsuccessful expedition to capture Constantinople.

1918 Recruiting began in Britain for the WRNS—Women's Royal Naval Service.

1921 Lloyd George became the first Prime Minister to occupy 'Chequers', a country mansion near Wendover in Buckinghamshire, given to the nation by Lord Lee of Fareham.

1935 Elvis Presley, born at Tupelo in Mississippi, the surviving brother of twins.

1937 Shirley Bassey, British singer and entertainer, born at Cardiff in South Wales.

1941 Robert Baden-Powell, British soldier, Boer War hero and founder of the Boy Scout movement in 1908, died aged 83.

1976 Chou En-Lai, Chinese Communist statesman and Prime Minister since 1949, died—succeeded by Hua Kuo-Feng.

9 JANUARY (9)

1788 Connecticut, the Constitution or Nutmeg State, became the 5th state of the Union.

1799 William Pitt the Younger introduced income tax, at 2 shillings in the £, to raise funds for the Napoleonic Wars.

1806 Lord Nelson was buried at St Paul's Cathedral.

1873 Napoleon III, Emperor of France and nephew of Bonaparte, died in exile, at Chislehurst in Kent.

1878 Victor Emmanuel, the first King of Italy in 1861, died and was succeeded by his son Humbert.

1898 Gracie Fields, English singer, comedienne and music-hall performer, born at Rochdale in Lancashire as Grace Stansfield.

1913 Richard Nixon, American Republican statesman and 37th President, born at Yorba Linda in California.

1914 Gypsy Rose Lee, American entertainer famed for her striptease act, born at Seattle in the State of Washington as Rose Louise Hovick.

1923 Juan de la Cierva, Spanish aeronaut and inventor of the autogyro, made the first successful flight, at Getafe in Spain.

1941 Joan Baez, American folk singer, born at Staten Island, New York.

1949 Tommy Handley, Liverpool comedian, died.

1960 Work began on the Aswan High dam in Egypt.

1969 The first trial flight of supersonic airliner 'Concorde' took place at Bristol.

1972 The liner 'Queen Elizabeth', after being removed to Hong Kong to serve as a floating marine university and renamed 'Seawise University', sank after catching fire.

10 JANUARY (10)

1645 William Laud, English churchman and Archbishop of Canterbury from 1633, was beheaded on Tower Hill for treason.

1769 Michel Ney, French Army marshal, the most famous of Napoleon's marshals, born at Saarlouis, the son of a cooper.

1778 Carl Linnaeus, Swedish botanist who devised a modern system of naming and classifying plants, died at Uppsala.

1840 The Penny Post came into force in Britain, as a result of the efforts of Sir Rowland Hill.

1862 Samuel Colt, American gunsmith and patentee in 1835 of a revolver that bears his name, died at Hartford in Connecticut.

1863 The first section of the London Underground Railway system was opened to passengers by Mr Gladstone—from Paddington to Farringdon Street.

1880 Grock, Swiss circus clown and entertainer, born as Adrien Wettach.

1903 Barbara Hepworth, English abstract sculptor, born at Wakefield in Yorkshire.

1917 William Frederick Cody, the army scout, Indian fighter and showman known as 'Buffalo Bill', died at Denver in Colorado.

1920 The League of Nations came into being, holding its first meeting at Geneva.

1946 The League of Nations was dissolved after 26 years, and was superseded by the United Nations.

1949 George Foreman, American heavyweight boxing champion, born at Marshall in Texas.

1951 Sinclair Lewis, American novelist, author of 'Babbitt' and Nobel Prize winner in 1930, died near Rome.

1952 The German freighter 'Flying Enterprise' finally sank off Falmouth, having been wrecked by enormous seas on the previous 27th December—Captain Kurt Carlsen remained on board until only minutes before it finally succumbed.

1957 Harold MacMillan was appointed British Prime Minister as a result of the resignation of Sir Anthony Eden.

11 JANUARY (11)

1753 Sir Hans Sloane, British physician and naturalist whose collection formed the nucleus of the British Museum, died.

1843 Francis Scott Key, American lawyer and poet who wrote the words of the US national anthem 'The Star-Spangled Banner' in 1814, died.

1857 Fred Archer, English champion jockey, born at Prestbury in Gloucestershire.

1864 Charing Cross railway station in London was formally opened.

1922 Leonard Thompson became the first diabetic patient treated with insulin, administered at Toronto General Hospital.

1928 Thomas Hardy, English poet and novelist, died in his native Dorset, aged 87.

1946 Albania was proclaimed a People's Republic, under General Enver Hoxha.

1974 The first sextuplets to survive were born, to Mrs Sue Rosenkowitz at Cape Town in South Africa.

12 JANUARY (12)

1628 Charles Perrault, French writer and collector of fairy tales, born at Paris.

1729 Edmund Burke, British statesman, orator and political writer, born in Dublin.

1746 Johann Pestalozzi, Swiss teacher and educational reformer, born at Zurich.

1852 Joseph Joffre, French Army marshal and commander-in-chief on the Western Front, born at Rivesaltes.

1876 Jack London, American novelist, notably 'Call of the Wild', born at San Francisco.

1893 Hermann Goering, German Nazi leader and creator of the Luftwaffe, born at Rosenheim in Bavaria.

1897 Sir Isaac Pitman, English inventor of a phonetic shorthand system of writing in 1837, died in Somerset aged 84.

1899 Paul Müller, Swiss chemist who formulated the insecticide DDT, born.

1907 Tex Ritter, American singing cowboy of stage and screen, born at Murvaul in Texas as Woodward Maurice Ritter.

1947 Joe Frazier, American world heavyweight boxing champion, born.

1948 The first full-size supermarket in Britain was opened—the London Co-op at Manor Park.

1950 The British submarine 'Truculent' sank in a Thames collision, with the loss of 65 lives.

1956 Nel Tarleton, British featherweight boxing champion, died.

1960 Nevil Shute, English novelist, author of 'A Town like Alice', died.

1976 Dame Agatha Christie, English mystery story writer and creator of the Belgian detective Hercule Poirot, died.

13 JANUARY (13)

1691 George Fox, English religious leader and founder of the Society of Friends, commonly called the 'The Quakers', died in London.

1864 Stephen Foster, American composer of minstrel songs and popular ballads, died in New York an alcoholic, in poverty and obscurity.

1884 Sophie Tucker, American singer and vaudeville star, born in Russia as Sophia Abuza.

1904 Richard Addinsell, English composer of music for films, notably the 'Warsaw Concerto' for 'Dangerous Moonlight', born.

1918 Lord Ted Willis, English scriptwriter for television and films, born.

1929 Wyatt Earp, American marshal famous for law enforcement by the use of a gun, died aged 80.

1941 James Joyce, Irish novelist, author of 'Ulysses', died in Zurich.

1978 Hubert Humphrey, US senator, Democratic Party leader and vice-President to Lyndon Johnson from 1965 to 1969, died.

14 JANUARY (14)

1741 Benedict Arnold, American general and traitor during the American Revolution, born at Norwich in Connecticut.

1742 Edmond Halley, English astronomer and Astronomer Royal, died at Greenwich aged 85.

1847 Wilson Carlile, English clergyman and founder of the Church Army, born at Buxton in Derbyshire.

1858 Felice Orsini, an Italian revolutionary, led an unsuccessful attempt on Napoleon III's life in Paris—an act for which he and another were executed.

1875 Albert Schweitzer, French medical missionary, born at Kaysersberg in Upper Alsace, the son of a Lutheran pastor.

1898 Lewis Carroll, English writer, author of 'Alice in Wonderland', died at Guildford in Surrey.

1904 Cecil Beaton, English photographer and theatrical designer, born in London.

1906 Nel Tarleton, British featherweight boxing champion, born.

1937 The first Gallup opinion poll in Britain took place, conducted by Dr Henry Durant.

1943 The Casablanca Conference, between President Roosevelt and Winston Churchill, began—ended on 26th.

1953 Tito assumed office as President of the Republic of Yugoslavia.

1957 Humphrey Bogart, American film actor and Academy Award (Oscar) winner in 1951 for his part in 'African Queen', died.

1972 Queen Margrethe II acceded to the throne of Denmark, in succession to her father King Frederick IX.

1977 Peter Finch, English film actor and posthumous Oscar winner for his part in 'Network', died in Los Angeles.
Sir Anthony Eden—Earl of Avon, British statesman and Conservative Prime Minister from 1955 to 1957, died aged 79.

15 JANUARY (15)

1559 The coronation of Queen Elizabeth I took place.

1622 Molière, French dramatist, born in Paris as Jean Baptiste Poquelin, the son of an upholsterer.

1759 The British Museum at Montague House in Bloomsbury, London, was opened to the public.

1815 Emma, Lady Hamilton, mistress of Lord Nelson, died in Calais in poverty.

1880 The first telephone directory in Britain was published, by the London Telephone Company, with 255 names.

1893 Ivor Novello, British actor, playwright and composer, born at Cardiff as David Ivor Davies.

1898 Uffa Fox, English yachtsman, born at Cowes on the Isle of Wight.

1906 Aristotle Onassis, Greek ship-owner, born at Smyrna in Turkey.

1913 The first sickness benefit (10 shillings per week), unemployment benefit (7 shillings) and maternity benefit (30 shillings) were introduced in Britain.

1918 Gamal Nasser, Egyptian statesman and his country's first President, born at Alexandria.

1929 Martin Luther King, American clergyman and Negro civil-rights leader, born at Atlanta in Georgia.

1943 The Pentagon, headquarters of the US Department of Defense, in Arlington County on the Virginia side of the Potomac River, was completed.

1971 ½p, 1p and 2p decimal coins were issued in Britain.

The Aswan High dam on the Nile, built with Soviet finance and technological assistance, was opened by Presidents Sadat and Podgorny.

16 JANUARY (16)

1547 Ivan the Terrible, the first to assume the title of 'Tsar', was crowned.

1794 Edward Gibbon, English historian and author of 'The Decline and Fall of the Roman Empire', died.

1809 The Battle of Corunna took place, in which the British won a rearguard action against the French under Nicolas Soult during the Peninsular War.

Sir John Moore, British commander, was killed during the above battle at Corunna.

1886 Amilcare Ponchielli, Italian composer of operas, notably 'La Gioconda', died.

1891 Léo Delibes, French composer, notably of ballet music including 'Coppelia', died in Paris.

1906 Diana Wynyard, British actress, born as Dorothy Cox.

1908 Baden-Powell's fortnightly magazine 'Scouting for Boys' first appeared in the shops.

1909 Ethel Merman, American singer in Broadway musicals, born at Astoria, New York as Ethel Zimmerman.

1920 Prohibition came into force in America, ratified by the 18th amendment to the Constitution—was repealed by the 21st amendment on 5th December 1933.

1929 The British periodical 'The Listener' was first published.

1957 Arturo Toscanini, Italian-born conductor and musical director, died in New York aged 89.

17 JANUARY (17)

1612 Thomas Fairfax, English commander of the Parliamentary Army in the Civil War, born at Denton in Yorkshire.

1706 Benjamin Franklin, American statesman, scientist and writer, born at Boston in Massachusetts, the 15th of 17 children.

1820 Anne Brontë, English novelist and youngest of the 3 literary sisters, born at Thornton in Yorkshire.

1860 Anton Chekhov, Russian dramatist and short-story writer, born at Taganrog, the son of a shopkeeper.

1863 David Lloyd George, British Liberal statesman and Prime Minister, born at Manchester.

1871 David, Earl Beatty, British admiral and fleet commander in World War I, born at Nantwich in Cheshire.

1880 Mack Sennet, film director in America, born at Richmond in the Canadian province of Quebec as Michael Sinnott.

1883 Compton Mackenzie, British writer, born at West Hartlepool as Edward Montague Compton, the older brother of actress Fay Compton.

1893 Rutherford Hayes, American Republican statesman and 19th President from 1877 to 1881, died at Fremont in Ohio.

1899 Al Capone, American gangster and racketeer in Chicago, born at Naples in Italy.
Nevil Shute, English novelist, born at Ealing in Greater London as Nevil Shute Norway.

1911 Sir Francis Galton, English anthropologist and writer on heredity and eugenics, died aged 88.

1918 Sir Keith Joseph, British politician and minister, born.

1926 Moira Shearer, British ballerina, born at Dunfermline in Scotland as Moira King, the daughter of a civil engineer.

1942 Muhammad Ali, American heavyweight boxing champion, born at Louisville in Kentucky as Cassius Clay.

1961 Ex-Premier Lumumba of independent Congo, was murdered at Katanga.

18 JANUARY   (18)

1778 Captain Cook discovered Hawaii (originally known as the Sandwich Islands).

1862 John Tyler, American Whig statesman and 10th President from 1841 to 1845, died at Richmond in Virginia.

1871 In the Hall of Mirrors at Versailles William I of Prussia was proclaimed the first Emperor of Germany—Deutscher Kaiser.

1879 The first England v Wales football international was played at Kennington Oval in London—England winning 2-1.

1882 A. A. Milne, English writer of children's books and creator of 'Winnie-the-Pooh', born at St John's Wood in London.

1892 Oliver Hardy, American comedian of Laurel and Hardy cinema fame, born at Atlanta in Georgia.

1904 Cary Grant, American film actor, born at Bristol in England as Alexander Archibald Leach.

1912 British explorer Captain Scott reached the South Pole with Lawrence Oates, Lieutenant Bowers, Edward Wilson and Edgar Evans—only to find that Amundsen had arrived 35 days earlier—all 5 died on the return journey.

1913 Danny Kaye, American comedy film actor, born at Brooklyn in New York as David Daniel Kaminsky.

1936 Rudyard Kipling, English poet and novelist and Nobel Prize winner in 1907, died.

1954 Sydney Greenstreet, British actor remembered in the film 'The Maltese Falcon', died.

1963 Hugh Gaitskell, British statesman and leader of the Parliamentary Labour Party from 1955 to 1963, died.

1972 The first plastic warship, minehunter HMS Wilton, was launched at Southampton.

1980 Cecil Beaton, English photographer and theatrical designer, died.

19 JANUARY (19)

1736 James Watt, Scottish engineer and inventor, born at Greenock.

1798 Auguste Comte, French philosopher, social reformer and founder of modern sociology, born at Montpellier.

1807 Robert E. Lee, American general and Confederate Army commander-in-chief in the Civil War, born at Stratford in Virginia.

1809 Edgar Allan Poe, American writer, best known for his macabre stories and poems, born at Boston in Massachusetts of theatrical parents.

1813 Sir Henry Bessemer, English metallurgist and inventor of a blast furnace method for converting cast iron into steel, born at Charlton in Hertfordshire.

1839 Paul Cézanne, French artist, born at Aix-en-Provence in the south of France.

1915 The first casualties were sustained in an air raid over Britain, when bombs were dropped on Great Yarmouth in Norfolk by the German L 3 Zeppelin.

1942 Michael Crawford, British comedy actor, born at Salisbury in Wiltshire as Michael Dumble-Smith.

1946 Dolly Parton, American 'country and western' singer and entertainer, born at Sevierville in Tennessee.

1966 Mrs Indira Gandhi became Prime Minister of India, following in the footsteps of her father, Jawaharlal Nehru.

20 JANUARY (20)

Terms of office of the US President and vice-President end at noon.

1779 David Garrick, English actor and theatre manager, died, and was buried in Westminster Abbey.

1837 Sir John Soane, English architect notably responsible for the design of the Bank of England building in Threadneedle Street, died in London.

1841 Hong Kong was acquired from China and first occupied by Britain.

1875 Jean Francois Millet, French painter of rural scenes, notably 'The Gleaners', died.

1886 The Mersey Railway tunnel was formally opened at James Street station by the Prince of Wales.

1892 The game of basketball, devised by Canadian doctor James Naismith, was first played, at the YMCA at Springfield in Massachusetts.

1896 George Burns, American comedy actor, born in New York City as Nathan Birnbaum.

1900 John Ruskin, English art and social critic, died near Coniston in the Lake District, aged 80.

1930 Edwin 'Buzz' Aldrin, American astronaut and the second man to set foot on the moon, born at Glen Ridge in New Jersey.

1936 Death of King George V at Sandringham in Norfolk, aged 70—accession of his eldest son as Edward VIII.

1937 Franklin D. Roosevelt began his record 4th term of office.

1961 John F. Kennedy, American Democrat statesman, was inaugurated as the 35th President—the first Roman Catholic.

1981 Ronald Reagan, American Republican statesman, was inaugurated as the 40th President—at 69, the oldest to take such office.

21 JANUARY   (21)

1793 Louis XVI, King of France since 1774, was guillotined in the Place de la Révolution after being found guilty of treason; the executioner was named Sanson.

1824 Thomas Jonathan Jackson, American soldier and Confederate general, called 'Stonewall', born at Clarksburg in West Virginia.

1901 Elisha Gray, American inventor who claimed to have invented the telephone, died.

1905 Christian Dior, French fashion designer, born at Granville.

1911 The first Monte Carlo Rally was held, won 7 days later by Henri Rougier.

1924 Lenin, Soviet Communist leader and founder of Bolshevism, died of a brain haemorrhage at Gorki outside Moscow.

1927 Telly Savalas, American film actor, best known as 'Kojak', born at Garden City in New York.

1940 Jack Nicklaus, American international golf champion, affectionately called 'The Golden Bear', born at Columbus in Ohio.

1950 George Orwell, British writer, notably 'Animal Farm' and 'Nineteen Eighty-four', died.

1954 'Nautilus', the first US nuclear submarine, was launched at Groton in Connecticut.

1959 Cecil B. De Mille, American film producer and director, died.

1976 'Concorde' airliner entered supersonic service with simultaneous take-offs, from London to Bahrain and Paris to Rio de Janeiro.

22 JANUARY (22)

1561 Francis Bacon, English statesman, essayist and philosopher, born at York House in London's Strand.

1775 André Ampère, French mathematician, physicist and founder of the study of electromagnetics, born at Lyons, the son of a rich merchant.

1788 Lord Byron, English poet, born in London.

1887 Sir Joseph Whitworth, English mechanical engineer who standardised screw threads, died at Monte Carlo.

1901 Death of Queen Victoria at Osborne House on the Isle of Wight, aged 81—the longest lived and longest reigning of all British monarchs, having reigned for over 63 years—accession of her eldest son as Edward VII.

1905 'Bloody Sunday', the massacre by troops of St Petersburg workers led by Priest Georgi Gapon.

1907 Dixie Dean, the legendary English footballer, born at Birkenhead on Merseyside as William Ralph Dean.

1909 U Thant, diplomat and later Secretary-General of the United Nations, born at Pantanaw in Burma.

1920 Sir Alf Ramsey, English international footballer and manager, born.

1924 Ramsay MacDonald took office as Britain's first Labour Prime Minister—on the resignation of Stanley Baldwin.

1944 The Allied Army landings at Anzio in Italy began.

1973 Lyndon Johnson, American Democrat statesman and 36th President from 1963 to 1969, died of a heart attack at San Antonio in Texas.

23 JANUARY (23)

1556 An earthquake took place in the Shensi Province of China, killing an estimated 830 000 people.

1571 The Royal Exchange in London, founded by financier Sir Thomas Gresham as a bankers' meeting house, was opened.

1783 Stendhal, French novelist, born at Grenoble as Marie Henri Beyle.

1806 William Pitt the Younger, British Tory statesman and Prime Minister on 2 occasions, first when only 25, died at Putney in Greater London, and was buried in Westminster Abbey.

1832 Edouard Manet, French painter and printmaker, born in Paris.

1875 Charles Kingsley, English clergyman and novelist, author of 'Westward Ho' and 'The Water Babies', died in London.

1903 Randolph Scott, American film actor, born in Orange County, Virginia as Randolph Crance.

1931 Anna Pavlova, Russian prima ballerina famous as the 'Dying Swan', died at The Hague.

1956 Sir Alexander Korda, Hungarian-born film producer and a major figure in the British film industry, died in London.

1976 Paul Robeson, American Negro bass baritone singer of stage and films, died.

24 JANUARY (24)

1712 Frederick the Great. Prussian king and military leader, born at Berlin.

1732 Pierre Beaumarchais, French playwright, best known for 'The Barber of Seville' and 'The Marriage of Figaro', born in Paris as Pierre Augustin Caron, the son of a watchmaker.

1749 Charles James Fox, British Whig statesman and brilliant orator, born in London.

1818 John Mason Neale, English churchman and hymn writer, born in London.

1848 Gold was first discovered in California, at Sutter's Mill near Coloma, by James Marshall.

1895 Lord Randolph Churchill, British statesman and Conservative Party leader, died.

1917 Ernest Borgnine, American film actor and Oscar winner in 1955, born at Hamden in Connecticut as Ermes Borgnino.

1965 Death of Sir Winston Churchill aged 90—exactly 70 years after his father—was buried in Bladon Churchyard, within view of Blenheim Palace, his birthplace.

1975 Dr Donald Coggan was enthroned as the 101st Archbishop of Canterbury, succeeding Michael Ramsey.

25 JANUARY (25)

Burns night.

1533 King Henry VIII and Anne Boleyn were secretly married by the Bishop of Lichfield—to become the parents of the future Queen Elizabeth I.

1627 Robert Boyle, Irish chemist and physicist, born at Lismore Castle in Munster in the Republic of Ireland.

1759 Robert Burns, Scottish poet, born at Alloway near Ayr in Ayrshire, the son of a poor farmer.

1874 W. Somerset Maugham, British novelist and short-story writer, born in Paris.

1882 Virginia Woolf, English novelist and playwright, born in London as Virginia Stephen.

1895 The first hockey international took place at Rhyl, with Ireland beating the hosts Wales by 3 goals to nil.

1917 USA purchased the Virgin Islands, formerly the Danish West Indies, for 25 million dollars.

1924 The first Winter Olympics were inaugurated at Chamonix in the French Alps.

1947 Al Capone, American gangster and leader of organised crime in Chicago during Prohibition, died as a result of a massive brain haemorrhage—and virtually penniless.

1971 Idi Amin became President of Uganda, deposing Milton Obote while he was absent abroad.

26 JANUARY (26)

National day of both Australia and India.

1788 The first consignment of convicts from England arrived in Australia, at Sydney Cove.

1823 Edward Jenner, English physician and pioneer in vaccination, died at Berkeley in Gloucestershire.

1828 The Duke of Wellington became Tory Prime Minister.

1837 Michigan, the Wolverine or Great Lake State, became the 26th state of the Union.

1871 The Rugby Football Union was founded in England, in London by 20 clubs.

1880 Douglas MacArthur, American general and commander in SW Pacific, born near Little Rock in Arkansas.

1885 General Gordon, British commander and Governor of the Sudan, was killed by a spear flung by a Muslim soldier while besieged at Khartoum.

1905 The Cullinan diamond, weighing over 1¼ pounds, was found at the Premier Mine at Pretoria in South Africa, by Captain Wells.
Cardinal Heenan, Roman Catholic Archbishop of Westminster, born.

1907 Henry Cotton, English golf champion, born at Holmes Chapel in Cheshire.

1908 The 1st Glasgow Boy Scout Troop was registered, to become the first such troop.

1922 Michael Bentine, British actor and comedian, born at Watford in Hertfordshire.

1925 Paul Newman, American film actor, born at Cleveland in Ohio.

1928 Eartha Kitt, American international singer and actress, born at North in South Carolina.

1950 India became a democratic Republic within the Commonwealth.

1973 Edward G. Robinson, Hungarian-born American film actor, usually in gangster roles, died aged 79.

1979 Nelson Rockefeller, American Republican politician, Governor of New York and vice-President to Gerald Ford, died.

27 JANUARY (27)

1731 Bartolommeo Cristofori, Italian harpsichord maker who developed the first pianos about 1710, died at Florence.

1756 Wolfgang Amadeus Mozart, Austrian composer, born at Salzburg, the son of a musician.

1832 Lewis Carroll, English mathematician and children's book author, born at the vicarage at Daresbury near Warrington as Charles Lutwidge Dodgson, the first son of a family of 12.

1859 Kaiser Wilhelm II born at Potsdam near Berlin, the son of the German Emperor and the grandson of Queen Victoria.

1885 Jerome Kern, American composer for Broadway musicals and films, born in New York City.

1901 Giuseppe Verdi, Italian opera composer, notably 'La Traviata' and 'Il Trovatore', died in Milan aged 87.

1926 Scottish inventor John Logie Baird gave the first public demonstration of true television, to members of the Royal Institution in his workshop in Soho, London.

1951 Carl Mannerheim, Finnish soldier, statesman and President who secured his country's independence from Russia, died aged 83.

1967 Queen Elizabeth conferred the knighthood on Francis Chichester at Greenwich, with Sir Francis Drake's sword.
Fire occurred aboard the spacecraft Apollo I during the ground test at Cape Kennedy, killing Virgil Grissom, Edward White and Roger Chaffee.

28 JANUARY (28)

1457 King Henry VII was born at Pembroke Castle—the founder of the Tudor dynasty.

1547 Death of King Henry VIII at Whitehall Palace aged 55— accession of his 9-year-old son as Edward VI.

1596 Sir Francis Drake, the most renowned seaman of the Elizabethan era, died of dysentery and was buried at sea off Porto Bello.

1725 Peter the Great, tsar of Russia from 1682, died at St Petersburg.

1791 Louis Hérold, French composer of operas and ballets, born at Paris.

1833 General Gordon, British Army commander and administrator, born at Woolwich in Greater London.

1841 Sir Henry Stanley, British journalist and explorer, born at Denbigh in North Wales as John Rowlands.

1884 Auguste Piccard, Swiss deep-sea explorer and balloonist, born at Basle.

The first Ireland v Scotland football international took place at Belfast—Scotland ending as winners by 5 goals to nil.

1887 Artur Rubinstein, concert pianist in America, born at Lodz in Central Poland.

1936 Alan Alda, American film actor, notably in 'M.A.S.H.', born in New York City.

1938 Jack Sharp, double English cricket and football international, died.

1939 (William Butler) W. B. Yeats, Irish poet, playwright and Nobel Prize winner in 1923, died in the South of France.

1965 Alfred Percy 'Tich' Freeman, Kent and England cricketer, died.

29 JANUARY (29)

1737 Thomas Paine, English social and political philosopher and pamphleteer, born at Thetford in Norfolk.

1782 Daniel Auber, French composer of operas, born at Caen.

1820 Death of George III at Windsor Castle aged 81—the longest-lived and the longest-reigning King—having reigned over 59 years. Accession of his son as George IV.

1843 William McKinley, American Republican statesman and 25th President, born at Niles in Ohio, the son of an iron manufacturer.

1856 The Victoria Cross, Britain's highest military decoration, was instituted by Queen Victoria.

1861 Kansas, the Sunflower State, became the 34th state of the Union.

1862 Frederick Delius, English composer, born at Bradford in Yorkshire.

1879 W. C. Fields, American comedy film actor, born at Philadelphia in Pennsylvania as William Claude Dukenfield.

1886 The first successful petrol-driven car, built by Karl Benz, was patented.

1916 British military tanks had their first trials, at Hatfield in Hertfordshire.

Victor Mature, American film actor, born at Louisville in Kentucky.

1928 Earl Haig, Army commander and founder of the British Legion in 1921, died in London and was buried at Dryburgh Abbey.

1942 'Desert Island Discs', a record programme on BBC's radio, began.

1950 Jody Scheckter, motor racing champion, born in South Africa.

1962 Fritz Kreisler, Austrian-born violin virtuoso, died in New York 4 days before his 87th birthday.

1964 Alan Ladd, American film actor, died.

1980 Jimmy Durante, American comedian and vaudeville performer, affectionately called 'Schnozzle', died aged 86.

30 JANUARY (30)

1649 King Charles I died on the scaffold outside the Banqueting House of London's Whitehall Palace, having been convicted of treason; the executioner was Richard Brandon.

1790 The first purpose-built lifeboat, appropriately called 'The Original', was launched at South Shields on the River Tyne.

1857 The naval uniform for ratings in the Royal Navy was authorised.

1882 Franklin Delano Roosevelt, American Democrat statesman and 32nd President, born near Hyde Park, New York.

1913 Percy Thrower, English gardener and broadcaster on the subject, born at Winslow in Buckinghamshire.

1933 Adolf Hitler was appointed German Chancellor by President von Hindenburg.

1948 Orville Wright, the younger of the two American airplane pioneers, died.

'Mahatma' Gandhi, Indian political and religious leader

was assassinated in his own garden in New Delhi by a Hindu fanatic, Nathuran Vinayak Godse—10 days after a previous attempt on his life.

1965 The state funeral of Sir Winston Churchill took place—was buried in Blaydon Churchyard, within view of Blenheim Palace, where he was born 90 years previously.

1972 'Bloody Sunday' in Londonderry in Northern Ireland, when 13 protest marchers were killed by British troops.

1982 Stanley Holloway, English actor and singer, best known for his role as Alfred Doolittle in 'My Fair Lady', died aged 91.

31 JANUARY (31)

1606 Guy Fawkes, English conspirator involved in the unsuccessful Gunpowder Plot to blow up the Parliament building, was executed.

1788 Bonnie Prince Charlie, leader of the Jacobite rebellion to depose King George II, died in Rome.

1797 Franz Schubert, Austrian composer, born near Vienna, the son of a schoolmaster.

1858 The 5-funnelled 692 foot long 'Great Eastern', designed by Isambard Brunel and John Scott Russell, was eventually launched at Millwall, after 3 months of setbacks.

1875 Zane Grey, American writer of western novels, notably 'Riders of the Purple Sage', born at Zanesville in Ohio.

1885 Anna Pavlova, Russian prima ballerina, born at St Petersburg.

1892 Eddy Cantor, American comedian and song-and-dance man, born in New York City as Edward Israel Iskowitz.

1903 Tallulah Bankhead, American actress, born at Huntsville in Alabama.

1910 Dr Crippen poisoned his wife Cora, for which he was executed at Pentonville on 23rd November.

1914 Jersey Joe Walcott, American heavyweight boxing champion, born at Merchantville in New Jersey as Arnold Raymond Cream.

1921 Mario Lanza, American tenor singer and actor, born at Philadelphia as Alfredo Arnold Cocozza.

1929 Jean Simmons, English film actress, born in London.
Leo Trotsky was exiled from Russia by Stalin, and found asylum in Mexico.

1931 Christopher Chataway, British athlete and later Conservative Member of Parliament, born.

1933 John Galsworthy, English novelist, noted for 'The Forsyte Saga' and Nobel Prize winner in 1932, died.

1956 A. A. Milne, English writer of children's books, notably 'Winnie-the-Pooh', died at Hartfield in Sussex.

1958 America's first earth satellite, Explorer I, was launched by the Army at Cape Canaveral.

1971 Apollo 14 was launched with Alan Shepard, Stuart Roosa and Edgar Mitchell—Shepard and Mitchell making the 3rd moon landing.

1974 Sam Goldwyn, Polish-born American film producer, died aged 91.

1983 In Great Britain the wearing of seat belts in cars became compulsory.

1 FEBRUARY (32)

The partridge and pheasant shooting season ends.

1851 Mary Shelley, English novelist, best known as the author of 'Frankenstein', died.

1859 Victor Herbert, Irish-American conductor and composer of light opera, born in Dublin.

1895 John Ford, American director of action-adventure and western films, born at Cape Elizabeth in Maine as Sean O'Feeney or O'Fearna.

1900 Stephen Potter, British writer of humorous books, born.

1901 Clark Gable, American film actor and Oscar winner, born at Cadiz in Ohio, the son of an oil man.

1908 Carlos I, King of Portugal, was assassinated.

1911 HMS Thunderer, the last battleship built on the Thames, was launched from the old Thames Ironworks at Silvertown.

1915 Stanley Matthews, the legendary English footballer, born at Hanley in Staffordshire.

1915 Passport photographs were first required in Britain.

1920 The North West Mounted Police changed their name to the Royal Canadian Mounted Police.

1966 Joseph Francis 'Buster' Keaton, American silent film comedian, died.

2 FEBRUARY (33)

Candlemas—feast of the purification of the Virgin Mary.

1650 Nell Gwyn, English comic actress, favourite and mistress of Charles II, by whom she had 2 children, born as Eleanor Gwyn, the daughter of a fishwife.

1875 Fritz Kreisler, Austrian-American violin virtuoso and composer, born in Vienna.

1880 The first frozen meat imported into Britain, arrived in London from Sydney, aboard SS Strathleven.

1882 James Joyce, Irish novelist, born at Dublin.

1901 Jascha Heifetz, violin virtuoso in America, born at Vilna in Russia.

1914 Cub Scouts were founded in England, at Robertsbridge in Sussex.

1918 John L. Sullivan, American boxer and world heavyweight champion from 1882 to 1892—the last bareknuckle champion—died.

1926 Giscard D'Estaing, French statesman and President, born.

1952 61 905 spectators attended Liverpool's FA Cup tie with Wolverhampton Wanderers, to create a club record.

1959 Buddy Holly, American singer, guitarist and major influence in early rock-and-roll, died aged 22.

1970 Bertrand Russell, British philosopher, mathematician and Nobel Prize winner in 1950, died aged 97.

1976 The Queen opened the 310-acre National Exhibition Centre at Bickenhill, Birmingham.

3 FEBRUARY (34)

1399 John of Gaunt, Duke of Lancaster, fourth son of Edward III and father of King Henry IV, died.

1809 Felix Mendelssohn, German composer and pianist, born at Hamburg, the son of a banker.

1811 Horace Greeley, American newspaper editor and founder of 'The New York Tribune', born at Amherst in New Hampshire.

1821 Elizabeth Blackwell, English-American physician, the first woman in US to gain an MD degree, born at Bristol.

1919 The League of Nations held its first meeting, in Paris, with Woodrow Wilson as chairman.

1924 Woodrow Wilson, American Democrat statesman and 28th President from 1913 to 1921 and Nobel Prize winner, died and was buried in Washington Cathedral.

1928 Frankie Vaughan, English singer and entertainer, born in Liverpool as Frank Abelson.

1929 Val Doonican, Irish singer and entertainer, born at Waterford in the Republic of Ireland.

1936 Bobby Simpson, Australian Test cricketer, born.

1960 Harold MacMillan made his 'wind of change' speech at Cape Town in South Africa.

1966 The first 'soft' landing on the Moon was made by Russia's Luna IX, in the area of the Ocean of Storms.

1969 Boris Karloff, London-born American actor, best known for horror-film roles, died aged 81.

4 FEBRUARY (35)

National day of Sri Lanka.

1881 Voroshilov, Russian Army marshal and political leader, born in the Ukraine.

1893 The first stretch of Liverpool's Overhead Railway—from Alexandra Dock to the Herculaneum Dock—was opened by Lord Salisbury.

1902 Charles Lindbergh, American aviator, noted for his historic solo flight across the Atlantic in 1927, born at Detroit in Michigan.

1912 Byron Nelson, American champion golfer, born at Fort Worth in Texas.

1918 Ida Lupino, English film actress, born in London.

1920 Norman Wisdom, English comedy actor, born as Norman Wisden.

1945 The Yalta Conference in the Crimea between Allied leaders Roosevelt, Churchill and Stalin, began.

1948 Ceylon became a self-governing dominion within the Commonwealth, having been a British Crown Colony since 1802.

1953 Sweet rationing ended in Britain.

1962 The 'Sunday Times' became the first British newspaper to issue a colour supplement.

1976 Roger Livesey, British actor, died.

5 FEBRUARY (36)

1788 Sir Robert Peel, British Tory statesman, Prime Minister and founder of the Metropolitan Police Force, born at Bury in Lancashire, the son of a cotton millionaire.

1840 Sir Hiram Stevens Maxim, American inventor of the first fully automatic machine-gun, named after him, born at Sangersville in Maine.
John Boyd Dunlop, Scottish veterinary surgeon and patentee of the pneumatic bicycle tyre, born at Dreghorn in Ayrshire.

1881 Thomas Carlyle, Scottish essayist and historian, called the 'sage of Chelsea', died at 5 Cheyne Row in Chelsea aged 85.

1889 Patsy Hendren, Middlesex and England cricketer and England football international, born at Chiswick.

1900 Adlai Stevenson, American Democrat statesman, born at Los Angeles in California, the grandson of a vice-President.

1920 Frank Muir, British comedy writer and broadcaster, born.
Royal Air Force College at Cranwell opened and had its first intake of apprentices.

1924 The BBC 'pips' were heard for the first time.

1946 George Arliss, British stage and film actor and Academy Award (Oscar) winner in 1930 for the leading role in 'Disraeli', died aged 77.

National day of New Zealand—Waitangi Day.

1564 Christopher Marlowe, English poet and dramatist, born at Canterbury in Kent, the son of a shoemaker.

1665 Queen Anne was born at St James's Palace, the second daughter of James II by his first wife Anne Hyde.

1685 Death of King Charles II, stricken with apoplexy— accession of his brother as James II.

1783 Lancelot Brown known as 'Capability' Brown, English landscape gardener, noted especially for the gardens at Blenheim and Kew, died.

1788 Massachusetts, the Bay State, became the 6th state of the Union.

1802 Sir Charles Wheatstone, English physicist and pioneer of telegraphy, born at Gloucester.

1804 Joseph Priestley, English clergyman and chemist who discovered oxygen, died at Northumberland in Pennsylvania.

1838 Sir Henry Irving, English actor, born at Keinton Mandeville in Somerset as John Henry Brodribb, the son of a shopkeeper.

1840 The Treaty of Waitangi was concluded by Captain Hobson, between Britain and the Maori chiefs of New Zealand— proclaiming British sovereignty and protection.

1895 'Babe' Ruth, the legendary American baseball player, born at Baltimore in Maryland as George Herman Ruth.

1911 Ronald Reagan, American Republican statesman and 40th President, born at Tampico in Illinois.

1918 A Parliamentary candidature deposit of £150 was introduced in Britain.
Women were first permitted to vote in elections to the Parliament at Westminster—their first vote actually came in the General Election on 14th December 1918.

1924 Billy Wright, English footballer and international with 105 caps, born at Ironbridge in Shropshire.

1931 Fred Trueman, Yorkshire and England cricketer, born at Scotch Springs.

1952 Death of King George VI at Sandringham aged 56—accession of his daughter as Elizabeth II.

1958 Manchester United lost 8 of their players when the aircraft bringing the team home from Belgrade crashed on take-off at Munich airport—also killed were 3 club officials and 8 sporting journalists.

7 FEBRUARY (38)

1301 The first Prince of Wales was created—Edward of Caernarvon, who later became King Edward II.

1478 Sir Thomas More, English statesman and Lord Chancellor to Henry VIII, born in London, the son of a judge.

1812 Charles Dickens, English novelist, born at Landport, Portsmouth, the son of a clerk in the Navy pay office.

1845 The Portland Vase, a 10-inch Roman dark blue cameo glass vessel, was smashed by a stone from a maniac, while on loan to the British Museum—has been skilfully restored.

1870 Alfred Adler, Austrian psychiatrist pioneer, born at Vienna.

1878 Pope Pius IX died after reigning for over 31½ years—was succeeded by Leo XIII (Gioacchino Vincenzo Pecci).

1885 Sinclair Lewis, American novelist and Nobel Prize winner, born at Sauk Centre in Minnesota.

1924 Dora Bryan, English comedy actress, born as Dora Broadbent.

1959 Daniel Malan, South African politician and creator of his country's apartheid policy, died at Stellenbosch in Cape Province aged 84.

1974 Grenada, in the Windward Islands of the West Indies, became a fully independent state within the Commonwealth, with Eric Gairy its first Prime Minister—having been a British colony since 1783.

8 FEBRUARY (39)

1587 After nearly 19 years of confinement Mary, Queen of Scots was executed in the Great Hall of Fotheringhay Castle in

Northamptonshire, for her implication in the Babington plot to overthrow Queen Elizabeth and restore Roman Catholicism in England.

1819 John Ruskin, English writer and art critic, born at Dulwich in Greater London, the son of a wine merchant.

1820 General William Sherman, American Union Army commander during the Civil War, born at Lancaster in Ohio.

1828 Jules Verne, French novelist and early exponent of science fiction, born at the seaport of Nantes.

1888 Dame Edith Evans, English actress, especially Shakespearean roles, born in London.

1904 The Russo-Japanese War broke out—provoked by Russian penetration into Manchuria and Korea.

1910 The Boy Scout movement in America was founded by W. Boyce.

1920 Lana Turner, American film actress, called the original 'sweater girl', born at Wallace in Idaho as Julia Turner.

1924 The gas chamber was used for the first time in America— at the Nevada State Prison at Carson City—the victim was Gee Jon.

1925 Jack Lemmon, American film actor and Oscar winner, born at Boston in Massachusetts.

1931 James Dean, American film actor, born at Marion in Indiana as James Byron.

1967 Sir Victor Gollancz, British writer and publisher, died.

1974 America's final Skylab mission, with Gerald Carr, Edward Gibson and William Pogue, returned after 84 days.

9 FEBRUARY (40)

1540 The first recorded horse race meeting in Britain was held, at the Roodeye Field, Chester—now called the Roodee.

1649 The funeral of King Charles I took place—was taken to his final resting place in the Garter Chapel in St George's, Windsor.

1773 William Henry Harrison, American Whig statesman and 9th President, born in Berkeley in Charles City County, Virginia.

1863 Anthony Hope, English novelist, author of 'The Prisoner of Zenda', born in London as Anthony Hope Hawkins.
1881 Fyodor Dostoyevsky, Russian novelist, born.
1891 Ronald Colman, film actor in America and Oscar winner, born at Richmond in England.
1894 Adolphe Saxe, Belgian musical instrument maker and designer of the saxophone, died in Paris.
1909 Dean Rusk, American government official and Secretary of State, born in Cherokee County, Georgia.
1916 Military conscription was first effective in Britain.
1922 Jim Laker, Surrey and England cricketer, born at Frizinghall in West Yorkshire.
1923 Brendan Behan, Irish playwright, born in the Dublin slums. The Soviet State Airline was instituted, called 'Dobrolet'—was re-named 'Aeroflot' in 1932.
1942 Soap rationing began in Britain. The French passenger liner 'Normandie' was gutted by fire.
1945 Mia Farrow, American film actress, born at Los Angeles in California, the daughter of Maureen O'Sullivan.
1958 Sandy Lyle, British golfer, born.

10 FEBRUARY (41)

1567 Lord Darnley, second husband of Mary Queen of Scots and father of James I of England, was murdered in the early hours of the morning at Kirk o' Field, a house near Edinburgh.
1763 Canada was ceded to Britain by the Peace of Paris.
1775 Charles Lamb, English essayist, born in the Temple, London, the son of a clerk.
1824 Samuel Plimsoll, British mercantile marine benefactor, born at Bristol.
1837 Alexander Pushkin, poet, novelist and a leading figure in Russian literature, was killed in a duel.
1840 Queen Victoria and Prince Albert were married at the Chapel Royal of St James's Palace, both aged 20.
1890 Boris Pasternak, Russian writer, author of 'Dr Zhivago', born in Moscow.

1893 Jimmy Durante, American vaudeville performer and comedian, born in New York City.

1894 Harold MacMillan, British statesman and Conservative Prime Minister, born in London.

1912 Lord Lister, English surgeon and founder of antiseptic surgery, died at Walmer in Kent aged 84.

1914 Larry Adler, American harmonica player and composer, born at Baltimore in Maryland.

1923 Wilhelm Konrad von Röntgen, German physicist who discovered X-rays in 1895, died at Munich.

1932 Edgar Wallace, English writer, noted as an author of thrillers, died at Hollywood.

1942 The first golden disc was presented to Glenn Miller, for 'Chattanooga Choo Choo'.

1950 Mark Spitz, American swimmer and Olympic champion of distinction, born at Modesto in California.

1966 Sophie Tucker, American singer known as 'the last of the red hot mammas', died aged 82.

11 FEBRUARY (42)

1800 William Fox Talbot, English photographic pioneer, born at Evershot.

1847 Thomas Alva Edison, prolific American inventor, born at Milan in Ohio.

1868 Jean Foucault, French physicist, inventor of the gyroscope and first to measure the speed of light, died in Paris.

1908 Sir Vivian Fuchs, English geologist and Antarctic explorer, born in Kent, the son of a farmer of German origin.

1920 Farouk, the last King of Egypt, born at Cairo, the son of King Fuad I.

1929 Vatican City became an independent Papal State within the city of Rome by the Lateran Treaty, signed by Benito Mussolini and Pietro Gasparri.

1931 Sir Charles Parsons, English engineer and inventor of the first practical steam turbine in 1884, died at Kingston in Surrey.

1934 John Surtees, British motor cycle and motor racing champion, born.

1934 Mary Quant, English fashion designer, including the mini skirt, born at Blackheath.

1936 Burt Reynolds, American film actor, born at Waycross in Georgia.

1940 John Buchan, Scottish novelist, ('The Thirty-Nine Steps' and others), latterly Governor-General of Canada, died.

1945 The Yalta Conference, in the Crimea, of Allied leaders ended, at which the final defeat of Germany was planned, together with agreement on the founding of the United Nations.

1970 Japan launched her first earth satellite.

12 FEBRUARY (43)

1554 Lady Jane Grey, Queen of England for 9 days, was executed on Tower Green for high treason.

1804 Immanuel Kant, German philosopher and idealist, died at Königsberg.

1809 Charles Darwin, English naturalist, born at Shrewsbury in Shropshire.
Abraham Lincoln, American Republican statesman and 16th President, born in a log cabin on a farm near Hodgenville in Hardin County, Kentucky, the son of a carpenter.

1818 Chile proclaimed independence from Spain after a revolutionary war led by San Martin and Bernardo O'Higgins.

1828 George Meredith, English novelist and poet, born at Portsmouth.

1851 The gold rush began in Australia, after Edward Hargraves made the discovery at Summerhill Creek, about 20 miles north of Bathurst in New South Wales.

1870 Marie Lloyd, English star of the music halls, born as Matilda Alice Victoria Wood.

1893 Omar Bradley, American general and commander, born at Clark in Missouri.

1915 Lorne Greene, film actor in America, born in Ottawa in Ontario, Canada.

1929 Lillie Langtry, British actress and entertainer, died in Monte Carlo.

1935 Escoffier, famous French chef known as the 'King of Cooks', died aged 88.

13 FEBRUARY (44)

1542 Catharine Howard, the fifth wife of Henry VIII, accused of adultery, was executed on Tower Green.

1689 William and Mary became joint sovereigns of Great Britain.

1692 The Glencoe massacre took place in the Scottish Highlands, in which the MacDonalds were massacred by their traditional enemies, the Campbells—38 butchered bodies were later found in the glen.

1849 Lord Randolph Churchill, British Conservative statesman and father of Winston, born at Blenheim Palace at Woodstock in Oxfordshire.

1859 The Corps of Commissionaires was founded in London by Captain Sir Edward Walter, for the employment of ex-regular service men.

1873 Fyodor Chaliapin, Russian operatic bass singer of great power, born at Kazan.

1883 Richard Wagner, German opera composer, died in Venice.

1885 Elizabeth Truman, wife of America's 33rd President, born at Independence in Missouri as Elizabeth Wallace.

1903 Georges Simenon, Belgian detective story writer and creator of 'Maigret' of the Paris police, born at Liège as Georges Sim.

1933 Kim Novak, American film actress, born at Chicago in Illinois as Marilyn Novak.

1943 The Nuffield Foundation for research was established in London.

1958 Dame Christabel Pankhurst, British suffragette and daughter of Emmeline, died.

14 FEBRUARY

St Valentine's Day.

1779 Captain Cook was stabbed to death by natives at Kealakekua Bay in the Sandwich Islands—now Hawaii.

1797 The naval Battle of St Vincent took place off SW Portugal, in which the British under Admiral Jervis defeated the Spanish fleet.

1852 The first patient, Eliza Armstrong, was admitted to the Children's Hospital in Great Ormond Street, London.

1859 Oregon, the Beaver State, became the 33rd state of the Union.

1891 William Sherman, Union Army general and military commander in the American Civil War, died in New York City.

1894 Jack Benny, American comedian and actor, born at Chicago in Illinois as Benjamin Kubelsky.

1912 Arizona, the Apache State, became the 48th state of the Union.

1916 Jimmy Wilde of Wales, nicknamed the 'mighty atom', won the world flyweight boxing title, which he held for over 7 years.

1938 The British naval base at Singapore opened.

1951 Kevin Keegan, English international footballer, born at Armthorpe in Yorkshire, the son of a miner.

1975 (Pelham Grenville) P. G. Wodehouse, English novelist and creator of the characters 'Bertie Wooster' and 'Jeeves', died aged 93.

15 FEBRUARY

1564 Galileo, Italian astronomer and physicist, born at Pisa as Galileo Galilei.

1809 Cyrus Hall McCormick, American inventor of the first reaper, born in Rockbridge County, Virginia.

1857 Mikhail Glinka, Russian composer, best known for his opera 'Russlan and Ludmilla', died in Berlin.

1874 Sir Ernest Shackleton, British Antarctic explorer, born at Kilkee in County Clare in the Republic of Ireland.

1882 The first shipment of frozen meat left New Zealand for England on SS Dunedin.
John Barrymore, American stage actor and star of the silent screen, born in Philadelphia as John Blythe, the younger brother of Lionel and Ethel.

1898 The US battleship 'Maine', sent to Havanna on a goodwill tour, was blown up by a mine—resulting in the short Spanish-American War.

1928 Herbert Henry Asquith, British Liberal Party leader and Prime Minister from 1908 to 1916, died.

1929 Graham Hill, British international motor racing champion, born in London.

1931 Claire Bloom, English actress, born in London as Claire Blume.

1933 Italian immigrant and anarchist Giuseppe Zangara failed in his attempt to assassinate President Franklin D. Roosevelt in Miami's Bayfront Park.

1942 The British naval base of Singapore surrendered to the Japanese forces.

1952 The funeral of King George VI took place at Windsor.

1965 Nat King Cole, American singer and pianist, died.

1970 Lord Dowding, British Air Chief Marshal and chief of Fighter Command during the Battle of Britain, died aged 87.

1971 The decimal currency system came into operation in Britain.

16 FEBRUARY (47)

1659 The date on the first cheque known to have been drawn on a British bank—the original cheque is preserved in the archives of the National Westminster Bank.

1740 Giambattista Bodoni, Italian printer and typographer, born at Saluzzo.

1822 Sir Francis Galton, English scientist famous for his pioneer work in eugenics, born at Birmingham, a cousin of Charles Darwin.

1937 Nylon, developed by a research team in America under the direction of Dr Carothers, was patented.

1940 HMS Cossack took off 299 British prisoners from the German naval auxiliary ship 'Altmark' in Norwegian waters.

1957 Sir Leslie Hore-Belisha, British statesman and Minister of Transport responsible for the introduction of Belisha beacons, the Highway Code and driving tests, died.

1959 Fidel Castro became Prime Minister of Cuba after overthrowing the regime of Fulgencio Batista.
John McEnroe, American international tennis champion, born in New York City.

17 FEBRUARY (48)

1673 Molière (Jean Baptiste Poquelin), French dramatist and writer of comedies, died of haemorrhage from the bursting of a blood vessel after a coughing fit on stage.

1781 René Laennec, French physician who invented and named the stethoscope, born at Quimper in Brittany.

1827 Johann Pestalozzi, Swiss educationalist and pioneer in progressive elementary school teaching, died at Brugg aged 81.

1862 Edward German, British composer, born at Whitchurch in Shropshire as Edward German Jones.

1863 The International Red Cross, an organisation for the prevention and alleviation of human suffering in time of war or disaster, was promoted in Geneva by Swiss philanthropist Jean Henri Dunant.

1909 Geronimo, the last Apache chief to surrender, died in custody at Fort Sill in Oklahoma.

1934 Albert I, King of the Belgians since 1909, was killed in a climbing accident near Namur.

1968 Sir Donald Wolfit, English stage and film actor, died.

National day of both Nepal and Gambia.

1455 Fra Angelico, Italian Dominican friar and painter of religious subjects, died in Rome.

1516 Queen Mary I, born at Greenwich Palace, the daughter of Henry VIII and Catharine of Aragon—became known as 'Mary Tudor' and 'Bloody Mary'.

1546 Martin Luther, German Augustinian friar and leader of the Protestant reformation, died at Eisleben.

1564 Michelangelo, Italian artist of the Renaissance, died in Rome aged 88.

1745 Alessandro Volta, Italian physicist, born at Como.

1882 England scored 13 goals against Ireland at Belfast—the highest margin in an international football match in the British Isles.

1892 Wendell Wilkie, American Republican politician, born at Elwood in Indiana.

1894 Andres Segovia, Spanish classical-guitar virtuoso, born at Linares.

1895 Timoshenko, Soviet Army marshal, born at Furmanka Village in Bessarabia.

1920 Jack Palance, American film actor, born at Lattimer in Pennsylvania as Walter Palanuik.

1933 James Corbett, American pugilist and world heavyweight champion from 1892 to 1897, known as 'Gentleman Jim', died.

1954 John Travolta, American film actor, born at Englewood in New York State.

1965 Gambia, the smallest country in Africa, became an independent monarchy within the Commonwealth—having been a British colony since 1843.

1967 Robert Oppenheimer, American physicist who developed the US atomic bomb, died at Princeton, New Jersey.

19 FEBRUARY (50)

1473 Nicolaus Copernicus, Polish astronomer, born at Torun.

1717 David Garrick, English actor and theatre manager, born at Hereford, the son of an Army captain.

1878 US patent number 200521 was issued to Edison for his phonograph.

1897 Charles Blondin, famous tightrope walker who crossed Niagara Falls many times, died aged 72.
The 'Women's Institute' organisation was founded at Stoney Creek in Ontario by Mrs Hoodless—its first meeting was held on 25th September. The idea was brought to England during World War I by a Mrs Watt.

1910 Manchester United played their first Football League game at their new ground at Old Trafford.

1911 Merle Oberon, film actress in America, born in Tasmania as Estelle Merle O'Brien Thompson.

1916 National Savings certificates first went on sale in Britain.

1924 Lee Marvin, American film actor and Oscar winner in 1965, born in New York City.

1960 Prince Andrew (Andrew Albert Christian Edward), third child and second son of Queen Elizabeth II, born at Buckingham Palace.

20 FEBRUARY (51)

1473 James I, King of Scotland, was murdered at Perth by a band of assassins led by Sir Robert Graham.

1547 The coronation of 9-year-old King Edward VI took place in Westminster Abbey.

1878 Pope Leo XIII (Gioacchino Vincenzo Pecci) was elected at the third ballot, upon the death of Pius IX.

1904 Alexei Kosygin, Soviet Communist leader and Premier, born at Leningrad.

1920 Robert Peary, American Arctic explorer and first man to reach the North Pole, in 1909, died at Washington, DC.

1927 Sidney Poitier, American film actor and first black Oscar winner, born at Miami in Florida.

1961 Percy Grainger, Australian-born composer and pianist, died.

1962 John Glenn became the first American in orbit when he circled the earth 3 times in the Mercury capsule 'Friendship 7'.

1966 Chester Nimitz, American admiral and Pacific fleet commander in World War II, died in San Francisco 4 days short of his 81st birthday.

1972 Walter Winchell, American journalist and gossip columnist, died.

21 FEBRUARY (52)

1728 Peter III, Tsar of Russia, born at Kiel, the grandson of Peter the Great.

1741 Jethro Tull, English agricultural pioneer and inventor of the seed drill about 1701, died near Hungerford in Berkshire.

1801 Cardinal Newman, English theologian, born in London, the son of a banker.

1836 Léo Delibes, French composer of opera and ballet music, born at St Germain-du-Val.

1852 Nikolai Gogol, Russian short-story writer and novelist, died at Moscow.

1859 George Lansbury, British Labour politician and Party leader, born near Lowestoft in Suffolk.

1910 Douglas Bader, World War II fighter pilot and squadron commander, born in London.

1941 Sir Frederick Banting, Canadian scientist who, with Charles Best in 1921, isolated insulin, was killed in an air crash.

1952 Identity cards were abolished in Britain.

1965 Malcolm X (Malcolm Little), American militant black Muslim leader, was murdered by persons unknown in New York City.

1968 Lord Florey, Australian-born British pathologist who helped to produce penicillin on a large scale, died.

22 FEBRUARY (53)

1512 Amerigo Vespucci, Italian navigator and explorer of the New World, died.

1732 George Washington, American soldier, Federalist statesman and President, born at Wakefield in Westmoreland County, Virginia.

1810 Frédéric Chopin, Polish composer and pianist, born at Zelazowa Wola near Warsaw, the son of a Frenchman.

1819 Florida was purchased by the United States from Spain.

1857 Lord Baden-Powell, British Army officer and founder of the Boy Scout movement in 1908, born in London, the son of an Oxford professor.

1879 F. W. Woolworth opened the first 'nothing over five cents' store, at Utica in New York.

1886 'The Times' became the first newspaper to institute a 'personal column' on its classified page.

1908 John Mills, English film actor, born at Felixstowe in Suffolk.

1932 Edward Kennedy, American senator and younger brother of President Kennedy, born at Brookline in Massachusetts.

1949 'Niki' Lauda, motor racing driver and world champion, born at Vienna in Austria.

23 FEBRUARY (54)

1468 Johann Gutenberg, German inventor of printing from movable type, died.

1633 Samuel Pepys, famous English diarist, born in Salisbury Court, Fleet Street in London, the son of a tailor.

1685 George Frederick Handel, German composer, born at Halle, the son of a barber-surgeon.

1792 Sir Joshua Reynolds, English portrait painter and first President of the Royal Academy, died in London.

1820 The Cato Street conspiracy—an unsuccessful plot to assassinate British Cabinet ministers—took place in London, led by Arthur Thistlewood.

1821 John Keats, English poet famous for his odes, died of tuberculosis in Rome, only 25 years of age.

1836 The Siege of the Alamo, a fort in San Antonio, Texas, by the Mexican Army under Santa Anna, began during the Texas Revolution.

1848 John Quincy Adams, American statesman and 6th President from 1825 to 1829, died in the White House.

1874 The game of lawn tennis was patented by Major Walter Wingfield, under the name of 'Sphairistike'.

1905 The Rotary Club was founded by Paul Harris and others, in offices in Dearborn Street, Chicago.

1931 Dame Nellie Melba (Helen Porter Mitchell), Australian operatic soprano, died.

1934 Sir Edward Elgar, English composer and a major figure in British music, died of pneumonia at Worcester.

1944 Leo Hendrik Baekeland, Belgian-born American chemist and inventor of one of the first plastics, Bakelite® , died.

1950 Election returns were televised in Britain for the first time.

1953 British World War II deserters were granted amnesty.

1965 Stan Laurel, English-born American film comedian with Oliver Hardy, died aged 74.

1970 Guyana, the former colony of British Guiana on the NE coast of South America, became a Republic, with Arthur Chung its first President.

1976 (Laurence Stephen) L. S. Lowry, English artist noted for his 'matchstick people', died at Glossop in Derbyshire.

1983 Sir Adrian Boult, English conductor, died at Tunbridge Wells in Kent aged 93.

24 FEBRUARY (55)

1582 Pope Gregory XIII announced the introduction of the new Gregorian calendar, replacing the Julian calendar—was not adopted by Britain until 1752, when it resulted in a loss adjustment of 11 days.

1786 Wilhelm Grimm, German philologist and collector of fairy tales with his brother Jacob, born at Hanau.
1810 Henry Cavendish, English scientist who discovered the properties of hydrogen and other gases, died.
1815 Robert Fulton, American engineer and designer of submarines and steamships, died.
1866 Sir Arthur Pearson, English newspaper owner, born at Wookey, near Wells in Somerset.
1885 Chester Nimitz, American admiral and commander of the Pacific fleet during World War II, born at Fredericksburg in Texas.
1887 The telephone link between Paris and Brussels was inaugurated—the first between capitals.
1914 David Langdon, British cartoonist, born.
1920 Viscountess Astor became the first woman to speak in the British Parliament.
1940 Denis Law, Scottish international footballer, born at Aberdeen.
1946 Juan Peron was elected President of Argentina.
1966 Kwame Nkrumah, President of Ghana since independence in 1957, was overthrown by an army coup, and went into exile in Guinea.
1975 Nikolai Bulganin, Soviet statesman and Prime Minister from 1955 to 1958, died.

25 FEBRUARY (56)

National day of Kuwait.

1308 The coronation of Edward II of England took place.
1723 Sir Christopher Wren, English architect and designer, notably of St Paul's Cathedral, died in London and was buried in the crypt of his Cathedral.
1841 Pierre Auguste Renoir, French Impressionist painter, born at Limoges, the son of a tailor.
1862 'Greenbacks', American bank notes, were first issued during the Civil War by Abraham Lincoln.
1873 Enrico Caruso, Italian operatic tenor, born at Naples.
1882 The first Wales—Ireland football international took place at Wrexham, the home side winning by 7 goals to 1.

1888 John Foster Dulles, American government official and diplomat, born at Washington, DC.

1890 Dame Myra Hess, English concert pianist, born in London.

1899 Paul Julius Reuter, German founder of the news agency that bears his name, died at Nice.

1901 'Zeppo' Marx, the youngest of the Marx Brothers who later became their agent, born in New York City as Herbert.

1914 John Arlott, British radio and television cricket commentator, born at Basingstoke in Hampshire.

1943 George Harrison of the pop group 'The Beatles', born in Liverpool.

1955 HMS Ark Royal, Britain's largest ever aircraft carrier, was completed.

1964 Cassius Clay (later Muhammad Ali) won the world heavyweight boxing title for the first time—knocking out Sonny Liston in round 7 at Miami.

1983 Tennessee Williams, American controversial playwright, died in a New York hotel.

26 FEBRUARY (57)

1797 £1 notes were first issued by the Bank of England.

1802 Victor Hugo, French poet and novelist, born at Besancon, the son of a professional soldier.

1815 Napoleon escaped from exile on the island of Elba and returned to France.

1839 The first official Grand National Steeplechase was run at Aintree, Liverpool—won by Jem Mason on 'Lottery'.

1846 'Buffalo Bill', American Army Scout and showman, born on a farm in Scott County in Iowa as William Frederick Cody.

1903 Richard Gatling, American inventor of the revolving battery gun that bears his name, died aged 84.

1922 Margaret Leighton, British stage and film actress, born.

1925 Everton Weekes, West Indian Test cricketer, born in Barbados.

1928 Fats Domino, American pianist, singer and songwriter, born at New Orleans in Louisiana as Antoine Domino.

1932 Johnny Cash, American 'country' singer, born at Kingsland in Arkansas, the son of a cotton farmer.

1935 'RADAR'—RAdio Detection And Ranging—was first demonstrated at Daventry, by Robert Watson-Watt.

1950 Sir Harry Lauder, Scottish music hall and vaudeville comedian, died aged 79.

1961 Hassan II acceded as King of Morocco on the death of his father, King Mohammad V.

27 FEBRUARY (58)

1706 John Evelyn, English writer whose diary covered the last 65 years of his life, died at Wotton near Dorking in Surrey.

1807 (Henry Wadsworth) H. W. Longfellow, American poet, born at Portland in Maine.

1847 Ellen Terry, English stage actress, born at Coventry, the daughter of a provincial actor.

1848 Sir Hubert Parry, English composer, born at Bournemouth in Dorset.

1879 The discovery of saccharin was reported by chemists Constantine Fahlberg and Ira Remsem of the John Hopkins University at Baltimore.

1899 Charles Best, Canadian co-discoverer of insulin for the treatment of diabetes, born at West Pembroke in Maine.

1902 John Steinbeck, American novelist and Nobel prize winner, born at Salinas in California.

1907 The Central Criminal Court, on the site of Newgate Prison, commonly called The Old Bailey, was opened.

1932 Elizabeth Taylor, English film actress and Oscar winner in 1960 and 1966, born in London.

1933 The Reichstag, the imposing German Parliament building in Berlin, was destroyed by fire, believed deliberately set by Nazis.

28 FEBRUARY (59)

1824 Charles Blondin, French tightrope walker famous for his crossings of Niagara Falls, born at Hesdin near Calais as Jean Francois Gravelet.

1854 The United States Republican Party was formed, at Ripon in Wisconsin.

1865 Sir Wilfred Grenfell, English medical missionary in Labrador, born.

1900 Ladysmith in West Natal was relieved by a force under Sir Redvers Buller—British troops having been besieged since the previous 2nd November by Transvaal forces during the Boer War.

1916 Henry James, American novelist, died at Rye in Sussex.

1922 The British Protectorate over Egypt ceased, when Ahmed Fuad was proclaimed King.

1940 Mario Andretti, motor racing champion, born at Trieste in Italy.

1941 Alfonso XIII, ex-King of Spain, died in Rome, having been forced into exile on the establishment of a Republic in 1931.

1975 Britain suffered its worst underground train disaster at London's Moorgate tube station, when 42 were killed.

29 FEBRUARY (60)

Leap Year day.

1792 Gioacchino Rossini, Italian composer of many operas, including 'The Barber of Seville' and 'William Tell', born at Pesaro on the Adriatic coast, the son of a strolling horn player.

1840 John Philip Holland, American inventor who pioneered the modern submarine, born in County Clare in the Republic of Ireland.

1880 The cutting of the 9¼ mile St Gotthard tunnel in Switzerland was completed—the work of engineer Louis Favre—linking the Swiss and Italian railways.

1960 Agadir, seaport of Morocco in North Africa, was devastated by an earthquake, with an estimated 12 000 deaths.

St David's day—national day of Wales.

1498 Mozambique, on the SE African coast, was discovered by Vasco de Gama.

1711 The first number of the British periodical 'Spectator' was published.

1803 Ohio, the Buckeye State, became the 17th state of the Union.

1867 Nebraska, the Cornhusker State, became the 37th state of the Union.

1872 Yellowstone, the oldest and largest park in America—over 2 million acres in Wyoming, Montana and Idaho—was designated.

1904 Glenn Miller, American band leader and trombonist, born at Clarinda in Indiana.

1910 David Niven, film actor in America and Oscar winner in 1958, born at Kirriemuir in Scotland.

1932 The 20-month-old son of Charles Lindbergh was kidnapped from the nursery of their home at Hopewell in New Jersey—was found dead on 12th May—Bruno Hauptmann was convicted and electrocuted.

1935 Herb Alpert, American musician and trumpeter, born at Los Angeles in California.

1940 David Broome, British show-jumping champion, born.

1946 The Bank of England passed to public ownership by Act of Parliament.

1947 The International Monetary Fund began operations.

1949 Joe Louis retired as world heavyweight boxing champion—having defended his title 25 times.

1980 William Ralph Dean, the legendary English footballer called 'Dixie', died, as a spectator at the ground of his old club Everton.

2 MARCH (62)

1791 John Wesley, English evangelist and theologian who founded the movement that became the Methodist Church, died in London aged 87.

1810 Pope Leo XIII was born at Carpineto as Gioacchino Vincenzo Pecci, the son of a Count.

1824 Bedrich Smetana, Czech composer, conductor and pianist, born at Litomysl in Bohemia.

1836 The first point-to-point meeting was held, at the Madresfield Estate, by the Worcester Hunt.

1855 Tsar Nicholas I of Russia died during hostilities in the Crimean War.

1876 Pope Pius XII was born in Rome as Eugenio Pacelli.

1882 An attempt to assassinate Queen Victoria was made at Windsor by R. MacLean.

1917 Nicholas II, the last Tsar, was forced to abdicate after Russian setbacks in World War I.

1919 Jennifer Jones, American film actress and Oscar winner in 1943, born at Tulsa in Oklahoma as Phyllis Isley.

1930 (David Herbert) D. H. Lawrence, English novelist and short story writer, died.

1939 Howard Carter, British Egyptologist who discovered the tomb of Tutankhamun in 1922, died.

1949 Captain James Gallagher, in a USAF B 50 'Lucky Lady II', completed the first non-stop round-the-world flight from Fort Worth in Texas—refuelling 4 times in flight.

1969 The French-built supersonic airliner 'Concorde' made its maiden flight from Toulouse.

1970 Rhodesia was declared a Republic.

3 MARCH (63)

National day of Morocco.

1703 Robert Hooke, English scientist, contributor to astronomy, chemistry and biology, died.

1792 Robert Adam, Scottish architect and interior designer, died.

1803 The Duke of Bridgewater, pioneer of British inland waterways, died.

1831 George Pullman, American inventor of Pullman railway carriages, born at Brocton in New York State.

1845 Florida, the Peninsular or Sunshine State, became the 27th state of the Union.

1847 Alexander Graham Bell, Scottish-American scientist and inventor of the telephone, born at Edinburgh, the son of a teacher of elocution.

1869 Sir Henry Wood, English conductor and founder of the Promenade Concerts, born in London.

1878 The Treaty of San Stefano was signed, ending the Russo-Turkish War.

1911 Jean Harlow, American film actress nicknamed the 'platinum blonde', born at Kansas City in Missouri as Harlean Carpentier.

1920 Ronald Searle, English artist and creator of the schoolgirls of 'St Trinians', born at Cambridge.

1923 The American magazine 'Time' was first issued.

1931 'The Star-Spangled Banner', written by Francis Scott Key on 14th September 1814, was designated the United States national anthem by Act of Congress. Music was adapted from an English song 'Anacreon in Heaven' written by John Stafford Smith.

1969 Apollo 9 was launched, with James McDivitt, David Scott and Russell Schweickart.

4 MARCH (64)

1789 The first meeting of Congress was held, at Federal Hall in New York City.

1791 Vermont, the Green Mountain State, became the 14th state of the Union.

1824 The Royal Naval Lifeboat Institution was founded by Sir William Hillary.

1882 The first electric tramcars ran in London, at Leytonstone.

1890 The 1710-foot Forth Railway cantilever bridge, the longest in Britain, designed and constructed by Benjamin Baker and John Fowler, was officially opened by the Prince of Wales—57 having been killed during its construction.

1923 Patrick Moore, English astronomer, born at Pinner in Middlesex.

1928 Alan Sillitoe, English author, especially 'Saturday Night and Sunday Morning', born at Nottingham.

1936 Jim Clark, British motor racing champion driver, born at Duns in Scotland.

1951 Kenny Dalglish, Liverpool and Scotland footballer and holder of the record number of appearances for his country, born at Glasgow.

1967 The first North Sea gas was pumped ashore, at Easington, Co. Durham.

1970 The 'Eurydice', a French submarine, was lost off the coast of Toulon in the Mediterranean, with the loss of its entire crew of 57.

1975 Charles Chaplin was knighted by the Queen.

5 MARCH (65)

1133 Henry II, the first Plantagenet King of England, born at Le Mans, the eldest son of Matilda, daughter of Henry I.

1461 Henry VI was deposed as King of England—accession of Edward IV.

1512 Gerardus Mercator, Flemish cartographer and mathematician, born in the Flanders region as Gerhard Kremer.

1575 William Oughtred, English mathematician and inventor of the slide rule, born at Eton in Berkshire.

1770 The Boston massacre took place, in which British troops fired into a mob, killing 5—one of the incidents leading up to the War of Independence.

1778 Thomas Arne, English composer, including 'Rule Britannia', died in London.

1790 Flora Macdonald, Scottish Jacobite heroine who helped the Young Pretender to escape from the Hebridean island of Benbecula, died.

1815 Friedrich Mesmer, German physician who developed the theory of animal magnetism (mesmerism) for curing disease, died aged 80.

1827 Alessandro Volta, Italian physicist who invented the first electric battery, died at Como in Lombardy aged 82.

1908 Rex Harrison, English stage and film actor and Oscar winner in 1964, born at Huyton in Liverpool as Reginald Carey.

1946 Winston Churchill made his 'iron curtain' speech at Westminster College, Fulton, in Missouri.

1953 Joseph Stalin, Soviet Communist leader, died in mysterious circumstances.
Sergei Prokofiev, Russian composer, notably the orchestral fairy tale 'Peter and the Wolf', died.

6 MARCH (66)

National day of Ghana.

1475 Michelangelo, Italian painter, sculptor, artist and poet, born at Capresse in Tuscany as Michelagniolo di Lodovico Buonarroti.

1619 Cyrano de Bergerac, French novelist and playwright, born in Paris.

1806 Elizabeth Barrett Browning, English poet and wife of Robert Browning, born at Coxhoe Hall in Durham.

1834 George du Maurier, English novelist and artist, born in Paris.

1836 The Siege of the Alamo ended after 12 days—the garrison included William Travis, Jim Bowie and Davey Crockett, who died defending the mission fort against Mexican forces under Santa Anna.

1888 Louisa M. Alcott, American novelist and author of 'Little Women' and 'Little Men', died at Concord.

1900 Gottlieb Daimler, German motor engineer who improved the internal combustion engine and made the first motorcycle, died.

1930 Frozen foods, developed by Clarence Birdseye, were first put on sale in stores in Springfield, Massachusetts.

1932 John Philip Sousa, American bandmaster and composer of famous marches, especially 'The Stars and Stripes forever' and 'El Capitan', died at Reading in Pennsylvania.

1937 Valentina Tereshkova, Russian astronaut and first woman in space in 1963, born.

1951 Ivor Novello, Welsh-born actor and composer, died in London.

1957 Ghana, formerly the Gold Coast, became the first British colony in Africa to achieve independence, with Kwame Nkrumah its first Premier.

1961 Mini cabs were first introduced in London.

1964 Constantine II acceded to the throne as King of the Hellenes, succeeding his father Paul.

1965 Herbert Morrison, British Labour statesman, died.

1967 Nelson Eddy, American singer, famed for operetta films with Jeanette MacDonald, died.

1973 Pearl Buck, American novelist, notably 'The Good Earth', and Nobel Prize winner in 1938, died aged 80.

7 MARCH (67)

1792 Sir John Herschel, English astronomer, born at Slough in Buckinghamshire.

1802 Sir Edwin Landseer, English painter, especially of animals, born in London, the son of an engraver.

1809 Jean Pierre Blanchard, French balloonist and first to cross the English Channel by air, from Dover to Calais in 1785, was killed at La Haye during practice jumps from a balloon.

1849 Luther Burbank, American botanist and plant breeder, born at Lancaster in Massachusetts.

1850 Thomas Masaryk, Czech statesman and his country's first President in 1918, born at Hodonin in Moravia.

1875 Maurice Ravel, French composer, born at Ciboure in the Basque country.

1917 Reginald Maudling, British Conservative statesman, born in London.

1930 The Earl of Snowdon, born, as Antony Charles Robert Armstrong-Jones.

1945 Allied troops crossed the Rhine, by the Ludendorff Bridge at Remagen.

8 MARCH (68)

1702 Death of King William III, caused by the stumbling of his horse Sorrel over a molehill in the Park at Hampton

Court—leaving no children; the crown passed to Anne, daughter of James II.

1717 Abraham Darby, English ironmaster and first to use coke to smelt iron, died at Worcester.

1726 Richard Howe, British admiral and commander of distinction, born in London.

1859 Kenneth Grahame, Scottish author of children's books, especially 'The Wind in the Willows', born in Edinburgh.

1869 Hector Berlioz, French composer, died in Paris.

1874 Millard Fillmore, American Whig statesman and 13th President from 1850 to 1853, died in Buffalo in the State of New York.

1889 John Ericsson, Swedish-born American ship designer and inventor of the first successful screw propeller, died.

1910 The first pilot's licence in Britain was issued by the Royal Aero Club to J. T. C. Moore Brabazon (later Lord Brabazon).

1917 Graf von Zeppelin, German airship pioneer, died at Charlottenburg near Berlin.

1930 William Howard Taft, American Republican statesman and 27th President from 1909 to 1913, died in Washington.

1961 Sir Thomas Beecham, English conductor and founder of the London Philharmonic Orchestra, died aged 81.

1974 The inauguration of the third Paris airport—the Charles de Gaulle—took place.

1983 Sir William Walton, English composer, died on the island of Ischia.

9 MARCH (69)

1454 Amerigo Vespucci, Italian explorer and navigator of many voyages to the New World, born at Florence.

1763 William Cobbett, English political journalist and historian, born at Farnham in Surrey, the son of a farmer.

1796 Napoleon Bonaparte married Josephine, the widow of the Vicomte de Beauharnais.

1831 The French Foreign Legion was founded by King Louis Philippe, with headquarters at Sidi-Bel-Abbes in Algeria— moved to Aubagne in France in 1962.

1876 Graham Bell filed his patent for the first telephone—only 3 hours ahead of a similar one by Elisha Gray.

1881 Ernest Bevin, British union leader, politician and minister, born at Winsford in Somerset.

1890 Molotov, Soviet political leader and diplomat, born at Kukaida with the surname Skriabin.

1934 Yuri Gagarin, Russian astronaut and the first man in space, born near Smolensk, the son of a collective farmer.

1943 Bobby Fischer, chess champion and first American to hold the world title, born at Chicago.

1946 Day of tragedy at Burnden Park, Bolton, before an English FA Cup tie against Stoke City, with 33 killed and over 400 injured, as a result of broken crush-barriers.

1956 Archbishop Makarios, implicated in terrorism in Cyprus, was deported by the British to the Seychelle Islands.

10 MARCH (70)

1863 King Edward VII, when he was Prince of Wales, married Princess Alexandra of Denmark in St George's Chapel, Windsor.

1872 Giuseppe Mazzini, Italian revolutionary who fought for his country's unity and independence, died at Pisa.

1876 Alexander Graham Bell transmitted the first coherent message from 5 Exeter Place, Boston, in Massachusetts to his assistant Thomas Watson, consisting of the words 'Come here, Watson, I want you'.

1886 The first Cruft's dog show was held, in London—the first ever took place in 1859 in Newcastle.

1906 The Bakerloo Line of London Underground was opened.

1935 Hitler renounced the Versailles Treaty of 1919 and ordered conscription in Germany.

1948 Jan Masaryk, Czech statesman and minister, died in Prague under suspicious circumstances after the Communists gained control.

1964 Prince Edward (Edward Antony Richard Louis), born at Buckingham Palace, the third son of Elizabeth II.

1969 Jimmy Wilde, Welsh flyweight boxer and world champion from 1916 to 1923, died aged 76.

11 MARCH

1702 The 'Daily Courant', the first successful English newspaper, published by E. Mallet as a single sheet, had its first issue.

1770 William Huskisson, British Tory statesman, born in Worcestershire.

1801 Paul I, Tsar of Russia, was strangled in a scuffle with his own officers who were conspiring to compel him to abdicate.

1819 Sir Henry Tate, English philanthropist whose money and pictures founded the Tate Gallery in 1897, born at Chorley.

1885 Sir Malcolm Campbell, English racing driver who established world records on land and water, born at Chislehurst in Kent.

1907 Jessie Matthews, English actress, born in London.

1916 Sir Harold Wilson, British statesman and Labour Prime Minister, born at Huddersfield in Yorkshire.

1936 Earl Beatty, British admiral and cruiser commander at the Battle of Jutland, died.

1941 The United States Lend Lease Bill was signed by President Roosevelt.

1955 Sir Alexander Fleming, Scottish bacteriologist, discoverer of penicillin in 1928 and Nobel Prize winner in 1945, died.

1957 Richard Byrd, American admiral, aviator and Polar explorer, died.

1970 Erle Stanley Gardner, American crime writer and creator of the character 'Perry Mason', died.

12 MARCH

1710 Thomas Arne, English composer, notably of 'Rule Britannia', born in London, the son of an upholsterer.

1789 The United States Post Office was established.

1881 Kemal Ataturk, Turkish general, statesman and President, born at Salonika in Greece as Mustafa Kemal Pasha.

1890 Vaslav Nijinsky, Russian ballet dancer and choreographer, born at Kiev.

1912 The Girl Scouts movement in America was founded by Juliette Gordon Low.

1914 George Westinghouse, American engineer, inventor and patentee of the Westinghouse railway brake in 1868, died in New York City.

1917 'Izvestia', the official daily newspaper of the USSR, was founded after the February Revolution.

1925 Sun Yat-Sen, Chinese revolutionary leader and national hero, died of cancer in Peking.

1935 A speed limit of 30 mph was introduced for towns and built-up areas in Britain.

1946 Liza Minnelli, American entertainer, film actress and Oscar winner in 1972, born at Los Angeles, the daughter of Judy Garland.

1968 The volcanic island of Mauritius in the Indian Ocean became an independent member of the Commonwealth, having been a British colony since 1810.

13 MARCH (73)

1733 Joseph Priestley, English scientist who discovered gases, notably oxygen, born at Leeds, the son of a cloth dresser.

1781 The planet Uranus, 7th in distance from the sun, was discovered by the German-born English astronomer Sir William Herschel.

1855 Percival Lowell, American astronomer, born at Boston in Massachusetts.

1858 Felice Orsini, Italian revolutionary, was executed for his part in the assassination attempt on the life of Napoleon III in Paris.

1873 The Scottish Football Association was formed at a meeting attended by the representatives of 8 clubs.

1881 Alexander II, Tsar of Russia from 1855, died from injuries received when a bomb was thrown at him near his Palace.

1884 Sir Hugh Walpole, British novelist, born at Auckland on the North Island of New Zealand.

1901 Benjamin Harrison, American Republican statesman and 23rd President from 1889 to 1893, died at Indianapolis in Indiana.

1930 The discovery of the planet Pluto, at the Lowell Observatory in Arizona, was announced by Clyde Tombaugh—although its existence had been predicted earlier by Percival Lowell.

1938 Nazi Germany invaded Austria, after which it was incorporated in the German Reich under the name of Ostmark.

1944 HMS Thunderbolt—the new name of the salvaged submarine 'Thetis'—was sunk off Sicily.

1948 The Lincolnshire Handicap, an English horse race, had a record 58 runners.

1950 Joe Bugner, British heavyweight boxing champion, born in Hungary.

1961 The old black and white Bank of England £5 notes ceased to be legal tender.

1967 Sir Frank Worrell, West Indian Test cricketer, died.

14 MARCH (74)

1757 Admiral John Byng was shot by a firing squad on the 'Monarque' at Portsmouth for his failure to relieve the island of Minorca, threatened by the French fleet.

1804 Johann Strauss the elder, Austrian composer and conductor, born in Vienna, the son of an inn-keeper.

1820 Victor Emmanuel II, the first king of united Italy, born.

1844 Umberto I, king of Italy, born in Turin the son of Victor Emmanuel above, whom he succeeded in 1878.

1879 Albert Einstein, German scientist known for his theory of relativity, born at Ulm in Bavaria of Jewish parents.

1883 Karl Marx, German social philosopher and radical leader, died in London and was buried in Highgate Cemetery.

1928 Frank Borman, American astronaut, born at Gary in Indiana.

1932 George Eastman, American photographic pioneer, died by his own hand.

1933 Michael Caine, English film actor, born in London as Maurice Micklewhite.

1936 The London to Hong Kong airline service was inaugurated.

1975 Susan Hayward, American film actress and Academy Award (Oscar) winner in 1958 for her part in 'I Want to Live', died.

15 MARCH (75)

1767 'Old Hickory', Andrew Jackson, American general, Democrat statesman and 7th President, born in the Waxhaws District in South Carolina, the son of Irish immigrants.

1779 Viscount Melbourne, British Whig statesman and Prime Minister, born in London as William Lamb.

1820 Maine, the Pine Tree State, became the 23rd state of the Union.

1877 Australia played England at Melbourne in the first cricket Test match—the hosts ended up winners by 45 runs.

1898 Sir Henry Bessemer, English metallurgist and inventor of an economical process for converting cast iron into steel in 1856, died aged 85.

1909 Selfridge's, American-owned department store in London's Oxford Street, was opened.

1919 The American Legion was founded.

1920 Billy Meredith became the oldest player to appear in a football international when he played for Wales against England at Highbury in London when well over 45.

1937 America set up its first blood bank, at Cook County Hospital in Chicago.

1947 Floods in England were the worst recorded.

1949 Clothes rationing ended in Britain.

1975 Aristotle Onassis, Greek shipping magnate and Olympic Airways operator, died.

16 MARCH (76)

1751 James Madison, American Republican statesman and 4th President, born at Port Conway in Virginia, the first of 12 children.

1774 Matthew Flinders, English naval officer and navigator, born at Donington near Boston in Lincolnshire, the son of a surgeon.

1787 Georg Ohm, German physicist specialising in electricity, born in Bavaria.

1802 The United States Military Academy was established at West Point in New York State.

1872 The first English FA Cup final took place, Wanderers, a team formed by ex-public school and university men, beating Royal Engineers 1-0 at the Oval in London.

1878 William Banting, English pioneer of slimming by diet control, died.

1904 Books of stamps were first issued in Britain by the GPO, containing 24 at one penny.

1912 Thelma Nixon, wife of America's 37th President, born at Ely in Nevada as Thelma Ryan.

1937 Sir Austen Chamberlain, British Conservative statesman who negotiated the signing of the Locarno Pact in 1925 and Nobel Prize winner in the same year, died.

1966 Spacecraft Gemini 8 was launched, with Neil Armstrong and David Scott.

17 MARCH (77)

St Patrick's Day—national day of Ireland.

1337 Edward, Duke of Cornwall, was the first to be created a Duke.

1787 Edmund Kean, English Shakespearean actor, born in London.

1834 Gottlieb Daimler, German engineer who improved the internal combustion engine, born at Schorndorf.

1846 Kate Greenaway, English artist and illustrator of children's books, born in London, the daughter of a wood engraver.

1861 Victor Emmanuel was declared King of Italy at Turin by the country's first Parliament.

1897 Bob Fitzsimmons became the only British-born boxer to win the world heavyweight title, defeating Jim Corbett at Carson City in Nevada.

1902 Bobby Jones, the legendary American golf champion, born at Atlanta in Georgia.

1912 Lawrence Oates, Putney-born explorer with Captain Scott, died on the return journey from the South Pole—on his 32nd birthday—'I am just going outside, and may be some time'.

1919 Nat 'King' Cole, American singer and entertainer, born at Montgomery in Alabama as Nathaniel Adams Coles.

1938 Rudolf Nureyev, Russian ballet dancer, born at Irkutsk in Siberia.

1958 Sir Hubert Wilkins, Australian Polar explorer and aviator, died.

1978 The oil-tanker 'Amoco Cadiz' ran aground on the coast of Brittany, broke in half and subsequently disgorged some 220 000 tons of crude oil.

18 MARCH (78)

1584 Ivan IV, called 'the Terrible', the first to assume the title of Tsar, died of sorrow for his son, whom he had killed in a mad fit of rage some 3 years earlier.

1745 Sir Robert Walpole, British Whig statesman and Chief Minister from 1721 to 1742, died in London, having been created Earl of Orford.

1768 Laurence Sterne, Irish-born clergyman and novelist, notably 'Tristram Shandy', died in poverty in London.

1837 Grover Cleveland, American Democrat statesman and President on two occasions, born at Caldwell in New Jersey, the son of a Presbyterian minister.

1844 Rimsky-Korsakov, Russian composer, born at Tikhvin, Novgorod.

1858 Rudolf Diesel, German engineer and inventor of the engine that bears his name, born in Paris.

1869 Neville Chamberlain, British statesman and Conservative Prime Minister, born at Birmingham.

1905 Robert Donat, English film actor and Oscar winner, born at Manchester.

1913 George I, King of Greece from 1863, was assassinated at Salonika.

1949 Alex 'Hurricane' Higgins, snooker champion, born in Northern Ireland.

1952 Pat Eddery, English champion jockey, born.

1965 Farouk I, King of Egypt from 1936 to 1952, died in exile in Italy.

Aleksei Leonov left 'Voshkod II' and made the first space walk, lasting about 10 minutes.

1967 The oil tanker 'Torrey Canyon' was wrecked on the Pollard Rock between the Isles of Scilly and Land's End.

1983 King Umberto II of Italy, in exile since 1946, died in a Geneva clinic aged 78.

19 MARCH (79)

1813 David Livingstone, Scottish explorer and medical missionary in Africa, born at 9 Shuttle Row, Blantyre, near East Kilbride.

1821 Sir Richard Burton, much-travelled English explorer and writer, born at Torquay in Devon, the son of a colonel.

1848 Wyatt Earp, American law officer and gunfighter, born at Monmouth in Illinois.

1872 Sergei Diaghilev, Russian ballet impresario and artistic director, born at Novgorod.

1906 Adolf Eichmann, German Nazi official responsible for the execution of millions of Jews during World War II, born at Solingen.

1930 Arthur James Balfour, British statesman and Conservative Prime Minister from 1902 to 1905, died aged 81.

1932 The 1650-foot-span Sydney Harbour Bridge—the world's widest—was officially opened.

1950 Edgar Rice Burroughs, American popular novelist, best known for the series of Tarzan books, died.

20 MARCH (80)

1413 King Henry IV died of a stroke in the Jerusalem Chamber at Westminster Abbey—having prophesied he would die in Jerusalem—accession of his eldest son as Henry V.

1602 The Dutch East India Company was founded by the Netherlands Government to trade with the East Indies— was wound up in 1798.

1727 Sir Isaac Newton, outstanding British scientist and mathematician, died in London aged 84 and was buried at Westminster Abbey.

1806 The foundation stone of Dartmoor Prison, at Princetown in Devon, was laid. Originally built to house French prisoners of war—was used as a convict prison from 1850.

1828 Henrik Ibsen, Norwegian playwright, the father of modern drama, born at the seaport of Skien.

1908 Michael Redgrave, English stage and film actor, born at Bristol.

1917 Dame Vera Lynn, English vocalist and 'Forces' Favourite', born in London as Vera Welch.

1929 Ferdinand Foch, French Army marshal and commander in chief of the allied armies in France, died.

1956 Tunisia became an independent sovereign state, after being a Protectorate of France since 1881.

1964 Brendan Behan, Irish playwright, notably 'The Quare Fellow', died in a Dublin hospital.

1974 An attempt to kidnap Princess Anne was made in The Mall in London.

21 MARCH (81)

1556 Thomas Cranmer, the first Protestant Archbishop of Canterbury in 1533, was condemned as a traitor and heretic and burnt at the stake at Oxford.

1685 Johann Sebastian Bach, German composer and organist, born at Eisenach, Thuringia, now in East Germany.

1839 Modest Moussorgsky, Russian composer, born at Karevo (now Pskov).

1843 Robert Southey, English poet and Poet Laureate from 1813, died at Keswick in Cumbria.

1869 Florenz Ziegfeld, American theatre manager, impressario and creator of the fabulous 'Follies', born at Chicago in Illinois.

1935 Brian Clough, English footballer and club manager, born.

1958 The London Planetarium in Marylebone Street was opened —the first of its kind in Britain.

1960 The Sharpeville shootings in the Transvaal, South Africa took place, when police fired on an African demonstration against Pass Laws—about 70 were killed.

1963 Davey Moore, defending his world featherweight boxing title against Sugar Ramos in Los Angeles, was taken to hospital after the fight—died 4 days later.

22 MARCH (82)

The earliest date on which Easter can fall.

1599 Sir Anthony van Dyck, Flemish artist and court painter to King Charles I, born at Antwerp, the son of a cloth manufacturer.

1832 Johann von Goethe, German poet and novelist, author of 'Faust', died aged 82.

1887 'Chico' Marx, the piano-playing member of the Marx brothers, born in New York City as Leonard.

1888 The English Football League was formed at a meeting at Anderton's Hotel in Fleet Street, London—with 12 clubs.

1895 The earliest demonstration of a celluloid cinematograph film was given at Paris by Auguste and Louis Lumière.

1896 Thomas Hughes, English reformer and author, known for his 'Tom Brown's Schooldays', died.

1903 Frederic William Farrar, English clergyman and writer of school stories, particularly 'Eric, or Little by Little', died.

1910 Nicholas Monsarrat, English author of sea novels, notably 'The Cruel Sea', born in Liverpool.

1929 The Grand National Steeplechase at Aintree, Liverpool had a record 66 runners.

1936 Roger Whittaker, British singer and song writer, born at Nairobi in Kenya.

1946 Jordan became an independent Kingdom, having been under British protection.

1948 Andrew Lloyd Webber, English songwriter, born in London.

23 MARCH (83)

National day of Pakistan.

1842 Stendahl (Marie Henri Beyle), French novelist, died in Paris.

1908 Joan Crawford, American film actress and dancer, born at San Antonio in Texas as Lucille Le Sueur.

1912 Wernher von Braun, German engineer and pioneer of rocketry in Germany and America, born at Wirsitz.

1919 The Fascist Party was founded by Benito Mussolini at Milan.

1921 (Ernest William) E. W. Hornung, English novelist and creator of 'Raffles' the gentleman burglar, died.

Donald Campbell, English racing driver and water speed record holder, born.

1929 Roger Bannister, British athlete and first to run a mile in under four minutes (3 minutes 59.4 seconds), born at Harrow in Greater London.

1956 Pakistan was proclaimed an Islamic Republic within the Commonwealth.

Queen Elizabeth laid the foundation stone of the new Coventry Cathedral.

1964 Peter Lorre, Hungarian-born American film character actor, died.

1965 Spacecraft Gemini 3 was launched, with Virgil Grissom and John Young.

24 MARCH (84)

1603 Queen Elizabeth died in Richmond Palace aged 69, after nearly 45 years as Queen—accession of James I, the son of Mary, Queen of Scots.

1776 John Harrison, English watchmaker and inventor of the chronometer, died in London.

1877 The only deadheat in the history of the Oxford—Cambridge University boat race took place.

1882 (Henry Wadsworth) H. W. Longfellow, American poet, author of 'The Song of Hiawatha', died at Cambridge in Massachusetts.

1905 Jules Verne, French novelist and pioneer of science fiction, died at Amiens aged 77.

1930 Steve McQueen, American actor in action-adventure films, born at Indianapolis in Indiana.

1944 Orde Wingate, British Army commander who created and led the famous Chindits in Burma, was killed in a plane crash in the jungle in Assam.

1953 Queen Mary, wife of George V, died at her London home, Marlborough House in Pall Mall.

1962 Benny Paret, defending his world welterweight boxing title against Emile Griffith in New York, was taken to hospital after the fight with brain injury sustained in the fight—died on 3rd April.
Auguste Piccard, French deep-sea explorer and balloonist, died at Lausanne.

1976 Isabel Peron was ousted as President of Argentina by a military coup.
Bernard, Viscount Montgomery, Irish-born British Army field marshal and successful commander, died aged 88.

25 MARCH (85)

National day of Greece.

1802 The Peace Treaty of Amiens was signed, settlement in which Britain returned most of its gains from the Revolutionary Wars.

1843 The 1300-foot Thames Tunnel, linking Wapping with Rotherhithe, was formally opened.

1867 Arturo Toscanini, Italian conductor and musical director, born at Parma, the son of a tailor.

1876 The first Scotland v Wales football international was played, at Glasgow—the hosts won easily by 4 goals to nil.

1881 Bela Bartok, Hungarian composer and pianist, born.
1906 A. J. P. Taylor, English historian, born.
1908 David Lean, British film director, born at Croydon in Greater London.
1918 Claude Debussy, French composer, including 'Clair de Lune' and 'La Mer', died of cancer in Paris.
1947 Elton John, British musician and pop singer, born at Pinner in Middlesex as Reginald Kenneth Dwight.
1957 European Economic Community, an organisation usually called the 'Common Market', was formed by the Treaty of Rome.
1975 King Faisal of Saudi Arabia was assassinated by his nephew Prince Museid, in the Royal Palace at Riyadh.
'Queen Elizabeth 2' ('QE 2') became the largest liner to pass through the Panama Canal.

26 MARCH (86)

1726 Sir John Vanbrugh, English architect of Blenheim Palace, died of a quinsy at Whitehall in London.
1827 Ludwig van Beethoven, German composer of outstanding genius, died at Bonn.
1839 The annual Henley Rowing Regatta at Henley-on-Thames in Oxfordshire, was inaugurated.
1885 The first cremation in Britain took place, at Woking Crematorium in Surrey.
1902 Cecil Rhodes, British statesman, financier and colonial administrator, died at Cape Town.
1914 Tennessee Williams, American playwright, born at Columbus in Mississippi as Thomas Lanier Williams.
1923 Sarah Bernhardt, versatile French actress, died aged 78.
1925 Hindenburg was elected President of the German Republic.
1945 David Lloyd George, British statesman and Liberal Prime Minister from 1916 to 1922, died at Llanystumdwy near Criccieth in North Wales aged 82.
1957 Edouard Herriot, French radical statesman and twice Prime Minister, died.
1959 Raymond Chandler, American detective story writer and creator of the character 'Philip Marlowe', died.

1973 Sir Noel Coward, English playwright, actor and songwriter, died.
Mrs Susan Shaw became the first woman to set foot on the floor of the London Stock Exchange in the 171 years of its existence.

27 MARCH (87)

1625 Death of King James I, the 'wisest fool in Christendom', at Theobalds Park, Cheshunt in Hertfordshire—accession of his son as Charles I.
1794 The United States Navy was created.
1845 Wilhelm von Röntgen, German physicist and discoverer of X-rays, born at Lennep in Prussia.
1863 Sir Frederick Henry Royce, English car manufacturer, of Rolls Royce Ltd, born at Alwalton, the son of a miller.
1871 The first Rugby International was played, Scotland defeating England at Edinburgh.
1889 John Bright, British radical statesman and reformer who worked with Richard Cobden for the repeal of the Corn Laws, died.
1912 James Callaghan, British statesman and Labour Prime Minister from 1976 to 1979, born at Portsmouth.
1917 Cyrus Vance, American Government official, born at Clarksburg in West Virginia.
1923 Sir James Dewar, Scottish chemist and physicist, inventor of the vacuum flask, died aged 80.
1931 Arnold Bennett, English novelist who wrote of the Staffordshire potteries, died of typhoid.
1961 The first women traffic wardens went on duty in Britain, at Leicester.
1968 Yuri Gagarin, the first man in space in 1961, was killed in a jet plane crash near Moscow on a routine training flight.
1975 Sir Arthur Bliss, English composer and Master of the Queen's Musick from 1953, died.
1977 The world's worst aviation disaster took place, when 2 aircraft collided and exploded on the foggy single airstrip at Los Rodeos Airport at Tenerife on the Canary Islands, with 582 deaths.

1483 Raphael, Italian painter, born at Urbino as Raffaello Sanzio or Santi.

1660 George I, the first Hanoverian King of Great Britain, born at Osnabrück Castle, Hanover.

1845 The oldest Beagle hunt—the Royal Rock Beagles, of Wirral, Merseyside—had its first outing.

1868 The Earl of Cardigan, British leader of the disastrous cavalry charge at Balaklava in the Crimean War in 1854, died.

1881 Modest Moussorgsky, Russian composer, died as a result of chronic alcoholism.

1902 Dame Flora Robson, English actress, born at South Shields on Tyneside.

1917 The Women's Army Auxiliary Corps was founded in Britain.

1921 Dirk Bogarde, English film actor, born at Hampstead in London.

1924 Freddie Bartholomew, English actor famed as a Hollywood child actor, born in London as Frederick Llewellyn.

1941 The Battle of Matapan took place off the south coast of Greece, with victory for the British Navy over an Italian fleet.

Virginia Woolf, English novelist and critic, died—ending her life by drowning near Rodmell in Sussex.

1942 British commandos made a dawn raid on the French port of St Nazaire—called 'Operation Chariot'—in which an old destroyer, the 'Campbeltown', full of explosives, rammed the main dock gate and put it out of action for the rest of the war.

1943 Sergei Rachmaninov, Russian-American composer and piano virtuoso, died at Beverly Hills in California.

1955 The lowest cricket Test score was recorded, 26 by New Zealand against England at Auckland.

1969 Dwight D. Eisenhower, American Army commander,

Republican statesman and 34th President from 1953 to 1961, affectionately called 'Ike', died at Washington.

1977 Eric Shipton, British mountaineer who made 5 assaults on Mount Everest, died at Salisbury in Wiltshire.

29 MARCH (89)

1461 The Battle of Towton took place in North Yorkshire in a snowstorm during the Wars of the Roses—the bloodiest battle fought on British soil, in which it was said that over 28 000 died.

1769 Nicolas Soult, French marshal serving under Napoleon, born.

1788 Charles Wesley, English evangelist, hymn writer and younger brother of John, died.

1790 John Tyler, American Whig statesman and 10th President, born at Greenway in Virginia.

1866 John Keble, English cleric who inspired the start of the Oxford Movement, died at Hursley in Hampshire.

1869 Sir Edwin Lutyens, English architect, born in London.

1871 The Royal Albert Hall at Kensington, built in memory of Prince Albert, was opened by Queen Victoria.

1902 Sir William Walton, English composer, born at Oldham in Lancashire to musical parents.

1912 Captain Scott perished in Antarctica returning from his expedition to the South Pole.

1920 After 42 years service in the British Army Sir William Robertson attained the rank of Field Marshal—the only British soldier to rise through the ranks from Private.

1939 The Spanish Civil War was declared to have ended, Franco was named Caudillo, or leader of the nation.

1940 Metal strips were introduced into the Bank of England £1 notes, as an anti-forgery device.

1980 Mantovani, Anglo-Italian conductor famous for his harmonious orchestral arrangements, died.

30 MARCH

1746 Francisco de Goya, Spanish painter, born at Fuendetodos near Saragossa, the son of a master gilder.

1820 Anna Sewell, English author, notably 'Black Beauty', born at Great Yarmouth in Norfolk.

1840 George Bryan ('Beau') Brummell, English dandy and leader of fashion, died at Caen in France, in the pauper lunatic asylum.

1853 Vincent van Gogh, Dutch painter, born in the village of Groot-Zundert, the son of a Lutheran pastor.

1856 The Treaty of Paris was signed, ending the Crimean War.

1867 Through the efforts of Secretary of State William H. Seward Alaska was acquired by America from Russia for 7.2 million dollars—the 375 million acres worked out at less than 2 cents an acre, including all rights.

1884 Sean O'Casey, Irish playwright, born in a poor part of Dublin.

1913 Frankie Laine, American singer, born at Chicago in Illinois as Frank Paul Lo Vecchio.

1930 Rolf Harris, Australian entertainer, born.

1938 Warren Beatty, American film actor and director, born at Richmond in Virginia, the older brother of Shirley MacLaine.

1950 Léon Blum, French Socialist statesman and Prime Minister, died.

1967 The wrecked oil tanker 'Torrey Canyon' off Land's End was bombed to destruction.

1981 An attempt to assassinate President Reagan was made by John Hinckley, outside Washington's Hilton Hotel.

31 MARCH

1732 Franz Joseph Haydn, Austrian composer, born at Rohrau, the son of a wheelwright.

1809 Edward Fitzgerald, English scholar and poet, born in Suffolk.

1809 Nikolai Gogol, Russian novelist, born at Sorochinsty in Poltava.

1811 Robert Bunsen, German chemist, physicist and inventor, born at Göttingen in Lower Saxony.

1837 John Constable, English landscape painter, notably 'The Hay Wain', died.

1855 Charlotte Brontë, the oldest of the 3 literary sisters, author of 'Jane Eyre', died during pregnancy.

1872 Sergei Diaghilev, Russian music and ballet impresario, born at Novgorod.
Arthur Griffith, Irish nationalist leader and President of the Irish Free State, born in Dublin.

1878 Jack Johnson, Negro American heavyweight boxing champion, born at Galveston in Texas.

1889 The 300-metre Eiffel Tower was completed in readiness for the Universal Exhibition in Paris, and inaugurated by Premier Tirard.

1900 Henry, Duke of Gloucester, third son of King George V, born.

1921 Gordon Richards rode 'Gay Lord' at Leicester, the first of 4870 winners in his career.

1938 David Steel, British politician and Liberal Party leader, born.

1970 Timoshenko, Soviet Army marshal of the Second World War, died.

1973 'Red Rum' won the Grand National Steeplechase of 30 jumps and 4½ miles, in a record time of 9 minutes 1.9 seconds.

1980 Jesse Owens, distinguished American athlete, died at Tucson in Arizona.

1 APRIL (92)

1578 William Harvey, English physician who discovered the circulation of the blood, born at Folkestone in Kent.

1815 Otto von Bismarck, German statesman and first Chancellor, born at Schönhausen in Brandenburg.

1875 'The Times' became the first newspaper to publish a daily weather chart.

1883 Lon Chaney, American silent-screen actor, born at Colorado Springs in Colorado.

1893 Cicely Courtneidge, British actress, born at Sydney in Australia.

1918 The Royal Air Force was formed, by the amalgamation of the Royal Flying Corps and the Royal Naval Air Service.

1932 Debbie Reynolds, American singer and film actress, born at El Paso in Texas as Mary Frances Reynolds.

1947 King George II of Greece died, and was succeeded by his brother as Paul I.
The school leaving age in Britain was raised to 15.

1948 Britain's electricity industry was nationalised.

1954 The US Air Force Academy was created at Colorado Springs in Colorado.

1960 America launched the first meteorological satellite, Tiros I.

1967 Sir Edmund Compton took office as Britain's first Ombudsman.

1973 Value Added Tax came into operation in Britain.

2 APRIL (93)

1725 Giovanni Casanova, Italian adventurer, born at Venice.

1792 The first United States Mint was established at Philadelphia, then the nation's capital.

1801 The naval Battle of Copenhagen took place, in the course of which Nelson, aboard the 'Elephant', put the telescope to his blind eye and so 'did not see' Admiral Parker's signal to break off the fight—the Danish fleet was destroyed.

1805 Hans Christian Andersen, Danish writer of fairy tales, born at Odense, the son of a shoemaker.

1827 Holman Hunt, English painter and member of the Pre-Raphaelite Brotherhood, born in London.

1840 Emile Zola, French novelist, born in Paris, the son of an Italian engineer.

1865 Richard Cobden, British statesman who worked for the repeal of the Corn Laws with John Bright, died in London.

1872 Samuel Morse, American inventor of the telegraphic Morse Code, died in New York City aged 80.

1873 Sergei Rachmaninov, Russian composer and piano virtuoso, born at Nijni-Novgorod.

1914 Sir Alec Guinness, English actor and Oscar winner in 1957, born at Marylebone in London.

1940 Metal strips were introduced into the Bank of England ten-shilling notes, as an anti-forgery device.
Mike Hailwood, British motor cycle racing champion, born at Oxford.

1946 The Royal Military Academy was established at Sandhurst in Berkshire, having been at Woolwich since 1741.

1966 (Cecil Scott) C. S. Forester, British novelist and writer of the 'Hornblower' series, died.

1974 Georges Pompidou, French statesman, Prime Minister and President from 1969, died in office.

1977 The English racehorse 'Red Rum' won the Grand National steeplechase for a record third time.

1982 Argentinian forces invaded and occupied the British Falkland Islands in the South Atlantic.

3 APRIL (94)

1367 Henry IV, the first Lancastrian King of England, born at Bolingbroke Castle in Lincolnshire, the son of John of Gaunt.

1721 Robert Walpole became Britain's first Prime Minister, an office he held continuously until 12th February 1742.

1783 Washington Irving, American writer, born in New York City.

1860 The Pony Express, founded by William Russell, was first run—1980 miles between St Joseph in Missouri and Sacramento in California—ended on 24th October 1861 when the first transcontinental telegraph line was completed.

1866 (James Barry) J. B. Hertzog, South African statesman and nationalist Prime Minister, born at Wellington in Cape Colony.

1882 Jesse James, American outlaw and robber, was shot in the back at close range by one of his own gang, Robert Ford, in St Joseph, Missouri.

1897 Johannes Brahms, German composer and pianist, died in Vienna.

1901 Richard D'Oyly Carte, English theatrical impresario who staged the Gilbert and Sullivan operettas, died.

1924 Marlon Brando, American film actor and twice Oscar winner, born at Omaha in Nebraska.
Doris Day, American singer and film actress, born at Cincinnati in Ohio as Doris Kappelhoff.

1925 Anthony Wedgwood Benn, British Labour politician, born.

1930 Haile Selassie was proclaimed Emperor of Ethiopia, a country he ruled for 44 years.

1933 Two British planes made history by becoming the first to fly over Mount Everest.

1954 Oxford won the 100th University Boat Race.

1982 Dick Saunders, at 48, became the oldest winner of the Grand National steeplechase, riding 'Grittar'—in the same race Geraldine Rees on 'Cheers' became the first female jockey to finish the 4½ mile course of 30 fences.

4 APRIL (95)

National day of Hungary.

1581 Francis Drake was knighted on board the 'Golden Hind' at Deptford, on the River Thames.

1617 John Napier, Scottish mathematician and first to publish logarithm tables, in 1614, died at Merchiston Castle, Edinburgh.

1774 Oliver Goldsmith, Irish writer, notably 'The Vicar of Wakefield', died in London.

1841 William Harrison, American statesman and 9th President, died after only 31 days in office, as a result of catching pneumonia during his inauguration—his term of office was finished by vice-President John Tyler.

1929 Karl Benz, German engineer and pioneer of early motor cars with internal combustion engines, died aged 84.

1933 America's helium-filled airship 'Akron' crashed into the sea off the coast of New Jersey during a violent storm.

1941 André Michelin, French industrialist who built the first factories for the mass-production of rubber motor tyres, died in Paris.

1949 The North Atlantic Treaty Organisation was created in a treaty signed at Washington.

1968 Martin Luther King, American Negro civil rights leader and Nobel Peace Prize winner in 1964, was assassinated at his motel at Memphis in Tennessee—the alleged assassin was James Earl Ray.

5 APRIL (96)

1614 The Addled Parliament began sitting—was dissolved on 7th June without having passed a Bill—hence its name.

1732 Jean Fragonard, French painter and engraver, born at Grasse.

1794 Georges Jacques Danton, French revolutionary leader, guillotined for treason.

1811 Robert Raikes, English philanthropist and founder of the Sunday School movement, died at Gloucester.

1818 Chile achieved independence from Spanish rule after a revolutionary war led by Bernardo O'Higgins.

1827 Joseph Lister, English surgeon and pioneer of disinfection and antiseptics, born in London.

1884 John Wisden, Sussex cricketer and compiler of the record books that bear his name, died in London.

1894 Chesney Allen, English comedian and member of the famous Crazy Gang, born.

1900 Spencer Tracy, American film actor, born at Milwaukee in Wisconsin.

1908 Bette Davis, American film actress and twice Oscar winner, born at Lowell in Massachusetts.

1916 Gregory Peck, American film actor, born at La Jolla in California.

1922 Tom Finney, English footballer with 76 international caps, born.

1955 Sir Winston Churchill resigned as Prime Minister.

1964 Douglas MacArthur, American general and commander in the Pacific in World War II, died at Washington, DC aged 84.

1975 Chiang Kai-Shek, Chinese military and political leader, died aged 87.

1976 Howard Hughes, American multi-millionaire industrialist, died on board his private jet en route to hospital at Houston, Texas.

6 APRIL (97)

1199 King Richard I, called the Lion Heart, died from a wound received while besieging the Castle of Chaluz.

1520 Raphael (Raffaello Sanzio or Santi), Italian Renaissance painter, died in Rome.

1528 Albrecht Dürer, German artist and engraver, died in Nuremberg.

1830 The Mormon Movement or Church of Jesus Christ of Latter Day Saints was founded by Joseph Smith at Fayette, New York.

1843 William Wordsworth was appointed Poet Laureate.

1874 Harry Houdini, American magician and escapologist, born at Appleton in Wisconsin as Ehrich Weiss, the son of a rabbi from Budapest.

1896 Modern Olympic Games were revived by Pierre de Coubertin, at Athens, with James Connolly of America winning the first Gold medal, in the triple jump event.

1906 Sir John Betjeman, English writer and Poet Laureate, born in London.

1909 Robert Peary became the first man to reach the North Pole—at his sixth attempt in 15 years—with his Negro servant Matthew Henson and 4 Eskimos.

1917 The United States of America declared war on Germany.

1926 Rev. Ian Paisley, British politician and MP for Antrim, born.

1929 André Prévin, conductor, composer and musical director, born in Berlin.

1944 PAYE income tax came into force in Britain. The system was devised by Sir Cornelius Gregg.
1955 Sir Anthony Eden succeeded Sir Winston Churchill as Prime Minister.
1965 The communications satellite 'Early Bird' was launched by USA.
1971 Igor Stravinsky, Russian-born composer best known for his ballets, died in New York City aged 88.

7 APRIL (98)

1506 St Francis Xavier, Spanish Jesuit missionary, born near Sanguesa.
1739 The notorious highwayman Dick Turpin was hanged at York for the murder of a keeper from Epping—was buried at York as 'John Palmer'.
1770 William Wordsworth, English poet, born at Cockermouth in Cumbria, the son of an attorney.
1891 Phineas T. Barnum, American showman who created 'The Greatest Show on Earth' in 1871, died aged 80.
     David Low, British political cartoonist, born at Dunedin on the South Island of New Zealand.
1897 Walter Winchell, American gossip columnist and radio commentator, born in New York City.
1928 James Garner, American film actor, born at Norman in Oklahoma as James Baumgarner.
1939 Italy invaded and seized Albania and placed it under the rule of the King of Italy.
1947 Henry Ford, American motor car manufacturer, the father of 'mass-production', died aged 83.
1948 WHO—the World Health Organisation—was established 'with the aim of attaining the highest possible level of health for all people', with headquarters at Geneva.
1968 Jim Clark, British motor racing champion driver, was killed during a race on the Hockenheim track in West Germany.

1614 El Greco, Greek-born Spanish painter, sculptor and architect, died.

1838 Brunel's 236 foot steamship 'Great Western' left Bristol for New York on her maiden voyage, under the command of Captain James Hosken.

1875 Albert I, King of the Belgians, born.

1889 Sir Adrian Boult, English conductor and musical director, born at Chester.

1893 Mary Pickford, American film actress, born at Toronto in the Canadian Province of Ontario as Gladys Marie Smith.

1908 Herbert Henry Asquith became Liberal Prime Minister and held the office until 7th December 1916, the longest tenure in modern times.

1912 Sonja Henie, Olympic and world skating champion and film actress in America, born at Oslo in Norway.

1918 Elizabeth Ford, wife of America's 38th President, born at Chicago in Illinois, née Bloomer.

1919 Ian Smith, Rhodesian Prime Minister, born at Selukwe in Southern Rhodesia.

1930 Dorothy Tutin, English actress, born.

1950 Vaslav Nijinsky, legendary Russian ballet dancer, died in London.

1973 Pablo Picasso, Spanish painter and founder of the Cubist movement, died aged 91.

1483 Death of King Edward IV—accession of his young son as Edward V.

1626 Francis Bacon, English philosopher and statesman, died near Highgate in London, as Lord Verulam.

1649 The Duke of Monmouth, son of King Charles II and Lucy Walter, born at Rotterdam.

1806 Isambard Brunel, English engineer, born at Portsmouth, the son of a refugee from the French Revolution.

1835 Leopold II, King of the Belgians, born in Brussels.

1838 The National Gallery in London's Trafalgar Square was opened.

1865 Confederate General Robert E. Lee surrendered to General Grant at Appomattox Court House in Virginia, bringing the American Civil War to an end.

1872 Léon Blum, French Socialist statesman and Prime Minister, born in Paris.

1882 Dante Gabriel Rossetti, English poet and painter, co-founder of the Pre-Raphaelite Brotherhood with Millais and Hunt, died in Kent.

1898 Paul Robeson, American Negro singer, born at Princeton in New Jersey, the son of a minister.

1906 Hugh Gaitskell, British politician and leader of the Labour Party, born in London.

1909 Robert Helpmann, Australian ballet dancer and choreographer, born at Mount Gambier in the State of South Australia.

1969 The British supersonic airliner 'Concorde' made its maiden flight, from Bristol to Fairford in Gloucestershire.

10 APRIL (101)

1820 The first British settlers arrived in South Africa, at Algoa Bay near Port Elizabeth in Cape Province.

1829 William Booth, English evangelist preacher and founder of the Salvation Army, born at Nottingham, the son of a builder.

1841 The American newspaper 'New York Tribune', founded by Horace Greeley, was first published.

1849 The safety pin was patented by New Yorker Walter Hunt.

1864 Maximilian, an Austrian Archduke, was made Emperor of Mexico.

1868 George Arliss, American film actor, born in London as Augustus George Andrews.

1870 Lenin, Russian Communist leader and founder of Bolshevism, born at Simbirsk (now Ulyanovsk) as Vladimir Ilyich Ulyanov, the son of a schools inspector.

1908 Vic Feather, British trade union leader, born.

1932 Omar Sharif, film actor, born at Alexandria in Egypt as Michel Shaboub (or Shalhouz).

1937 Stan Mellor, English National Hunt jockey, born at Manchester.

1954 Auguste Lumière, French pioneer of cinematography with his brother Louis, died at Lyons.

1963 The US Navy atomic submarine 'Thresher' sank off Cape Cod, with the loss of 129 lives.

1966 Evelyn Waugh, English novelist, died near Taunton in Somerset.

11 APRIL (102)

1689 King William III and Queen Mary II were crowned as joint sovereigns of Great Britain by the Bishop of London—the Archbishop of Canterbury refused to perform the service.

1713 The Treaty of Utrecht was signed, ending the hostilities in the War of the Spanish Succession.

1770 George Canning, British Tory statesman and Prime Minister, born in London.

1814 Napoleon abdicated as Emperor, and was exiled to the island of Elba—Louis ascended the throne of France on his return from refuge in England.

1819 Sir Charles Hallé, British pianist, conductor and founder of the famous Hallé orchestra, born at Hagen in Germany.

1884 Charles Reade, English novelist, notably 'The Cloister and the Hearth', died.

1893 Dean Acheson, American politician and Secretary of State, born at Middletown in Connecticut.

1926 Luther Burbank, American botanist and plant breeder, died.

1930 The British newspaper 'Daily Express' became the first to publish television programmes.

1961 The trial of the Nazi war criminal Adolf Eichmann opened in Jerusalem.

1970 Apollo 13 was launched, with James Lovell, Fred Halse and John Swigert.

The English FA Cup final at Wembley Stadium, between Leeds United and Chelsea, ended in a draw—the first since 1912.

12 APRIL

1606 The Union Jack was adopted as the flag of England.

1684 Niccolo Amati, the most famous of a family of violin makers at Cremona, died.

1709 The English magazine 'The Tatler' was first published.

1861 The American Civil War, a conflict between the 23 northern states and the 11 southern states, began with the bombardment of Fort Sumter in South Carolina by the Confederate Army under General Pierre Beauregard.

1938 Fyodor Chaliapin, Russian operatic bass singer considered one of opera's greatest performers, died.

1941 Bobby Moore, English international footballer with a record 108 appearances for his country, born at Barking in London.

1945 Franklin D. Roosevelt, American Democrat statesman and 32nd President from 1933, died of cerebral haemorrhage at Warm Springs in Georgia—the remainder of his term of office was completed by vice-President Harry S. Truman.

1961 Yuri Gargarin was launched in Vostok I from Tyuratam in Kazakhstan and made a single orbit of the earth, and landed near Engels in the Saratov region.

1981 Joe Louis, American legendary heavyweight boxing champion, died in a Las Vegas hospital.

The United States launched its pioneering space shuttle 'Columbia' from Cape Canaveral, with Robert Crippen and John Young.

13 APRIL

1668 John Dryden was appointed the first Poet Laureate, an appointment he kept until 1689.

1732 Lord North, British statesman and Tory Prime Minister, born in London.

1741 The Royal Military Academy was established at Woolwich—is now at Sandhurst in Berkshire.

1743 Thomas Jefferson, American statesman and 3rd President, born at Shadwell in Virginia, the son of a civil engineer.

1771 Richard Trevithick, English engineer and designer of steam engines, born at Illogan, Redruth in Cornwall.

1852 Frank Winfield Woolworth, American merchant and founder of the chain of stores which bears his name, born at Rodman, Jefferson County in the State of New York.

1892 Sir Arthur Harris, British wartime bomber commander, born.

1919 The Amritsar massacre took place in the Punjab, in which General Dyer's British troops shot 380 of Gandhi's followers and wounded over 1200.

1922 John Braine, English author, born at Bradford in Yorkshire.

1935 The London to Australia airline service was inaugurated by Imperial Airways and QANTAS.

1936 Joe Payne scored a record 10 goals, for Luton Town against Bristol Rovers—on his debut as a centre forward.

1951 The Coronation Stone (Stone of Destiny), stolen on the previous Christmas Day by Scottish nationalists, was returned to Westminster Abbey.

1964 Ian Smith became Prime Minister of Southern Rhodesia on the resignation of Winston Field.

14 APRIL (105)

1629 Christian Huygens, Dutch scientist and astronomer, born at The Hague, the son of a poet.

1759 George Frederick Handel, German composer, best known for his 'Messiah', died in London aged 74.

1828 'Webster's Dictionary' was first published—properly named 'American Dictionary of the English language'.

1865 Abraham Lincoln, America's 16th President from 1861, was shot in Ford's Theatre by John Wilkes Booth. He died the following day—the remainder of his term of office was completed by vice-President Andrew Johnson, sworn in as President.

1904 Sir John Gielgud, English Shakespearean actor, born in London.

1917 Dr Zamenof, Polish linguist and creator of the international language of Esperanto, died.

1925 Rod Steiger, American film actor and Oscar winner in 1967, born at Westhampton in the State of New York.

1929 The Monaco Grand Prix was first run, 76 laps round the narrow streets and the harbour of Monte Carlo.

1931 The Highway Code was first issued in Britain by the Ministry of Transport.
Alfonso XIII, the last king of Spain, abdicated in favour of a Republic.

1951 Ernest Bevin, British Labour statesman and trade union leader, died.

1975 Fredric March, American film actor and twice Academy Award (Oscar) winner, in 1932 and 1946, died.

1981 The first American space shuttle landed at Edwards Air Force Base in California after a successful mission.

15 APRIL (106)

1764 Madame de Pompadour, French courtier and mistress of Louis XV, died at Versailles.

1793 The first Bank of England £5 notes were issued.

1797 British naval personnel mutinied at Spithead, in the Solent off Portsmouth.

1843 Henry James, American novelist, born in New York.

1865 Andrew Johnson was sworn in as President of the United States on the death of Abraham Lincoln.

1888 Matthew Arnold, English poet and educationalist, died suddenly at Liverpool.

1889 Father Damien, Belgian RC priest and missionary, died on the Hawaiian island of Molokai.

1901 Joe Davis, many times world snooker and billiards champion, born at Whitwell, near Chesterfield in Derbyshire.

1912 The 'unsinkable' White Star passenger liner 'Titanic' sank in 2½ hours on her maiden voyage from Southampton to New York City, hitting an iceberg off Newfoundland, with the loss of over 1500 lives.

1942 The island of Malta was awarded the George Cross for its heroism during heavy German and Italian bombardments.

1949 Wallace Beery, American film actor and Academy Award (Oscar) winner for his part in 'The Champ', died.

16 APRIL (107)

1746 The Battle of Culloden took place near Inverness—the last battle in Britain—in which the Jacobites were defeated by the Duke of Cumberland's forces, terminating attempts of the Stuarts to regain the English throne.

1828 Francisco de Goya, Spanish painter and etcher, died in France aged 82.

1850 Madame Tussaud, Swiss founder of the famous wax museum in London, died.

1867 Wilbur Wright, the elder of the 2 American aviation pioneers, born near Millville in Indiana.

1875 The English Hockey Association was founded at Cannon Street Hotel in London.

1881 Earl of Halifax, British Conservative statesman and diplomat, born in Devon as Edward Frederick Lindley Wood.

1889 Charlie Chaplin, film actor, producer and director, born at Kennington in London, the son of two music hall entertainers.

1912 American pilot Harriet Quimby became the first woman to fly the English Channel, from Dover to Hardelot.

1918 Spike Milligan, English comedy actor, born at Ahmaddnagar in India as Terence Alan Milligan.

1921 Peter Ustinov, English actor and producer, born in London.

1922 Kingsley Amis, English novelist, born in London.

1940 Queen Margrethe II, Queen of Denmark, born.

1951 The British submarine 'Affray' sank in the English Channel, with the loss of 75 lives.

1953 The Royal yacht 'Britannia' was launched.

1954 Stock car racing was seen for the first time in Britain, at the Old Kent Road Stadium, New Cross in London.

1972 Apollo 16 was launched with John Young, Charles Duke and Thomas Mattingley—Young and Duke making the 5th moon landing.

17 APRIL (108)

National day of Syria.

1790 Benjamin Franklin, American scientist and statesman who helped draft the Declaration of Independence, died in Philadelphia aged 84.

1876 Ian Hay, Scottish writer, born as John Hay Beith.

1894 Nikita Khrushchev, Russian political leader, born at Kalinovka, near Kursk.

1897 Thornton Wilder, American novelist and playwright, born at Madison in Wisconsin.

1916 Sirimavo Bandaranaike, Sri Lankan stateswoman and Prime Minister, born at Ratnapura.

1937 A British attendance record at a football match was set when 149 547 watched Scotland v England at Hampden Park, Glasgow.

1946 Clare Francis, British round-the-world yachtswoman, born.

1961 An attempt by Cuban exiles and US forces to invade Cuba at the Bay of Pigs and overthrow Castro's Communist regime, was repulsed.

1969 All women in Britain over the age of 18 were allowed to vote—21 having been the age since 1928.

18 APRIL (109)

1689 Judge Jeffreys, Lord Chancellor notorious for his harshness at the 'Bloody Assizes' following the

Monmouth Rebellion of 1685, died in the Tower of London.

1775 The night of Paul Revere's famous ride from Charlestown to Lexington, accompanied by William Dawes, to warn the Massachusetts colonists of the arrival of British troops at the outbreak of the War of American Independence.

1820 Franz von Suppé, Austrian composer, born at Spalato.

1867 Sir Robert Smirke, British architect who designed the front facade of the British Museum at Bloomsbury, died.

1874 David Livingstone's remains were interred at Westminster Abbey—he having died in Africa on 1st May 1873.

1882 Leopold Stokowski, American conductor and musical director, born in London of Polish origin.

1906 The San Francisco earthquake and resulting fire started just before dawn.

1932 Business reply-paid envelopes were introduced in Britain by the GPO.

1949 The start of the first Scout 'Bob-a-job' week in Britain. The Republic of Ireland was proclaimed, severing ties with Britain by leaving the Commonwealth.

1955 Albert Einstein, naturalised-American physicist who propounded the theory of relativity and Nobel prize winner in 1921, died at Princeton in New Jersey.

19 APRIL (110)

1661 Postmarks were introduced in Britain by the post office.

1775 The Battle of Lexington, the opening engagement in the War of American Independence, took place near Boston.

1824 Lord Byron died of marsh fever at Missolonghi while aiding the Greek insurgents who had risen against the Turks in their fight for independence, aged only 36.

1873 Sydney Barnes, Lancashire and England cricketer, born at Smethwick in the West Midlands.

1881 Benjamin Disraeli, British Conservative statesman, twice Prime Minister and as a novelist wrote 'Coningsby', died and was buried at Hughenden near High Wycombe in Buckinghamshire. The date became known as 'Primrose Day' from his liking for this flower.

1882 Charles Darwin, English naturalist who developed the theory of evolution, died near Orpington in Kent and was buried in Westminster Abbey.

1903 Eliot Ness, American Government special agent, born at Chicago in Illinois.

1905 Jim Mollison, Scottish aviator, born at Glasgow.

1906 The San Francisco earthquake ended, resulting in 452 deaths.
Pierre Curie, French physicist who discovered radium, was run over and killed in Paris.

1932 Jayne Mansfield, American film actress, born at Bryn Mawr in Pennsylvania as Vera Jane Palmer.

1951 The initial Miss World contest took place, at the Lyceum Ballroom off the Strand in London—the winner was Miss Sweden—Kiki Haakonson.

1956 Prince Rainier of Monaco married Grace Kelly.

1958 Bobby Charlton made the first of his 106 football international appearances for England—against Scotland—and scored the first of his record 49 goals.

1967 Konrad Adenauer, West German statesman and Chancellor from 1949 to 1963, died aged 91.

1971 Russia launched the first space station, 'Salyut'.

20 APRIL (111)

1768 Canaletto, Italian painter and a pioneer of architecturally accurate cityscapes, died in Venice.

1889 Adolf Hitler, German dictator and Nazi leader, born at Braunau in Austria, the son of a Customs official, who had changed his name from Schicklgrüber.

1893 Harold Lloyd, American comedian of the silent film era, born at Burchard in Nebraska.

1902 Sir Donald Wolfit, English actor, born at Newark-on-Trent in Nottinghamshire.

1912 Bram Stoker, Dublin-born writer of the classic horror tale 'Dracula' in 1897, died in London.

1939 Battledress blouses and gaiters were first issued in the British Army.

1947 Christian X, King of Denmark since 1912, died.

1949 The first 3-day Badminton horse trials were held, at that village in Gloucestershire, the seat of the Duke of Beaufort —won by John Shedden on 'Golden Willow'.

21 APRIL (112)

1509 Death of King Henry VII at Richmond in Surrey—accession of his second son as Henry VIII.

1634 Jan van Riebeck, Dutch surgeon and founder of Cape Town, born in the Netherlands.

1782 Friedrich Froebel, German educational pioneer and founder of the kindergarten system, born at Oberweissbach.

1816 Charlotte Brontë, English novelist, born at Thornton, the eldest of 3 literary daughters of a Yorkshire clergyman.

1910 Mark Twain, American writer, especially of 'Tom Sawyer' and 'Huckleberry Finn', died at Reading in Connecticut.

1916 Anthony Quinn, American film actor, born at Chihuahua in Mexico.

1918 The legendary German air ace Manfred von Richthofen, known as the 'Red Baron', was shot down in his bright red tri-plane, and died behind the British lines.

1926 Queen Elizabeth II was born at 17 Bruton Street in London —Elizabeth Alexandra Mary—the elder daughter of King George VI.

1952 Sir Stafford Cripps, British statesman, died in Switzerland.

1960 Brasilia was inaugurated as the new capital of Brazil— planned by Lucio Costa.

1964 BBC's second television channel opened.

1966 The opening of British Parliament was televised for the first time.

1970 Bobby Charlton made his 100th football international appearance for England—against Northern Ireland at Wembley Stadium—and scored a goal.

1977 Milton 'Gummo' Marx, a Marx brother who became the family's agent and manager, died at Palm Springs in California.

1500 Brazil was discovered by Pedro Alvarez Cabral, who claimed it on behalf of the King of Portugal.

1662 The Royal Society was constituted by Royal Charter from Charles II.

1707 Henry Fielding, English novelist, born at Sharpham Park, Glastonbury, the son of an Army general.

1724 Immanuel Kant, German philosopher, born at Königsberg in East Prussia, the son of a saddler.

1778 James Hargreaves, English inventor of the spinning jenny in 1764, died at Nottingham.

1806 Villeneuve, French admiral, died at Rennes, having stabbed himself on his way home after captivity in England.

1833 Richard Trevithick, English engineer and pioneer of the steam railway locomotive, died at Dartford in Kent.

1838 The British ship 'Sirius' reached Sandy Hook, New York to become the first to cross the Atlantic under steam power only—having left Queenstown, now Cobh, on 4th April.

1881 Alexander Kerensky, Russian politician and Prime Minister until overthrown by the Bolsheviks, born at Simbirsk (now Ulyanovsk).

1884 An earthquake occurred in East Anglia, killing 4.

1904 Robert Oppenheimer, American physicist who developed the US atomic bomb at Los Alamos, born in New York City.

1908 Sir Henry Campbell-Bannerman, British statesman and Liberal Prime Minister, died.

1912 Kathleen Ferrier, British contralto singer, born at Higher Walton in Lancashire.

1915 Germany introduced poison gas, at Ypres.

1916 Yehudi Menuhin, American violin virtuoso and child prodigy, born in New York City.

1933 Sir Frederick Henry Royce, English car manufacturer of Rolls Royce Ltd., died.

1938 Glen Campbell, American singer and entertainer, born at Billstown in Arkansas.

1969 Robin Knox Johnston arrived back at Falmouth in his yacht 'Suhaili' after 312 days, having completed the earliest non-stop solo circumnavigation of the earth.

23 APRIL (114)

St George's Day—national day of England.

1564 The traditional date of the birth of William Shakespeare at Stratford-on-Avon, the third of 8 children of a tanner.

1616 Miguel de Cervantes, Spanish novelist, best known for his masterpiece 'Don Quixote', died at Madrid.
William Shakespeare, playwright and poet, died.

1661 The coronation of King Charles II took place.

1702 The coronation of Queen Anne took place.

1775 Joseph Turner, English landscape and seascape painter, born at Covent Garden in London, the son of a barber.

1791 James Buchanan, American Democrat statesman and 15th President, born at Stony Batter near Mercersburg in Pennsylvania, the son of a farmer.

1850 William Wordsworth, English poet and Poet Laureate from 1843. died at Rydal Mount, Grasmere in the Lake District aged 80.

1861 Viscount Allenby, British Army commander, born at Brackenhurst in Nottinghamshire.

1891 Sergei Prokofiev, Russian composer of 'Peter and the Wolf', born at Sontsovka in the Ukraine.

1897 Lester Pearson, Canadian statesman and Liberal Prime Minister, born at Newtonbrook in Ontario.

1915 Rupert Brooke, English poet, died of blood poisoning on the Greek island of Skyros on his way to the Dardanelles.

1924 The Empire Exhibition opened at the Wembley Stadium in London.

1928 Shirley Temple, American child film star, born at Santa Monica in California—is now Mrs Charles Black.

1965 The Pennine Way—250 miles long from Edale in Derbyshire to Kirk Yetholm in Roxburghshire—opened.

1967 Russian Soyuz I was launched, and after completing 17 orbits crashed on re-entry, 'on the Steppes of Orenburg', killing Vladimir Komarov.

1968 5p and 10p decimal coins were issued in Britain.

24 APRIL

1743 Edmund Cartwright, British inventor of the power loom in 1785, born at Marnham in Nottinghamshire.

1800 The United States Library of Congress, the largest in the world, was founded, on Capitol Hill at Washington, DC.

1815 Anthony Trollope, English post-office official and novelist, born in London.

1856 Philippe Pétain, French statesman and Army marshal, born at Cauchy-à-la-Tour.

1882 Lord Dowding, British Air Force commander, responsible for victory in the Battle of Britain, born at Moffat, Scotland

1889 Sir Stafford Cripps, British statesman, born in London.

1892 Jack Hulbert, English actor, born at Ely in Cambridgeshire.

1895 Captain Joshua Slocum set out on his single-handed voyage round the world, from Boston in the 36 ft sloop 'Spray'—completed the circumnavigation on 27th June 1898.

1906 William Joyce, British traitor and Nazi collaborator, born at Brooklyn, New York City.

1916 Roger Casement was arrested in Ireland after landing from a German submarine.
The Easter rebellion took place in Dublin against British rule in Ireland—ended on 29th—was followed by reprisals by British troops, called the 'Black and Tans'.

1927 The English Table Tennis Association was formed.

1934 Shirley MacLaine, American film actress, born at Richmond in Virginia as Shirley Beaty *(sic)*, the younger sister of fellow actor Warren Beatty.

1942 Barbra Streisand, American singer and film actress, born at Brooklyn, New York.

1970 After a national referendum Gambia became a Republic within the Commonwealth—having been a British colony since 1843.

China launched her first satellite.

25 APRIL

Anzac day.

The last date on which Easter can fall.

1284 King Edward II born in Caernarvon Castle, the third son of Edward I.

1599 Oliver Cromwell, British soldier, statesman and Lord Protector of England, born at Huntingdon in Cambridgeshire.

1744 Anders Celsius, Swedish astronomer who devised the centigrade temperature scale in 1742, died.

1769 Sir Marc Isambard Brunel, British engineer, born at Hacqueville near Rouen in France.

1792 The guillotine was first used, in Paris at the Place de Grève —the victim was a young highwayman named Pelletier.

Rouget de Lisle, a French Army captain, completed the words and music for his country's national anthem 'La Marseillaise', when stationed at Strasbourg.

1800 William Cowper, English poet and writer of hymns, died at East Dereham in Norfolk.

1843 The Royal yacht 'Victoria and Albert' was launched at Pembroke in South Wales.

1859 Work began on the construction of the 100-mile Suez Canal, under the direction of its planner Ferdinand de Lesseps—was opened on 16th November 1869.

1872 C. B. Fry, English all-round sportsman, born at Croydon in Surrey.

1873 Walter de la Mare, English poet and novelist, born at Charlton in Kent.

1874 Guglielmo Marconi, Italian physicist and radio pioneer, born at Bologna.

1878 Anna Sewell, English authoress, best remembered for her book 'Black Beauty', died.

1895 Sir Stanley Rous, English football administrator, born.

1908 Ed Murrow, American broadcaster, born at Greensboro in North Carolina.

1918 Ella Fitzgerald, American jazz singer, born at Newport News in Virginia.

1947 Johann Cruyff, Dutch international footballer, born.

1959 The St Lawrence Seaway, linking the Great Lakes to the Atlantic, was opened jointly by Queen Elizabeth II and President Eisenhower.

1960 US nuclear submarine 'Triton' surfaced at St Paul's Rock after a 3-month submerged circumnavigation of the earth.

1976 Sir Carol Reed, British film director, died.

26 APRIL (117)

1731 Daniel Defoe, English writer, best known as author of 'Robinson Crusoe' and 'Moll Flanders', died.

1765 Emma, Lady Hamilton, mistress of Lord Nelson, born as Emily Lyon at the village of Ness in Cheshire.

1812 Alfred Krupp, German armaments manufacturer, born at Essen in the Ruhr.

1865 John Wilkes Booth, the assassin of Abraham Lincoln, died of a bullet wound resisting arrest in a burning barn on a farm near Bowling Green in Virginia.

1880 Michel Fokine, Russian-American dancer, choreographer and founder of modern ballet, born at St Petersburg.

1894 Rudolf Hess, Nazi leader and Hitler's deputy, born at Alexandria in Egypt.

1918 Fanny Blankers-Koen, Dutch athlete of distinction, born at Amsterdam.

1923 King George VI, then the Duke of York, married Lady Elizabeth Bowes-Lyon in Westminster Abbey.

1942 The world's worst mine disaster took place, in Honkeiko Colliery in China, resulting in 1572 deaths.

1964 The Republic of Tanzania was formed by the union of Tanganyika and Zanzibar, with Julius Nyerere as its first President.

1970 Gypsy Rose Lee, American entertainer famed for her striptease act, died.

1980 Cicely Courtneidge, British actress, died aged 87.

27 APRIL (118)

National day of both Sierra Leone and Togo.

1521 Ferdinand Magellan, Portuguese navigator, was killed by natives on the island of Mactan in the Philippines on his voyage round the world.

1737 Edward Gibbon, English historian, born at Putney in London, the son of a country gentleman.

1791 Samuel Morse, American portrait painter and inventor of the famous code, born at Charlestown in Massachusetts.

1822 Ulysses Grant, American general of the Union Army, Republican statesman and 18th President, born at Point Pleasant in Ohio, the son of a tanner.

1828 Regent's Park of 464 acres in North West London was opened.

1840 Edward Whymper, English mountaineer and first to climb the Matterhorn in 1865, born in London.

1882 Ralph Waldo Emerson, American philosopher and poet, died at Concord in Massachusetts.

1904 C. Day-Lewis, British novelist, poet and Poet Laureate, born at Sligo in the Republic of Ireland.

1908 The annual Football Association Charity Shield was first played for—Manchester United being the initial winners.

1927 Coretta King, civil-rights leader and wife of Martin Luther King, born at Marion in Alabama, née Scott.

1932 The London to Cape Town airline service was inaugurated.

1961 Sierra Leone, Republic of West Africa, achieved full independence within the Commonwealth.

1972 Kwame Nkrumah, ex-Ghanaian Prime Minister and President, died.

1442 King Edward IV born at Rouen, the son of Richard, Duke of York.

1603 The funeral of Queen Elizabeth I took place at Westminster Abbey.

1758 James Monroe, American Republican statesman and 5th President, born in Westmoreland County, Virginia.

1770 Captain Cook in the 'Endeavour' reached Australia, at a point in New South Wales they named Sting Ray Bay—found to be a botanist's paradise, it was later re-named Botany Bay.

1788 Maryland, the Old Line or Free State, became the 7th state of the Union.

1789 The mutiny on the 'Bounty' took place in the early hours off Tofua in the Friendly Islands in the South Seas, led by Fletcher Christian. Captain Bligh and 17 men reached Timor—the mutineers settled on and colonised Pitcairn Island.

1801 Lord Shaftesbury, British social reformer, born in London as Anthony Ashley Cooper.

1878 Lionel Barrymore, American film actor, born at Philadelphia as Lionel Blythe—the eldest of the acting trio.

1889 Antonio Salazar, Portuguese long-serving Prime Minister and dictator, born at Vimiero near Coimbra.

1923 The first English FA Cup final at Wembley Stadium in London was staged—Bolton Wanderers defeating West Ham United 2-0.

1924 Kenneth Kaunda, Zambia's first President, born at Lubwa.

1936 Farouk became King of Egypt on the death of his father, King Fuad I.

1942 Mike Brearley, Middlesex and England cricketer, born.

1945 Benito Mussolini, Italian dictator and creator of Fascism, was executed with his mistress Claretta Petacci near Azzano by Italian partisans as they tried to flee the country.

1967 Muhammad Ali was stripped of his title by the World Boxing authorities for refusing to serve in the US forces.

National day of Japan.

1769 The Duke of Wellington, British soldier of distinction, statesman and public official, born at Dublin as Arthur Wellesley.
(Some authorities say 1st May.)

1818 Alexander II, Tsar of Russia, born at St Petersburg, the son of Tsar Nicholas I.

1879 Sir Thomas Beecham, English conductor, born at St Helens in Lancashire, the son of a manufacturer of patent medicines.

1895 Sir Malcolm Sargent, English conductor, born.

1899 'Duke' Ellington, American jazz musician and composer, born at Washington, DC as Edward Kennedy Ellington, the son of a butler in the service of the White House.

1901 Hirohito, Emperor of Japan, born in Tokyo.

1913 The improved version of the zip fastener as we know it today, was patented by a young Swedish engineer Gideon Sundback from Hoboken, New Jersey.

1929 Jeremy Thorpe, British politician and leader of the Liberal Party, born.

1933 Players were first numbered, in the English FA Cup final at Wembley Stadium—the numbers running from 1 to 22— with Manchester City having the higher set of numbers.

1947 Johnny Miller, American golf champion, born at San Francisco.

1980 Sir Alfred Hitchcock, London-born director known for suspense thriller films, died in Hollywood aged 80.

30 APRIL (121)

National day of the Netherlands.

1789 George Washington was inaugurated as the first President of the USA, on the balcony of New York's Federal Hall, with John Adams as vice-President.

1803 USA purchased Louisiana from France, the deal was completed by President Thomas Jefferson—working out at a little under 3 cents an acre.

1804 Shrapnel was first used in warfare, by the British against the Dutch in Surinam.

1812 Louisiana, the Pelican State, became the 18th state of the Union.

1870 Franz Lehar, Hungarian composer, born at Komarom, the son of a military bandmaster.

1883 Edouard Manet, French Impressionist painter, died in Paris.

1909 Juliana, Queen of the Netherlands, born at The Hague.

1938 The English FA Cup final at Wembley Stadium, between Preston North End and Huddersfield Town, was the first to be televised live.

1945 Adolf Hitler committed suicide with his wife Eva Braun, in his underground bunker beneath the Chancellory in Berlin.

1980 Juliana abdicated as Queen of the Netherlands in favour of her daughter Beatrix.

1 MAY (122)

1672 Joseph Addison, English poet, essayist and co-founder of 'The Spectator', born the son of the rector of Milston in Wiltshire.

1700 John Dryden, English poet and Poet Laureate for over 20 years, died in London.

1707 The Union of Scotland and England was proclaimed.

1841 47 persons left Independence in Missouri on the first emigrant wagon train—reached Stanislaus River in California on 4th November.

1851 The Great Exhibition, housed in the Crystal Palace in London's Hyde Park, was opened by Queen Victoria.

1873 David Livingstone was found dead at Chitambo—kneeling by his bedside in an attitude of prayer.

1896 General Mark Clark, US Army commander, born at Madison Barracks, New York of a military father.

1904 Antonin Dvorak, Czech composer, noted for his symphony 'From the New World', died.

1916 Glenn Ford, American film actor, born at Quebec in Canada.

1931 The Empire State Building on New York's 5th Avenue was completed—its 102 floors rising to 1250 feet.

1933 The Britain to India telephone service was inaugurated.

1945 Joseph Goebbels, Nazi leader and propagandist, committed suicide in a Berlin bunker after killing his wife and 6 children.

1949 Britain's gas industry was nationalised.

1952 William Fox, American film impresario and founder of 20th Century Fox, died in New York.

1961 Betting shops opened in Britain.

2 MAY (123)

1519 Leonardo da Vinci, Italian artist and man of science, noted for his painting of the 'Mona Lisa', died at the Château Cloux near Amboise.

1729 Catharine the Great, Empress of Russia, born at Stettin in Germany.

1859 Jerome K. Jerome, English humorous writer, born at Walsall in Staffordshire.

1860 Theodor Herzl, Hungarian Jew, founder of Zionism, born in the capital Budapest.

1892 Baron Manfred von Richthofen, German air ace of World War I, known as the 'Red Baron', born in Schweidnitz in Prussia to aristocratic parents.

1903 Dr Benjamin Spock, American pediatrician, born at New Haven in Connecticut.

1904 Bing Crosby, born at Tacoma in Washington as Harry Lillis Crosby.

1926 Clive Jenkins, British trade union leader, born.

1953 King Hussein II formally acceded as King of Jordan, succeeding his father, King Talal, deposed the previous August.

1957 Senator Joe McCarthy, American politician and Republican Senator noted for his campaign against Communism, died.

1959 Chapelcross nuclear power station, the first in Scotland, opened.

1964 Nancy, Lady Astor, the first woman to sit in the House of Commons, in 1919, died aged 84.

1969 The British passenger liner 'QE 2' ('Queen Elizabeth 2') went on its maiden voyage.

1972 J. Edgar Hoover, American founder and head of the FBI from 1924, died at Washington, DC.

3 MAY (124)

1844 Richard D'Oyly Carte, English theatrical impresario, known for his productions of Gilbert and Sullivan operettas, born.

1845 Thomas Hood, English poet and humorist, died at Finchley Road in London after a long illness.

1898 Golda Meir, Israeli Prime Minister, born at Kiev in Russia as Golda Mabovitch (Mabovitz), the daughter of a carpenter.

1903 The first electric train ran in the Mersey Railway tunnel.

1920 Sugar Ray Robinson, American boxer and world champion, born at Detroit in Michigan as Walker Smith.

1934 Henry Cooper, British long-reigning heavyweight boxing champion, born at Camberwell in London.

1936 Engelbert Humperdinck, British pop singer, born at Madras in India as Arnold George Dorsey.

1948 Peter Oosterhuis, British golfer, born.

1951 The Festival of Britain in London was opened by King George VI—ended on 30th September.

4 MAY (125)

1471 The Battle of Tewkesbury took place in Gloucestershire, the scene of a Yorkist victory in the last encounter in the War of the Roses.

1494 The West Indian island of Jamaica was discovered by Columbus.

1655 Bartolommeo Cristofori, Italian craftsman who developed the first piano, born in Padua.

1780 The first Derby horse race classic for 3-year-olds over a distance of 1½ miles was run at Epsom—won by Sir Charles Bunbury's 'Diomed'.

1820 Joseph Whitaker, English publisher, born in London, the son of a silversmith.

1896 The British newspaper 'Daily Mail', founded by Lord Northcliffe, was first published.

1926 The General Strike in England started, in response to the national lockout of the coalminers—ended on 12th.

1929 Audrey Hepburn, British actress and Oscar winner in 1953, born at Brussels in Belgium.

1953 The Duke of Edinburgh received his pilot's wings.

1979 Margaret Thatcher became Britain's first female Prime Minister.

1980 Marshal Tito, President of Yugoslavia since 1953, died after a long illness aged 87.

5 MAY (126)

1760 The hangman's drop was used for the first time, at Tyburn in London, for the execution of Earl Ferrers.

1818 Karl Marx, German social philosopher, radical leader and 'Father of Communism', born at Trier, the son of a Jewish lawyer.

1821 Napoleon Bonaparte died of cancer in exile on the Atlantic island of St Helena.

1835 Belgium's national railway first ran—from Brussels to Malines.

1904 Sir Gordon Richards, 26 times English champion jockey, born at Oakengates in Shropshire, the son of a miner.

1906 Mary Astor, American film actress, born at Quincy in Illinois as Lucille Langehanke.

1913 Tyrone Power, American film actor, born at Cincinnati in Ohio.

1915 Alice Faye, American singer and film actress, born in New York City as Alice Leppert.

1923 Roy Dotrice, British actor, born on the Channel Island of Guernsey.

1928 Dixie Dean of Everton scored 3 goals against Arsenal to take his season's total to a record 60.

1930 Amy Johnson took off from Croydon on her historic solo flight to Australia in a Gipsy Moth named 'Jason'—arrived on 24th.

1941 Emperor Haile Selassie returned to Ethiopia from exile in England after the liberation of his country by British forces.

1961 Alan Shepard became the first American spaceman, in a Mercury capsule Freedom VII.

1967 Britain's first satellite Ariel III was launched from Vandenburg Air Base in California.

6 MAY (127)

1626 Manhattan Island, a borough of New York City, was bought from the local Red Indians by Peter Minuit for goods and trinkets to the equivalent value of 24 dollars.

1758 Robespierre, French Revolutionary leader, born at Arras.

1840 The first adhesive British stamps, the penny black and the twopenny blue, introduced by Sir Rowland Hill, were officially issued by the GPO.

1851 Linus Yale patented the lock that bears his name.

1856 Robert Peary, American Arctic explorer, born at Cresson Springs in Pennsylvania.
Sigmund Freud, Austrian neurologist and pioneer of psychoanalysis, born at Freiburg in Moravia.

1882 Epping Forest in Essex, was opened as a Park by Queen Victoria.
The Phoenix Park murders by the 'Irish Invincibles' took place in Dublin—the victims were Lord Cavendish and Thomas Burke.

1894 Sir Alan Cobham, British aviator, born.

1895 Rudolph Valentino, American film actor and romantic idol, born at Castellaneta in Southern Italy, the son of a vet.

1910 Death of King Edward VII after a short illness—accession of his son as George V.

103

1913 Stewart Granger, British film actor, born in London as James Stewart.

1915 Orson Welles, American film actor, director and producer, born at Kenosha in Wisconsin.

1937 The 804-foot German airship 'Hindenburg' was burned at its moorings at Lakehurst, New Jersey, killing 36 of the 97 people aboard.

1954 Roger Bannister ran the first sub four-minute mile, on the Iffley Road track at Oxford, in 3 minutes 59.4 seconds.

1960 Princess Margaret was married to Antony Armstrong-Jones in Westminster Abbey.

7 MAY (128)

1812 Robert Browning, English poet, born at Camberwell in London.

1832 Greece was proclaimed an independent kingdom, with Otto I as King.

1833 Johannes Brahms, German composer and pianist, born at Hamburg, the son of a poor orchestral musician.

1840 Peter Ilyich Tchaikovsky, Russian composer, born at Votkinsk, the son of a Government mines inspector.

1847 Lord Rosebery, British Liberal statesman and Prime Minister, born in London.

1890 James Nasmyth, Scottish engineer and inventor of the first steam hammer, died in London.

1901 Gary Cooper, American film actor and twice Oscar winner, born at Helena in Montana as Frank James Cooper.

1909 Edwin Land, American inventor of the Polaroid lens and the instant camera, born at Bridgeport in Connecticut.

1915 The 762-foot Cunard passenger liner 'Lusitania', captained by William Thomas Turner, was torpedoed by a German submarine about 10 miles off Old Head of Kinsale, Ireland, and sank in 18 minutes with the loss of 1198 lives.

1925 William Lever, English manufacturer and builder of the great Lever Brothers enterprise, died as Viscount Leverhulme.

1932 French President Paul Doumer was assassinated by a Russian émigré.

1940 George Lansbury, British politician and Labour Party leader, died in London aged 81.

1957 Eliot Ness, US Government agent, best known as the special FBI agent who headed the investigation of Al Capone in Chicago, died.

8 MAY (129)

The festival of the Floral Dance is held annually at Helston in Cornwall.

1701 'Captain' Kidd was tried at London's Old Bailey for piracy—was hanged on 23rd.

1794 Antoine Lavoisier, French chemist who identified and named oxygen, was guillotined in Paris.

1828 John Henri Dunant, Swiss philanthropist and founder of the International Red Cross, born at Geneva.

1884 Harry S. Truman, American Democrat statesman and 33rd President, born at Lamar in Missouri.

1886 Dr John Pemberton first produced the world's top-selling soft drink Coca-Cola® at Atlanta in Georgia.

1896 Yorkshire's score against Warwickshire at Edgbaston reached 887 to record the highest innings total in a county cricket championship game.

1902 The volcano of Mount Pelée on the French Caribbean island of Martinique erupted—within 3 minutes the town of St Pierre was totally destroyed and about 30 000 people killed.

1903 Paul Gauguin, French post-Impressionist painter, died.

1921 Sweden abolished capital punishment.

1926 David Attenborough, British broadcaster, born.

1927 Speedway racing took place in Britain for the first time, at Camberley Heath.

1932 Sonny Liston, American heavyweight boxing champion, born.

1936 Jack Charlton, English football international and club manager, born at Ashington in Northumberland.

1945 The war in Europe officially ended.

1955 The European Cup for the football league champions of the respective nations was approved by FIFA.

1962 Trolleybuses ran for the last time in London.

9 MAY

National day of Czechoslovakia.

1671 Disguised as a clergyman, Colonel Thomas Blood attempted to steal the Crown jewels from the Tower of London.

1800 John Brown, American anti-slavery crusader, born at Torrington in Connecticut.

1850 Joseph Gay-Lussac, French chemist and physicist, died.

1860 (James Matthew) J. M. Barrie, Scottish playwright and novelist, born at 9 Brechin Road, Kirriemuir, the son of a weaver.

1873 Howard Carter, English Egyptologist who discovered the tomb of King Tutankhamun in 1922, born at Swaffham in Norfolk.

1926 Richard Byrd, American explorer, made the first flight over the North Pole, with pilot Floyd Bennett.

1927 Canberra was inaugurated as the new capital of Australia, replacing Melbourne.

1936 Glenda Jackson, English film actress and Oscar winner, born at Hoylake in Merseyside.
Terry Downes, British boxer and former world lightweight champion, born at Paddington in London.

1946 Victor Emmanuel III, King of Italy since 1900, abdicated—the monarchy being replaced by a Republic.

1949 Prince Rainier III became Head of State of Monaco, succeeding his grandfather Prince Louis II.
The first self-service launderette was opened in Britain, at Queensway in London.

10 MAY

1798 George Vancouver, British navigator, explorer and surveyor of the Pacific coast of North America, died.

1818 Paul Revere, American patriot famed for his night ride in 1775 to warn of the advance of British troops, died at Boston in Massachusetts aged 83.

1838 John Wilkes Booth, American actor and assassin of President Abraham Lincoln, born at Baltimore in Maryland.

1857 The Indian Mutiny or Sepoy Rebellion, against biting off the greased end of the cartridges for the new Lee Enfield rifles, broke out at Meerut—ended in July 1858.

1863 Thomas Jonathan 'Stonewall' Jackson, American Confederate general, was killed by his own soldiers near Chancellorsville in Virginia.

1886 The issuing of football international caps was approved by the FA Council.

1899 Fred Astaire, American film actor and dancer, born at Omaha in Nebraska as Frederick Austerlitz, the son of Austrian immigrants.

1904 Sir Henry Morton Stanley, British journalist and explorer in Africa, died in London.

1907 Mother's Day, initiated in America by Miss Anna Jarvis, was first held at Philadelphia.

1920 John Wesley Hyatt, American inventor and discoverer of celluloid, the first synthetic plastic, died.

1934 The Police Training College at Hendon in London was opened.

1940 Neville Chamberlain resigned as Prime Minister.
Belgium was invaded and occupied by German forces.

1941 Rudolf Hess, German Nazi leader and Hitler's deputy, parachuted and landed at Eaglesham in Scotland, apparently hoping to negotiate a separate peace, but was imprisoned.

1954 George Hirst, Yorkshire and England cricketer, died at Huddersfield.

1977 Joan Crawford, American film actress and Academy Award (Oscar) winner in 1945 for her part in 'Mildred Pierce', died in New York.

1978 Liverpool won the European Cup at football for the second successive year.

1980 Paul Allen, at 17 years and 256 days, became the youngest footballer to appear in a FA Cup final, playing for West Ham United against Arsenal.

11 MAY (132)

National day of Laos.

1745 The Battle of Fontenoy took place in Belgium, the scene of Marshal de Saxe's French victory over British and allied forces during the War of the Austrian Succession.

1778 William Pitt the Elder, British statesman and chief minister who became Earl of Chatham, died at Hayes.

1812 Spencer Perceval, British Tory Prime Minister from 1809, was assassinated in the Lobby of the House of Commons by a merchant named Francis Bellingham.

1858 Minnesota, the Gopher or North Star State, became the 32nd state of the Union.

1871 Sir John Herschel, English astronomer and pioneer of celestial photography, died in London.

1888 Irving Berlin, American composer, born at Tyumen in Eastern Russia as Israel Baline.

1892 Margaret Rutherford, English stage and film actress, born in London.

1904 Salvador Dali, Spanish Surrealist painter, born at Figueras in Upper Catalonia.

1912 Phil Silvers, American comedy film actor, born at Brooklyn in New York as Philip Silversmith.

1922 The British radio station '2LO' was established, at Marconi House in London's Strand.

1940 Winston Churchill became head of the wartime Coalition Government.

12 MAY (133)

1812 Edward Lear, English 'nonsense' poet and artist, born at Highgate in London.

1820 Florence Nightingale, English hospital reformer and founder of the modern nursing profession, born in Italy at Florence—after which place she was named.

1828 Dante Gabriel Rossetti, English poet and painter, born in London to exiled Italian parents as Gabriel Charles Dante.

1860 Sir Charles Barry, English architect responsible for the new Palace of Westminster, died.

1870 Manitoba, previously called the Red River Colony and controlled by the Hudson Bay Company, was purchased by Canada and made a province.

Rules were drafted for the game of water polo, by the London Swimming Association.

1871 Daniel Auber, French composer of operas, died in Paris.

1884 Bedrich Smetana, Czech composer, notably the opera 'The Bartered Bride', died in a Prague mental hospital.

1903 Wilfrid Hyde White, British film actor, born.

1906 Horatio Bottomley began the publication of the British weekly magazine 'John Bull'.

1926 The General Strike in England ended after 9 days.

1928 Burt Bacharach, American pianist and composer, born at Kansas City in Missouri, the son of a newspaper columnist.

1935 'Alcoholics Anonymous', a self-help organisation, was founded by William Wilson at Akron in Ohio.

1937 The coronation of King George VI took place.

1967 John Masefield, English poet and Poet Laureate from 1930, died.

13 MAY (134)

1607 Captain John Smith and 105 Cavaliers in 3 ships landed on the Virginia coast and started the first permanent English settlement in the New World, at Jamestown.

1717 Maria Theresa, Empress of Austria, born in Vienna.

1835 John Nash, English architect, especially of Regent's Park and Brighton Pavilion, died on the Isle of Wight.

1842 Sir Arthur Sullivan, English composer of light operas in collaboration with W. S. Gilbert, born at Lambeth in London, the son of a bandmaster.

1884 Cyrus Hall McCormick, American inventor of the first successful reaping machine, died at Chicago.

1907 Daphne du Maurier, British novelist, author of 'Rebecca', born in London.

1914 Joe Louis, American heavyweight boxer and world champion known as 'The Brown Bomber', born in Lafayette, Alabama as Joseph Louis Barrow.

1930 Fridtjof Nansen, Norwegian Arctic explorer and later statesman and Nobel Prize winner in 1922, died at Lysaker in Norway.

1949 Britain's first jet bomber, the 'Canberra', was test flown at Warton in Lancashire.

1961 Gary Cooper, American film actor and twice Academy Award (Oscar) winner--1941 for the title role in 'Sergeant York' and 1952 for his part in 'High Noon'—died.

1981 An attempt was made on the life of Pope John Paul II in St Peter's Square in Rome—the would-be assassin was Nehmet Ali Hagca.

14 MAY (135)

National day of Paraguay.

1643 Louis XIV ascended the throne of France, aged 4 years 231 days, on the death of his father Louis XIII—and reigned for over 72 years.

1686 Gabriel Fahrenheit, German physicist and inventor of the mercury thermometer, born at Danzig.

1727 Thomas Gainsborough, English landscape and portrait painter, born at Sudbury in Suffolk, the son of a cloth merchant.

1771 Robert Owen, British industrialist and social reformer, born at Newtown in Wales, the son of a saddler.

1796 Edward Jenner made his first vaccination against smallpox, and laid the foundation for modern immunology.

1842 The British periodical 'Illustrated London News' was first published.

1885 Otto Klemperer, German musical director and conductor, born at Breslau.

1912 The Royal Flying Corps was created.

1919 Henry John Heinz, American food manufacturer and founder of the company that bears his name, died.

1921 The British Legion was founded in London by Earl Haig—became the Royal British Legion in 1971.

1925 Sir Rider Haggard, English novelist, notably 'King Solomon's Mines', died.

1926 Eric Morecambe, English comedian of the Morecambe and Wise team, born at Morecambe in Lancashire as Eric Bartholomew.

1936 Viscount Allenby, British army commander in Palestine in World War I, died.

1940 Local Defence Volunteers (later called Home Guard) was formed in Britain as a makeshift anti-invasion force.

1948 Israel was established as a Jewish state following the partition of Palestine.

1967 Liverpool's Roman Catholic Cathedral was opened.

1973 America's Skylab I was launched—eventually returning to earth on 11th July 1979, after 34 981 orbits.

1977 Bobby Moore retired from professional football on his 1000th appearance in all matches, for West Ham United, Fulham and England.

15 MAY (136)

1800 At the theatre in Drury Lane an attempt to assassinate King George III was made by James Hatfield.

1847 Daniel O'Connell, Irish Catholic political leader, called 'The Liberator', died at Genoa.

1858 The present Royal Opera House at Covent Garden in London (the third) was opened.

1859 Pierre Curie, French physicist, born in Paris the son of a French physician.

1892 Jimmy Wilde, British flyweight boxing champion known as the 'Mighty Atom', born in Wales.

1895 Joseph Whitaker, English publisher who founded 'Whitaker's Almanack' in 1869, died.

1909 James Mason, British film actor, born at Huddersfield in Yorkshire.

1928 The Flying Doctor Service was inaugurated in Australia, at Cloncurry in Queensland—Dr Vincent Welsh was the first.

1937 Philip Snowden, British Labour statesman, died at Tilford in Surrey.

1940 Nylon stockings were first launched in the United States.

1941 Britain's first jet-propelled aircraft, designed by Frank Whittle, flew for the first time, at Cranwell.

1948 In one day's cricket Australia scored a record 721 runs, against Essex at Southchurch Park, Southend.

1957 Britain dropped her first hydrogen bomb, over Christmas Island in the South Pacific.

1972 Governor George Wallace of Alabama was seriously crippled after being shot in an assassination attempt at Laurel in Maryland.

16 MAY (137)

1568 Mary, Queen of Scots sailed from Port Mary across the Solway Firth to begin her exile in England.

1703 Charles Perrault, French author and writer of fairy tales, including 'Little Red Ridinghood' and 'Cinderella', died in Paris.

1811 The Battle of Albuera took place in Spain, the scene of a combined English, Portuguese and Spanish victory over the French under Marshal Soult.

1831 David Hughes, Anglo-American inventor of the teleprinter and the microphone, born in London.

1835 Felicia Hemans, English poet who wrote 'The boy stood on the burning deck', died in Dublin.

1905 Henry Fonda, American film actor, born at Grand Island in Nebraska.

1908 Britain's first diesel submarine, appropriately called D 1, was launched at Barrow.

1913 Woody Herman, American jazz clarinettist and bandleader, born at Milwaukee in Wisconsin as Woodrow Charles.

1919 Liberace, American pianist and entertainer, born into a musical family at West Allis in Wisconsin as Wladziu Valentino Liberace.

1929 Film Academy Awards were first presented in Hollywood—the name 'Oscar' for the trophy was first used in 1931, after a Mr Oscar Pierce of Texas.

1938 The WVS (Women's Voluntary Service) was started in Britain by the Marchioness of Reading—it became 'Royal' in 1966.

1943 The Mohne, Eder and Sorpe dams in Germany were breached by 19 Lancaster bombers of 617 Squadron from Scampton, led by Guy Gibson, using special 'skip' bombs invented by Dr Barnes Wallis.

17 MAY (138)

National day of Norway.

1749 Edward Jenner, English physician and pioneer in vaccinations, born at Berkeley vicarage in Gloucestershire.

1875 The first Kentucky Derby was run, at Churchill Downs, Louisville in Kentucky.

1889 'Tich' Freeman, Kent and England cricketer, born at Lewisham.

1890 'Comic Cuts', the first comic paper, was issued in London.

1900 A small British force under Baden-Powell at Mafeking, in the Cape Province of South Africa, was relieved after holding out for 217 days during the siege by the Boers under General Piet Cronje.

1911 Maureen O'Sullivan, American film actress, born at Bayle in Ireland.

1920 KLM, the national airline of the Netherlands, opened its first scheduled service—Amsterdam to London.

1935 Paul Dukas, French composer, best known for 'The Sorcerer's Apprentice', died in Paris.

1960 The Kariba Dam, on the Zambesi River, was opened by Queen Elizabeth, the Queen Mother.

1970 Nigel Balchin, English novelist, died.

1804 Napoleon Bonaparte was proclaimed Emperor of France.

1868 Nicholas II, the last Tsar of Russia, born the son of Alexander III.

1872 Bertrand Russell, British philosopher and mathematician, born at Ravenscroft near Trelleck, Monmouthshire in Wales.

1905 Hedley Verity, Yorkshire and England cricketer, born at Headingley, Leeds.

1909 Fred Perry, English tennis champion, born at Stockport in Cheshire.

George Meredith, English novelist and poet, died at Boxhill in Surrey aged 81.

1911 Gustav Mahler, Czech-Austrian composer, conductor and musical director, died in Vienna.

1912 Perry Como, American singer and entertainer, born at Canonsburg in Pennsylvania.

1919 Margot Fonteyn, English prima ballerina, born at Reigate in Surrey as Margaret Hookham.

1920 Pope John Paul II was born as Karolum Wojtyla in the market town of Wadowice near Cracow in Poland, the son of a junior officer in the Polish army.

1969 Apollo 10 was launched with Thomas Stafford, John Young and Eugene Cernan.

1536 Anne Boleyn, the second of Henry VIII's wives and mother of Queen Elizabeth I, was executed on Tower Green for alleged adultery.

1795 James Boswell, Scottish diarist and biographer of Dr Johnson, died in London.

1799 Pierre Beaumarchais, French playwright, notably 'The Marriage of Figaro', died in Paris.

1802 The French 'Légion d'Honneur', an order of distinction for civil or military service, was created by Napoleon.

1849 An attempt to assassinate Queen Victoria was made by William Hamilton.

1861 Dame Nellie Melba, Australian operatic singer, born at Melbourne as Helen Mitchell, the daughter of a brick-maker.

1864 Nathaniel Hawthorne, American novelist and short story writer, died at Plymouth in New Hampshire.

1879 Lady Astor, English politician and the first lady to take a seat in the House of Commons, born at Greenwood in Virginia—née Langhorne.

1898 William Ewart Gladstone, British statesman and 4 times Liberal Prime Minister, died at Hawarden Castle in North Wales aged 88.

1906 The 20 kilometre Simplon rail tunnel, between Switzerland and Italy, was officially opened.

1912 Aeroplane International Registration numbers were introduced.

1935 (Thomas Edward) T. E. Lawrence, known as Lawrence of Arabia, died as a result of a motor cycle accident 6 days previously in a Dorset country lane.

1958 Ronald Colman, British-born film actor and Academy Award (Oscar) winner in 1947 for his part in 'A Double Life', died.

1971 Ogden Nash, American poet known for his humorous verse, died at Baltimore in Maryland.

20 MAY (141)

1506 Christopher Columbus, Italian navigator and discoverer of the New World in 1492, died at Valladolid in Spain.

1588 The Spanish Armada, comprising 129 ships, under the command of the Duke of Medina, sent by Philip II in an attempt to invade England, set sail from Lisbon.

1799 Honoré de Balzac, French novelist, born at Tours, the son of the deputy Mayor.

1818 William George Fargo, co-founder of Wells-Fargo Express Co., born at Pompey in the State of New York.

1834 Lafayette, French general and statesman, died aged 76.
1867 The foundation stone of the Royal Albert Hall in London was laid.
1881 Wladyslaw Sikorski, Polish general and Prime Minister, born in the Galicia region.
1908 James Stewart, American film actor and Oscar winner, born at Indiana in Pennsylvania.
1913 The first Chelsea Flower Show opened in London.
1915 Moshe Dayan, Israeli military commander and minister, born at Deganya.
1941 The island of Crete in the East Mediterranean was invaded by German airborne forces.
1956 Sir Max Beerbohm, English writer and caricaturist, died aged 83.
1962 Bobby Moore made the first of his record 108 football international appearances for England, against Peru at Lima.
1970 Bobby Charlton scored his record 49th goal for England, against Colombia in the World Cup competition.
1975 Barbara Hepworth, English abstract sculptor, died at St Ives in Cornwall.

21 MAY (142)

1471 Albrecht Dürer, German artist and engraver, born at Nuremberg, the son of a goldsmith.
Henry VI, King of England, was murdered in the Tower of London.
1502 The South Atlantic island of St Helena was discovered by the Portuguese explorer Joao de Nova.
1688 Alexander Pope, English poet, born in London, the son of a linen draper.
1780 Elizabeth Fry, English prison reformer, born at Norwich, the daughter of a Quaker banker John Gurney.
1840 New Zealand was declared a colony of Britain.
1844 Henri Rousseau, French painter known as 'Le Douanier', born at Laval.
1894 The 35-mile Manchester Ship Canal was formally opened by Queen Victoria.

1895 Franz von Suppé, Austrian composer who wrote the overture 'Poet and Peasant', died in Vienna.

1904 The Football Federation FIFA was founded in Paris, for the better control of the game on an international basis.

1916 Daylight saving, advocated by William Willett, was introduced in Britain.

1917 Raymond Burr, American film actor, born at New Westminster in the Canadian province of British Columbia.

1927 Charles Lindbergh, US air-mail pilot, became the first to fly the Atlantic solo—from Roosevelt Field, Long Island, New York to Le Bourget airfield, Paris in 33½ hours in a single-engine monoplane 'Spirit of St Louis', to win a prize of 25 000 dollars.

1929 Lord Rosebery, British statesman and Liberal Prime Minister, died.

1930 Malcolm Fraser, Australian politician and Liberal Prime Minister, born at Melbourne in the State of Victoria.

1932 Amelia Earhart became the first woman to fly the Atlantic solo—flying from Harbor Grace in Newfoundland to Londonderry in Ireland in just under 15 hours.

22 MAY (143)

1783 William Sturgeon, English scientist who built the first practical electromagnet, born at Whittington in Lancashire.

1813 Richard Wagner, German operatic composer, born at Leipzig.

1859 Sir Arthur Conan Doyle, British novelist, creator of Sherlock Holmes, born of Irish parents at Edinburgh.

1874 Daniel Malan, South African politician responsible for the country's apartheid policy, born at Riebeck West in Cape Province.

1880 Sir Ernest Oppenheimer, South African mining magnate and philanthropist, born at Friedberg in Germany, the son of a Jewish cigar merchant.

1885 Victor Hugo, French poet and novelist, author of 'Les Misérables', died in Paris aged 83.

1897 The Blackwall tunnel under the Thames was officially opened by the Prince of Wales.

1906 Wilbur Wright patented his airplane.

1907 Laurence Olivier, English stage and film actor, born at Dorking in Surrey.

1915 The worst train disaster in the United Kingdom took place—a triple collision at Quintins Hill, near Gretna Green, Dumfries, killing 227.

1923 Stanley Baldwin began the first of his 3 terms as Conservative Prime Minister.

1925 Sir John French, British general and commander of the British Expeditionary Force in France and Belgium, died.

1972 Ceylon became the Republic of Sri Lanka within the Commonwealth.

C. Day-Lewis, English poet and Poet Laureate from 1967, died.

Margaret Rutherford, British character actress, died aged 80.

23 MAY (144)

1701 'Captain' William Kidd, Scottish privateer, was hanged at Execution Dock in London for piracy.

1706 The Battle of Ramillies took place near Louvain in Belgium, the scene of the French defeat by the allied British, Dutch and Danish armies under Marlborough in the War of the Spanish Succession.

1707 Carl Linnaeus, Swedish botanist, born as Carl Linné, the son of the parish clergyman of Rashult.

1734 Franz Anton Mesmer, Austrian physician and founder of mesmerism, born near Constance, the son of a gamekeeper.

1788 South Carolina, the Palmetto State, became the 8th state of the Union.

1795 Sir Charles Barry, English architect and designer of the new Palace of Westminster, born in London.

1797 The Nore mutiny, led by Richard Parker, against bad food and inadequate pay was started—collapsed on 30th June.

1799 Thomas Hood, English poet, born in London, the son of a bookseller.

1868 Kit Carson, American frontiersman, soldier and Indian agent, died.

1873 The North West Mounted Police were established in Canada—their name was changed to The Royal Canadian Mounted Police on 1st February 1920.

1883 Douglas Fairbanks, American film actor, born at Denver in Colorado as Douglas Elton Thomas Ullman.

1890 Herbert Marshall, American film actor, born in London.

1906 Henrik Ibsen, Norwegian playwright, best known for 'Peer Gynt', died aged 78.

1910 Artie Shaw, American clarinettist and bandleader, born in New York City as Arthur Jacob Arshawsky.

1918 Denis Compton, English international cricketer and footballer, born at Hendon in London.

1931 Whipsnade Zoo, a park in the Chiltern Hills in Bedfordshire, was opened.

1934 Bonnie and Clyde (Bonnie Parker and Clyde Barrow), notorious murderers and outlaws, were killed in an ambush near Gibland in Louisiana.

1937 John D. Rockefeller, American philanthropist and founder of the Standard Oil Company, died in Florida aged 97.

1944 John Newcombe, international tennis champion, born at Sydney in Australia.

1945 Heinrich Himmler, German Nazi leader and notorious chief of police, committed suicide.

24 MAY (145)

1543 Nicolas Copernicus, Polish founder of modern astronomy, died of apoplexy.

1743 Jean Paul Marat, French revolutionary, born at Boudry, near Neuchâtel in Switzerland.

1792 Lord Rodney, British admiral and victorious commander, died at Hanover Square in London.

1809 Dartmoor Prison at Princetown was opened—was built originally to house French prisoners of war—used for convicts from 1850.

1819 Queen Victoria was born at Kensington Palace, granddaughter of King George III and niece of King William IV.

1830 The first passenger railroad was opened in America—the Baltimore & Ohio.

1844 The first morse message over the first telegraph line was sent, from Washington to Baltimore, by its inventor Samuel Morse—'What hath God wrought'.

1870 Jan Christiaan Smuts, South African soldier, statesman and Prime Minister, born at Malmesbury in Cape Colony.

1883 The 1595-foot Brooklyn Bridge over the East River, designed by John Augustus Roebling, was opened.

1895 The first stage knighthood was conferred, on Sir Henry Irving in the Birthday Honours.

1899 Suzanne Lenglen, French tennis player and 6 times Wimbledon winner, born at Compiègne in Picardy.

1902 Empire Day was first celebrated in Britain.

1912 Joan Hammond, New Zealand soprano, born.

1930 Amy Johnson landed at Darwin in Northern Australia, having flown solo from London—in her Gipsy Moth, 'Jason'—the first woman to do so.

1941 The battle cruiser HMS Hood was sunk by the 'Bismarck' 13 miles off the coast of Greenland—only 3 of her 1421 crew survived.
Bob Dylan, American singer, born at Duluth in Minnesota as Robert Zimmerman—chose the name in honour of Dylan Thomas.

1959 Empire Day was renamed Commonwealth Day.
John Foster Dulles, American Government official and diplomat, died.

1974 'Duke' Ellington, American jazz musician, composer and pianist, died aged 75.
Giscard D'Estaing became President of France.

25 MAY (146)

National day of Jordan.

1803 Ralph Waldo Emerson, American poet and essayist, born at Boston in Massachusetts the son of a minister.

1871 The Bank Holiday Act was passed in the House of Commons.
1879 Lord Beaverbrook, English statesman and newspaper owner, born at Maple in the Canadian province of Ontario as William Maxwell Aitken.
1889 Igor Sikorsky, American aviation engineer and pioneer of the helicopter, born at Kiev.
1892 Josip Broz (Marshal Tito), Yugoslav Communist leader and President, born at Kumrovec near Klanjec.
(Some sources quote 7th May).
1898 Gene Tunney, American heavyweight boxing champion, born at Greenwich Village, New York City as James Joseph Tunney.
1913 Richard Dimbleby, English broadcaster, born.
1934 Gustav Holst, English composer of 'The Planets', died, and was buried in Chichester Cathedral.
1935 Jesse Owens, American athlete, set 6 world records within 45 minutes, at Ann Arbor in Michigan.
1939 Sir Frank Dyson, English astronomer and director of Greenwich Observatory, died.
1962 Coventry's new Cathedral was consecrated—after 6 years of building.
1967 Celtic, the Scottish champions, became the first British football club to win the European Cup—beating Internazionale 2-1 in Lisbon.

26 MAY (147)

1650 The Duke of Marlborough, British general and statesman, born as John Churchill at Ashe in Devon.
(Some sources quote 24th June).
1703 Samuel Pepys, famous English diarist, died at Clapham in London.
1799 Aleksander Pushkin, Russian poet and novelist, born at Moscow.
1805 Napoleon was crowned King of Italy, in Milan Cathedral.
1865 The American Civil War ended, with the surrender of General Kirby Smith in Texas.

1867 Queen Mary, wife of King George V, born in Kensington Palace as Princess Mary of Teck.

1868 The last public execution in England took place—Michael Barrett—outside Newgate Prison in London.

1886 Al Jolson, American entertainer, often in blackface, born at Srednik in Lithuania as Asa Yoelson.

1904 George Formby, English comedy actor and entertainer, born.

1906 Vauxhall Bridge, over the river Thames, was officially opened.

1907 John Wayne, American film actor, born at Winterset in Iowa as Marion Michael Morrison.

1908 Robert Morley, English actor, born at Semley in Wiltshire.

1909 Sir Matt Busby, Scottish international footballer and club manager, born.

1923 The annual Le Mans 24-hour race for sports cars was first held, on the old Sarthe circuit.
James Arness, American film actor, born in Minneapolis, the elder brother of fellow actor Peter Graves.

1924 Victor Herbert, Irish-born American cellist, conductor and composer, died.

1939 Charles Mayo, American surgeon and co-founder of the Mayo Clinic Foundation, died aged 78.

1950 Petrol rationing ended in Britain.

1966 British Guiana, under Burnham, became fully independent and a member of the British Commonwealth, changing its name to Guyana.

27 MAY (148)

National day of Afghanistan.

1564 John Calvin, French theologian who spread the Protestant Reformation, died.

1818 Amelia Bloomer, American campaigner for women's rights who popularised 'bloomers', born at Homer in New York.

1837 'Wild Bill' Hickok, American scout and frontier marshal, born at Troy Grove in Illinois as James Butler Hickok.

1840 Niccolo Paganini, Italian violin virtuoso and composer, died at Nice.

1863 Broadmoor Asylum, for the criminally insane, was established at Crowthorne in Berkshire.

1867 Arnold Bennett, English novelist, born near Hanley in Staffordshire the son of a solicitor.

1878 Isadora Duncan, American dancer, born at San Francisco.

1887 Frank Woolley, Kent and England cricketer, born at Tonbridge.

1897 Sir John Cockcroft, English nuclear physicist, born in Yorkshire.

1910 Robert Koch, German bacteriologist and Nobel Prize winner who discovered the bacillus of tuberculosis, died.

1911 Vincent Price, American actor best known for his roles in horror movies, born at St Louis in Missouri.
Hubert Humphrey, American Democrat politician and vice-President to Lyndon Johnson, born at Wallace in South Dakota.

1912 Sam Snead, American champion golfer, born at Hot Springs in Virginia.

1914 Sir Joseph Swan, English chemist, physicist and inventor, died in Surrey aged 85.

1922 Christopher Lee, British actor, mainly in horror films, born in London.

1923 Henry Kissinger, American Secretary of State, born at Furth in Germany.

1936 The open prison at New Hall near Wakefield in Yorkshire was opened, as the first of its kind in Britain.

1937 The 4200 foot Golden Gate Bridge, over the Golden Gate waterway at San Francisco, was opened.

1940 'Operation Dynamo', the evacuation of British and French troops from the Dunkirk beaches began—ended on 4th June.

1941 The German battleship 'Bismarck' was sunk by the battleships 'Prince of Wales', 'King George V' and 'Rodney' after torpedo attacks by Swordfish aircraft from the carrier 'Ark Royal'.

1943 Cilla Black, English pop singer, born in Liverpool as Priscilla White.

1964 Pandit Nehru, Indian statesman and first Prime Minister of independent India in 1947, died.

1981 Willie Shoemaker rode 'War Allied' to victory at Hollywood Park in California to record his 8000th winner.

28 MAY (149)

1759 William Pitt the Younger, British statesman and Tory Prime Minister, born at Hayes, near Bromley in Kent.

1843 Noah Webster, American lexicographer and originator of 'Webster's Dictionary' in 1828, died at New Haven in Connecticut aged 84.

1849 Anne Brontë, English novelist, author of 'The Tenant of Wildfell Hall', died at Scarborough in Yorkshire aged 29.

1884 Eduard Benes, Czech statesman and founder of modern Czechoslovakia, born at Kozlany in Bohemia.

1907 The first Isle of Man motor cycle TT race was held.

1908 Ian Fleming, English novelist and creator of the character 'James Bond', born in London.

1934 The Dionne quins (Emilie, Yvonne, Cécile, Marie and Annette) were born at Callender in Ontario to Mrs Oliva Dionne.

1937 Alfred Adler, Austrian psychiatrist and psychologist, died.

1940 Belgian King Leopold III surrendered to Germany.

1959 The Mermaid Theatre in London opened at Puddle Dock.

1967 Francis Chichester arrived back at Plymouth after sailing around the world single-handed in Gipsy Moth IV.

1972 The Duke of Windsor, the abdicated King Edward VIII, died in Paris aged 77.

1982 When John Paul II arrived at Gatwick airport he became the first reigning Pope to visit Great Britain.

29 MAY (150)

Oak apple day.

1500 Bartolomeu Diaz, Portuguese explorer who discovered the Cape of Good Hope in 1488, was drowned during a storm at sea.

1630 King Charles II was born at St James's Palace, the son of Charles I and Henrietta Maria of France.

1790 Rhode Island, the Ocean State, became the 13th state of the Union—and the smallest.

1829 Sir Humphry Davy, English chemist who invented the miners' safety lamp in 1815, died in Geneva.

1848 Wisconsin, the Badger State, became the 30th state of the Union.

1871 Whit Monday became the first Bank Holiday in Britain.

1874 (Gilbert Keith) G. K. Chesterton, English novelist and poet, born at Kensington in London.

1898 Beatrice Lillie, American actress, born at Toronto in the Canadian province of Ontario as Constance Sylvia Munston.

1903 Bob Hope, American comedian and film actor, born at Eltham, London as Leslie Townes Hope—emigrated to USA when he was 4.

1911 Sir William Gilbert, English writer of comic operas in collaboration with Sir Arthur Sullivan, died.

1917 John F. Kennedy, American Democrat statesman and 35th President, born at Brookline in Massachusetts, the second of 9 children.

1942 John Barrymore, American film actor, called the 'Great Profile', died.

1953 Everest, the world's highest mountain, was conquered by Edmund Hillary and Sherpa Tensing.

1968 Manchester United became the first English football club to win the European Cup—beating Benfica of Portugal 4-1 at Wembley Stadium in London.

1979 Mary Pickford, Canadian-born film actress and Academy Award (Oscar) winner in 1929 for her part in 'Coquette', died aged 86.

30 MAY (151)

1431 Joan of Arc, French peasant girl of Domrémy who became a national heroine, was burned at the stake at Rouen for heresy—was made a saint in 1920.

1536 King Henry VIII married Jane Seymour, the third of his six wives, in the Queen's Chapel, Whitehall—11 days after the execution of Anne Boleyn.

1593 Christopher Marlowe, English poet and playwright, author of 'Doctor Faustus', was mysteriously killed in a tavern brawl at Deptford, London aged 29.

1640 Peter Paul Rubens, Flemish baroque painter, died at Antwerp.

1656 The Grenadier Guards, the senior regiment of the British Army, was formed.

1672 Peter the Great, Tsar and Emperor of Russia, born at Moscow the son of Tsar Alexei.

1744 Alexander Pope, English poet, died at Twickenham in London.

1766 The 'Royal' at Bristol, the oldest theatre still in use in Britain, was opened.

1778 Voltaire, the name adopted by Francois Marie Arouet, French philosopher and historian, died in Paris aged 83.

1842 An attempt was made on the life of Queen Victoria as she was driving down Constitution Hill with Prince Albert—the would-be assassin was John Francis.

1909 Benny Goodman, American clarinettist and band leader, born at Chicago in Illinois.

1911 The 'Indianapolis 500' car race of 200 laps was inaugurated in the USA.

1912 Wilbur Wright, American airplane pioneer and first to make a controlled flight in 1903, died at Dayton in Ohio.

1922 The Lincoln Memorial in West Potomac Park was dedicated. It was designed by Henry Bacon, and the statue was made by Daniel Chester French.

1959 Auckland Harbour bridge on New Zealand's North Island was officially opened.

1960 Boris Pasternak, Russian poet and novelist, author of 'Dr Zhivago' and Nobel Prize winner in 1958 (declined), died near Moscow.

1967 Claude Rains, British-born film actor, died aged 77.

31 MAY (152)

National day of South Africa.

1594 Tintoretto, the name adopted by Jacopo Robusti, one of the greatest of Italian painters, died in Venice.

1669 Samuel Pepys discontinued his diary, which began on 1st January 1660.

1809 Franz Josef Haydn, Austrian composer, died in Vienna.

1837 Joseph Grimaldi, English clown of Italian parentage, died.

1859 'Big Ben', in the clock tower of the Houses of Parliament in London, first began recording time.

1872 Heath Robinson, British humorous artist of complex machinery which performed simple tasks, born in London.

1902 The Peace of Vereeniging was signed, ending the Boer War.

1908 Don Ameche, American film actor, born at Kenosha in Wisconsin as Dominic Felix Amici.

1910 The colonies of the Cape of Good Hope, Natal, the Transvaal and the Orange River Colony became united to form the Union of South Africa.
Elizabeth Blackwell, English-born American physician, the first woman to gain an MD degree, in 1849, died.

1911 The ill-fated British liner 'Titanic' was launched at the Harland and Wolff shipyard at Belfast.

1915 The first air raid on London took place.

1916 The Battle of Jutland was fought in the North Sea between the British fleet under Jellicoe and Beatty and the German fleet commanded by Scheer and von Hipper.

1923 Prince Rainier III, the ruling Prince of the House of Grimaldi, born at Monaco.

1930 Clint Eastwood, American film actor and director, born in San Francisco.

1961 South Africa became a Republic and withdrew from the Commonwealth.

1962 Adolf Eichmann was executed inside Ramleh Prison near Tel Aviv for his part in the wartime mass execution of millions of Jews.

1970 The famous British steeplechaser 'Arkle' was put down.

1983 Jack Dempsey, world heavyweight boxing champion, died.

1 JUNE (153)

National day of Tunisia.

1792 Kentucky, the Blue Grass State, became the 15th state of the Union.

1796 Tennessee, the Volunteer State, became the 16th state of the Union.

1801 Brigham Young, American influential Mormon religious leader, born at Whittingham in Vermont.

1804 Mikhail Glinka, Russian composer of operas, born at Novospasskoi, Smolensk.

1868 James Buchanan, American Democrat statesman and 15th President from 1857 to 1861—the only bachelor—died at Wheatland, near Lancaster in Pennsylvania aged 77.

1874 Pullman carriages were introduced in Britain, by the Midland Railway, from London to Bradford.

1878 John Masefield, English poet and Poet Laureate, born at Ledbury in Herefordshire.

1907 Sir Frank Whittle, English inventor and pioneer of jet propulsion, born at Coventry.

1926 Marilyn Monroe, American film actress and sex symbol, born at Los Angeles in California as Norma Jean Baker.

1927 Lizzie Borden, the alleged axe murderess, died.

1935 Driving tests in Britain were introduced by Leslie Hore Belisha, and 'L' plates were made compulsory.

1939 The British naval submarine 'Thetis' sank while on trials in Liverpool Bay, with the loss of 99 lives. Was later raised and put back into service as HMS Thunderbolt.

1946 The first television licences were issued in Britain, at a fee of £2.

1957 The first Premium Bond prize winners were drawn by the computer 'ERNIE'—with a first prize of £1000.

1968 Helen Keller, American author and lecturer, blind and deaf from the age of 2, died aged 87.

2 JUNE (154)

National day of Italy.

1840 Thomas Hardy, English novelist and poet, born at Higher Bockhampton in Dorset, the son of a stonemason.

1857 Sir Edward Elgar, English composer, born at Broadheath near Worcester, the son of a music-seller and organist.

1868 The first Trades Union Congress was held, at Manchester—finished on 6th.

1882 Giuseppe Garibaldi, Italian soldier and patriot who helped to form the Kingdom of Italy, died.

1896 Marconi was granted the first patent (numbered 12039) for a system of communication by means of electro-magnetic waves.

1903 Johnny Weissmuller, American swimmer, holder of many world records and 'Tarzan' in 19 movies, born at Windber in Pennsylvania.

1938 Regent's Park Children's Zoo in London was opened by Robert and Edward Kennedy.

1940 Constantine II, King of the Hellenes, born the son of King Paul.

1941 Clothes rationing started in Britain.

1953 The coronation of Queen Elizabeth II took place.

1970 Bruce McLaren, New Zealand motor racing driver, accidentally killed.

3 JUNE (155)

1657 William Harvey, English anatomist and physician who discovered and demonstrated the circulation of the blood, died near Saffron Walden in Essex.

1804 Richard Cobden, British statesman and economist, born at Heyshott, near Midhurst in Sussex, the son of a farmer.

1808 Jefferson Davis, American statesman and President of the Confederate States in the American Civil War, born at Fairview in Kentucky.

1865 King George V, the second son of Edward VII and Queen Alexandra, born at Marlborough House in London.

1875 Georges Bizet, French composer, notably the opera 'Carmen', died at Bougival near Paris.

1898 Samuel Plimsoll, English social reformer, known as 'The Sailors' Friend', who devised the Plimsoll line for the safe loading of ships, died at Folkestone in Kent.

1899 Johann Strauss the Younger, Austrian composer of light music, notably the 'Blue Danube', died in Vienna.

1915 Paulette Goddard, American film actress, born at Great Neck in the State of New York as Marion Levy.

1925 Tony Curtis, American film actor, born in New York City as Bernard Schwartz, the son of Hungarian-Jewish immigrant parents.

1937 The Duke of Windsor, the abdicated King Edward VIII, married Mrs Wallis Warfield Simpson at Monts in France.

1945 Hale Irwin, American golf champion, born at Joplin in Missouri.

1956 Third class rail travel was abolished on British Rail, to conform with continental practice.

1963 Pope John XXIII, Angelo Giuseppe Roncalli, died.

1965 Gemini 4 was launched, with James McDivitt and Edward White—during the flight Ed White became the first American to walk in space.

4 JUNE (156)

1703 Samuel Pepys was buried at St Olave's in London's Hart Street.

1738 King George III, the grandson of George II, was born in lodgings at St James's Square in London.

1798 Giovanni Casanova, Italian adventurer, lover and romancer, died at his Castle of Dux in Bohemia.

1805 The first 'Trooping of the Colour' took place, at Horse Guards Parade in London.

1831 Prince Leopold of Saxe-Coburg was chosen as the first sovereign of independent Belgium.

1832 The Great Reform Bill passed into law.

1867 Carl Mannerheim, Finnish soldier, statesman and President, born at Vilnas.

1910 Christopher Cockerell, British engineer and inventor of the amphibious Hovercraft, born at Cambridge.

1913 The 'Suffragette' Derby took place, during which Emily Davidson was trampled to death when she threw herself in front of the King's horse 'Anmer' at Tattenham Corner.

1940 The evacuation of allied forces from Dunkirk and St Valéry was completed—having started on 27th May.

1941 Kaiser Wilhelm II, German Emperor, died in exile in the Netherlands.

1944 Allied forces entered and liberated the city of Rome.

1958 The first Duke of Edinburgh Awards were presented, at Buckingham Palace.

1970 Tonga or Friendly Islands became completely independent and a member of the Commonwealth, having been a British Protectorate since 1900.

5 JUNE (157)

National day of Denmark.

1723 Adam Smith, Scottish economist and philosopher, born at the seaport of Kirkcaldy, the son of a Customs officer.

1819 John Couch Adams, English astronomer, co-discoverer of the planet Neptune, born near Launceston in Cornwall.

1826 Carl von Weber, German composer, pianist and musical director, died in London.

1878 'Pancho' Villa, Mexican guerilla leader and revolutionary, born at San Juan del Rio as Doroteo Arango.

1916 Lord Kitchener, British general and conqueror of the Sudan, was lost at sea when HMS Hampshire struck a mine off Orkney, en route to Russia.

1947 Marshall Aid by America was inaugurated, for European post-war recovery.

1964 Britain made its first flight into space, with 'Blue Streak' rocket, launched from Woomera in Australia.

1968 Robert Kennedy, American Senator and younger brother of the late President, was shot in the Hotel Ambassador in Los Angeles by a Jordanian-Arab, Sirhan Bishara Sirhan—died the following day.

1975 President Sadat re-opened the Suez Canal to all but Israeli shipping, after 8 years of closure.

British citizens voted in a referendum on the entry into the European Community—result 17 378 581 YES and 8 470 073 NO.

National day of Sweden.

1599 Diego Velasquez, Spanish court painter, born at Seville.

1683 The first museum in Britain, the Ashmolean Museum in Broad Street, Oxford, founded by Elias Ashmole, was opened to the public.

1727 The first boxing title fight took place, in London—James Figg defeating Ned Sutton.

1755 Nathan Hale, American soldier and Revolutionary hero, born at Coventry in Massachusetts.

1861 Count Cavour, Italian statesman primarily responsible for the unification of Italy, died.

1868 Robert Falcon Scott, British Antarctic explorer, born near Devonport in Devon.

1875 Thomas Mann, German novelist, born at the port of Lübeck.

1882 The three-mile coastal limit for territorial waters was established by the Hague Convention.

1900 Arthur Askey, English comedian, born at Liverpool.

1908 England played their first football international against a foreign country—winning 6-1 in Vienna against Austria.

1944 The allied landings on the coast of Normandy, called 'Operation Overlord', took place—the start of the biggest sea-borne invasion in history.

1953 Gordon Richards, at his 28th attempt, rode his first Derby winner, 'Pinza', at the odds of 5-1.

1954 The Eurovision television link-up was inaugurated.

1956 Bjorn Borg, Swedish international tennis champion, born at Stockholm.

1961 Carl Jung, Swiss psychologist, psychiatrist and associate of Freud, died aged 85.

1976 Paul Getty, American oil businessman and reputed to be the richest man in the world, died aged 83.

1329 Robert the Bruce, King of Scotland from 1306, died of leprosy at Cardross Castle, on the Firth of Clyde, and was buried in Dunfermline Abbey under the High Altar.

1614 The Addled Parliament was dissolved without having passed a Bill since it first sat on 5th April—hence its name.

1761 John Rennie, Scottish civil engineer, responsible for several bridges and docks in London, born at East Linton.

1778 'Beau' Brummell, English dandy and leader of fashion, born in London as George Bryan Brummell.

1848 Paul Gauguin, French painter, born in Paris, the son of a journalist.

1905 Norway gained independence from Sweden.

1906 The British Atlantic passenger liner 'Lusitania' was launched.

1910 Pietro Annigoni, Italian painter, born at Milan.

1917 Dean Martin, American actor, singer and entertainer, born as Dino Paul Crocetti, at Steubenville in Ohio.

1929 The Papal State, extinct since 1870, was revived as the State of Vatican City, as a result of the Lateran Treaty.

1937 Jean Harlow, American film actress, died aged 26.

1940 Tom Jones, British entertainer, born at Pontypridd in South Wales as Thomas Jones Woodward.

1950 The BBC radio serial 'The Archers', created by Godfrey Baseley, was first broadcast.

1970 (Edward Morgan) E. M. Forster, English novelist, died aged 91.

1980 Henry Miller, American novelist, author of 'Tropic of Cancer' and 'Tropic of Capricorn', died in California.

8 JUNE (160)

1695 Christiaan Huygens, Dutch physicist and astronomer who invented the pendulum clock, died.

1724 John Smeaton, English civil engineer, born at Austhorp near Leeds in Yorkshire.

1809 Thomas Paine, English radical and political reformer, author of 'The Rights of Man', died in poverty in New York.

1810 Robert Schumann, German composer, born at Zwickau where his father kept a book shop.

1814 Charles Reade, English novelist, born at Ipsden House, Oxfordshire, the youngest of 11 children.

1829 Sir John Millais, English painter who helped to form the Pre-Raphaelite brotherhood, born at Southampton.

1845 Andrew Jackson, American general, Democrat statesman and 7th President from 1829 to 1837, nicknamed 'Old Hickory', died at The Hermitage in Nashville, Tennessee.

1865 Sir Joseph Paxton, English ornamental gardener and architect who designed the Crystal Palace for the 1851 Great Exhibition, died in London.

1876 George Sand (Armandine Dupin), French novelist and mistress of Chopin and Musset, died at Nohant.

1940 Nancy Sinatra, American entertainer, born at Jersey City in New Jersey, the daughter of Frank Sinatra.

1969 Robert Taylor, American film actor, died.

9 JUNE (161)

1549 The Book of Common Prayer, compiled by Thomas Cranmer, was adopted in England.

1781 George Stephenson, English locomotive engineer, builder of the 'Rocket', born at Wylam-on-Tyne near Newcastle, the son of a colliery engine keeper.

1870 Charles Dickens, English novelist, author of many famous works, died at Gadshill near Rochester in Kent after a brain haemorrhage the previous evening.

1874 Cochise, Apache chief and war leader against white settlers, died.

1892 Cole Porter, American lyricist and composer of musicals, born at Peru in Indiana.

1898 Hong Kong was leased by Britain from China for 99 years.

1915 The British troops in France were first issued with hand grenades.

1958 Gatwick Airport in Sussex was opened by the Queen.
Robert Donat, British film actor and Academy Award (Oscar) winner in 1939 for his part in 'Goodbye, Mr Chips', died.

1959 The first Polaris submarine, 'George Washington', was launched at Groton in Connecticut.

1964 Lord Beaverbrook, Canadian-born statesman and newspaper magnate, died aged 85.

1976 Dame Sybil Thorndike, British stage and film actress, died aged 93.

10 JUNE (162)

1688 James Stuart, the 'Old Pretender', born at St James's Palace, the only son of King James II and his second wife, Mary of Modena.

1727 King George I died on his way to Hanover in the castle at Osnabrück—in the very room in which he had been born.

1829 The first Oxford and Cambridge University boat race took place, 2¼ miles from Hambledon Lock to Henley Bridge— won easily by Oxford.

1836 André Ampère, French physicist noted for his work on electrodynamics, died.

1901 Frederick Loewe, musical comedy composer of Lerner and Loewe fame, born in Vienna.

1909 The SOS distress signal was transmitted for the first time when the Cunard liner 'Slavonia' was wrecked off the Azores.

1911 Terence Rattigan, English playwright, born in London.

1921 Royal Consort Prince Philip, Duke of Edinburgh, born on the Greek island of Corfu.

1922 Judy Garland, American film actress and singer, born in Minnesota as Frances Ethel Gumm, of vaudeville parents.

1934 Frederick Delius, English composer, died.

1943 Ball-point pens, devised by Hungarian Laszlo Biro, were patented in the United States.

1946 Jack Johnson, American boxer, the first black to hold the world heavyweight title, died.

1967 Spencer Tracy, American film actor and twice Academy Award (Oscar) winner, died.

1974 Henry, Duke of Gloucester, son of King George V, died.

11 JUNE (163)

1509 Henry VIII married Spanish Princess Catharine of Aragon —the first of his six wives.

1572 Ben Jonson, English poet and dramatist, born at Westminster in London.

1727 Accession of King George II on his father's death the previous day.

1776 John Constable, the greatest of English landscape painters, born at East Bergholt in Suffolk, the son of a landowner and miller.

1847 Sir John Franklin, English Arctic explorer, died in Canada in an attempt to discover the Northwest Passage.

1864 Richard Strauss, German composer, born at Munich where his father was a horn player.

1895 Nikolai Bulganin, Russian military and political leader, born at Gorki.

1907 Northamptonshire scored a record low of 12, against Gloucestershire at Gloucester in the County Cricket Championship.

1910 Jacques Cousteau, French underwater explorer and inventor of the aqualung, born at Saint-André in Gironde.

1919 Richard Todd, British film actor, born at Dublin.

1930 The luxury liner 'Empress of Britain' was launched at Clydebank in Scotland, by the Prince of Wales.

1939 Jackie Stewart, British motor racing driver and world champion, born at Milton in Dunbartonshire.

1967 'Bombardier' Billy Wells, British heavyweight boxer, died.

1970 Alexander Kerensky, Russian political leader overthrown by the Bolsheviks in 1917, died in New York City aged 89.

1975 The first oil was pumped ashore from Britain's North Sea oilfields.

1979 John Wayne, American film actor and Academy Award (Oscar) winner in 1969 for his part in 'True Grit', died.

12 JUNE (164)

National day of the Philippines.

1819 Charles Kingsley, English clergyman-author, born at Holne vicarage, Dartmoor.

1842 Thomas Arnold, English educationalist who reformed the Public School system, died one day before his 47th birthday, and was buried in Rugby Chapel.

1897 Anthony Eden, later Earl of Avon, British statesman and Tory Prime Minister, born at Windlestone Hall at Bishop Auckland in County Durham.
Leon Goossens, English oboist, born in Liverpool of a musical family.

1901 Norman Hartnell, English couturier and court dressmaker, born.

1921 The last occasion postmen in Britain delivered mail on a Sunday.

1930 Germany's Max Schmelling won the vacant world heavyweight boxing title, against Jack Sharkey in New York on a disqualification in round 4—the only man to win this title in such a manner.

1944 The first flying bomb fell in England.

1980 Sir Billy Butlin, the holiday camp promoter, died in Jersey.

13 JUNE (165)

1752 Fanny Burney, English novelist and diarist, born at King's Lynn in Norfolk, the daughter of a musician.

1795 Thomas Arnold, English educationalist, born at East Cowes on the Isle of Wight.

1854 Sir Charles Parsons, English engineer who developed the steam turbine, born in London.

1865 (William Butler) W. B. Yeats, Irish poet and playwright, born at Sandymount near Dublin, the son of an artist.

1892 Basil Rathbone, English stage and film actor, best known for his role as Sherlock Holmes, born at Johannesburg.

1893 The first women's golf championship took place, at Royal Lytham—won by Lady Margaret Scott.
Dorothy L. Sayers, English writer of detective novels, born at Oxford.

1897 Paavo Nurmi, Finnish distance runner and world record holder, born at Turku.

1900 The Boxer Rebellion in China began—an uprising by the Boxers, a secret society dedicated to the removal of foreign influence.

1915 Donald Budge, American international tennis champion, born at Oakland in California.

1930 Sir Henry Segrave, British racing driver, was killed when his speed boat 'Miss England' crashed at nearly 100 mph on Lake Windermere—it was Friday the 13th.

1956 The last British troops were removed from the Suez Canal zone.

14 JUNE (166)

1645 The Battle of Naseby took place in Northamptonshire during the Civil War, with the Parliamentarians, under Cromwell and Fairfax, victorious over the Royalists under the command of Prince Rupert.

1777 The 'Stars and Stripes' was adopted by Congress as the flag of the United States of America.

1800 The Battle of Marengo took place near Alessandria in NW Italy, in which a French army under Napoleon crushed the Austrians during the French Revolutionary Wars.

1801 Benedict Arnold, American general best known as a traitor during the Revolution, died in obscurity in London.

1811 Harriet Beecher Stowe, American novelist noted for 'Uncle Tom's Cabin', born at Litchfield in Connecticut.

1839 The first Henley Regatta on the Thames took place.
1883 Edward Fitzgerald, English poet and translator of the 'Rubaiyat of Omar Khayyam', died in Suffolk.
1884 John McCormack, Irish operatic tenor, born in Athlone in the Republic of Ireland.
1894 French President Sadi Carnot was assassinated by Italian anarchists at Lyons.
1909 Burl Ives, American folk singer and film actor, born at Hull in Illinois as Burl Icle Ivanhoe.
1919 Sam Wanamaker, American actor, born at Chicago.
1927 Jerome K. Jerome, English author, notably 'Three Men in a Boat', died.
1928 Emmeline Pankhurst, English suffragette and founder of Women's Social and Political Union, died in London.
Ernesto 'Che' Guevara, Cuban Communist revolutionary leader, born at Rosario in Argentina.
1936 G. K. Chesterton, English author of the 'Father Brown' detective stories, died.
1940 Paris was captured and occupied by German forces.
1946 John Logie Baird, Scottish inventor and pioneer in the development of television, died.
1970 Bobby Charlton played his 106th and last football game for England, in the World Cup in Mexico City—his first having been on 19th April 1958 against Scotland.
1982 Argentinian forces formally surrendered to troops of the British task force in the Falkland Islands.

15 JUNE (167)

1215 King John stamped the Royal seal on the Magna Carta at Runnymede, near Windsor.
1381 Wat Tyler, English rebel and leader of the Peasants' Revolt against the poll tax imposed by Richard II, was beheaded at a meeting at Smithfield in London.
1836 Arkansas, the Wonder State, become the 25th state of the Union.
1843 Edvard Grieg, Norwegian composer, born at Bergen of Scots descent.

1849 James Knox Polk, American Democrat statesman and 11th President from 1845 to 1849, died at Nashville in Tennessee.

1869 Thermoplastic called celluloid, a technically improved version of that invented by the English chemist Alexander Parkes, was patented by American inventor John Wesley Hyatt of Albany, New York.

1884 Harry Langdon, American silent film comedian, born in Iowa.

1905 James Robertson-Justice, British film actor, born.

1910 Captain Scott set out on his second and fatal expedition to the South Pole, in the 'Terra Nova'.

1919 John Alcock and Arthur Whitten Brown completed the first non-stop Transatlantic flight, from Lester's Field, St Johns in Newfoundland to Derrygimla Bog near Clifden in County Galway, in a Vickers Vimy in just over 16 hours.

1925 Richard Baker, BBC television news reader, born at Willesden in London.

1940 Ken Fletcher, Australian tennis champion, born.

1945 Family allowance payments were introduced in Britain— 5 shillings per week per child, after the first.

16 JUNE (168)

1722 The Duke of Marlborough, British general famed for his victories in the War of the Spanish Succession, died at Windsor.

1743 The Battle of Dettingen took place in Bavaria, with King George III's forces defeating the French in the War of the Austrian Succession.

1858 Gustav V, King of Sweden from 1907 to 1950, born the son of Oscar II.

1890 Stan Laurel, of Laurel and Hardy fame, born at Ulverston in Lancashire as Arthur Stanley Jefferson.

1892 Lupino Lane, English music hall entertainer, born in London as Henry Lupino.

1912 Enoch Powell, British politician, born at Stechford, Birmingham.

1930 Elmer Sperry, American inventor of the gyroscopic compass and a wide variety of electrical devices, died at Brooklyn, New York.

1932 At cricket Holmes and Sutcliffe made an English record first-wicket partnership of 555, for Yorkshire against Essex at Leyton.

1942 Giacomo Agostini, motor cycle champion, born at Lovere in Italy.

1963 Valentina Tereshkova blasted off from Tyuratam in Vostok 6 to become the first woman in space—landed on 19th June after 48 orbits.

1969 Earl Alexander of Tunis, British army commander and leader of the invasion of Italy, died.

1977 Leonid Brezhnev became President of USSR.
Werner von Braun, German-born pioneer of rocketry in America's manned flights to the moon, died at Alexandria in Virginia.

17 JUNE

National day of Iceland.

1239 King Edward I was born at Westminster in London, the elder son of Henry III and Eleanor of Provence.

1703 John Wesley, English evangelist and founder of the Methodist movement, born at Epworth in Lincolnshire, the 15th of the rector's 19 children.

1719 Joseph Addison, English poet, essayist and founder of the 'Spectator' in 1711 with Sir Richard Steele, died at Holland House.

1775 The Battle of Bunker Hill, actually fought on nearby Breed's Hill, took place, with victory for the British under General Howe over American rebel troops in the War of Independence.

1818 Charles Gounod, French composer of operas, born in Paris the son of a portrait painter.

1845 Richard Barham, English author of the 'Ingoldsby Legends', died.

1860 The 692-foot liner 'Great Eastern', designed by Brunel and Russell, began its first Transatlantic voyage.

1867 Joseph Lister performed the first operation under antiseptic conditions—on his sister Isabella, at the Glasgow Infirmary.

1882 Igor Stravinsky, American composer, born at Oranienbaum near St Petersburg in Russia.

1939 German multiple-murderer Eugen Wiedmann was the last to be publicly guillotined—outside Versailles prison in Paris.

1940 The British troopship 'Lancastria' was sunk by enemy bombing action off St Nazaire, when some 2500 crew and troops perished.

1944 Iceland became an independent Republic.

1970 Decimal postage stamps (10p, 20p, 50p) went on sale in Britain.

18 JUNE (170)

1769 Viscount Castlereagh, British statesman, born in Ireland.

1812 American Congress, by a small majority, voted a declaration of war against Great Britain.

1815 The Battle of Waterloo took place south of Brussels, the scene of Napoleon's defeat by the troops of Wellington and Blücher.

1817 London's Waterloo Bridge, built by John Rennie, was opened.

1835 William Cobbett, English political journalist and radical reformer, died near Guildford in Surrey.

1884 Edouard Daladier, French statesman and Premier, born at Carpentras, Vaucluse.

1902 Samuel Butler, English novelist, best known for 'The Way of all Flesh', died.

1915 Arthur Fagg, Kent cricketer and the only batsman to score double centuries in both innings, born.

1920 Ian Carmichael, English film actor, born at Hull on Humberside.

1928 Roald Amundsen, Norwegian explorer and first to reach the South Pole in 1911, was lost in the North Sea after a flying accident.

1929 Eva Bartok, film actress in America, born at Budapest as Eva Sjoke.

1942 Paul McCartney of the 'Beatles' pop group, born in Liverpool.

1953 On Farouk's abdication Egypt was proclaimed a Republic, with General Neguib its first President.

1959 Ethel Barrymore, American actress, sister of John and Lionel, called the 'First Lady of American Theatre', died aged 79.

19 JUNE (171)

1566 King James I of England and Scotland, born at Edinburgh Castle, the only son of Mary, Queen of Scots and Lord Darnley.

1623 Blaise Pascal, French mathematician and philosopher, born at Clermont.

1820 Sir Joseph Banks, English botanist who accompanied Cook on his voyage round the world in the 'Endeavour', died.

1829 The London Metropolitan Police was founded, and set up by Sir Robert Peel.

1846 The first baseball game was played at the Elysian Fields at Hoboken in New Jersey—New York Nine against Knickerbockers.

1861 Earl Haig, British army commander, born at Edinburgh.

1867 Emperor Maximilian of Mexico was shot by the troops of Juarez.

1895 The 61-mile Kiel Canal, connecting the North Sea with the Baltic, was formally opened by the German Emperor Wilhelm II.

1896 Bessie Wallis Warfield, later the Duchess of Windsor, born at Blue Ridge Summit in Pennsylvania.

1903 Walter Hammond, Gloucestershire and England cricketer, born at Dover.

1906 Ernst Boris Chain, British biochemist noted for his work on penicillin with Fleming and Florey, born in Berlin.

1910 'Deutschland', the first zeppelin airliner, was launched—crashed on 28th.

1910 Father's Day was initiated in America by Mrs John Bruce Dodd.

1937 (James Matthew) J. M. Barrie, Scottish writer best known for 'Peter Pan', died.

20 JUNE (172)

1756 146 British subjects were imprisoned in a dungeon by the Nawab of Bengal—only 23 survived overnight—known as the 'Black Hole of Calcutta'.

1789 The French Revolution began.

1819 Jacques Offenbach, French-Jewish composer of light operas, born at Cologne as Jakob Eberst.
The 'Savannah' arrived in Liverpool to become the first steamship to cross the Atlantic, having left Savannah in Georgia on 24th May, under the command of Captain Moses Rogers.

1837 Death of William IV, the 'Sailor King', at Windsor—accession of his 18-year old niece as Queen Victoria.

1863 West Virginia, the Panhandle or Mountain State, became the 35th state of the Union.

1887 The second Tay Bridge, the longest railway bridge in Britain, was opened.

1909 Errol Flynn, actor in action-adventure films, born at Hobart in Tasmania.

1911 The city of Leeds introduced Britain's first trolley-bus service.

1923 General 'Pancho' Villa, Mexican guerrilla leader and revolutionary, was assassinated at Parral (Chihuahua) in Mexico.

1960 Floyd Patterson defeated Ingemar Johansson by a knock-out in round 5 to become the first heavyweight in boxing history to regain the world title—having lost it to the Swede some 12 months earlier.

1973 Juan Peron returned to his former office as President of Argentina after almost 20 years of exile.

1377 King Edward III of England died.

1652 Inigo Jones, designer and the first of the great English architects, died.

1675 Work began on the rebuilding of St Paul's Cathedral.

1788 New Hampshire, the Granite State, became the 9th state of the Union.

1813 The Battle of Vitoria took place, the scene of Wellington's decisive victory over the French in the Peninsular War.

1843 The Royal College of Surgeons was founded in London.

1852 Friedrich Froebel, German educationalist and founder of the kindergarten system in 1837, died.

1854 20-year-old Irishman Charles Lucas won the first VC, for his action aboard HMS Hecla at Bomarsund in the Baltic—throwing an unexploded Russian bomb over the side.

1908 Nikolai Rimsky-Korsakov, Russian composer, died at Lyubensk.

1919 72 warships of the German Fleet were scuttled in Scapa Flow in the Orkneys.

1921 Jane Russell, American film actress, born in Minnesota.

1937 Lawn tennis at Wimbledon was televised for the first time.

1963 Giovanni Battista Montini was elected as Pope Paul VI.

1969 Maureen Connolly, American international tennis champion, affectionately called 'Little Mo', died aged 34.

1970 Brazil beat Italy at football in Mexico City to become World champions and win the Jules Rimet trophy for a record third time.

Tony Jacklin became the first Englishman since Ted Ray in 1920 to win the US Open golf championship, played at Chaska in Minnesota.

1977 Menachem Begin became Prime Minister of Israel.

1982 Prince William (Arthur Philip Louis) born in London to the Prince and Princess of Wales.

1377 King Richard II acceded to the throne of England on the death of his grandfather Edward III the previous day.

1757 George Vancouver, English naval captain and surveyor of the Pacific coast of North America, born at King's Lynn in Norfolk.

1805 Giuseppe Mazzini, Italian patriot and revolutionary, born at Genoa.

1814 The first cricket match was played at the present Lord's Ground in London.

1856 Rider Haggard, English novelist known for adventure stories in African settings, born at Bradenham Hall, Norfolk.

1910 John Hunt, leader of the successful British Everest climbing expedition in 1953, born.

1911 The coronation of King George V took place.
Liverpool's Liver clock—'Great George'—first began recording time.

1937 Joe Louis won the world heavyweight boxing title by knocking out James J. Braddock in round 8 at Chicago—the title he successfully defended 25 times before announcing his retirement on 1st March 1949.

1956 Walter de la Mare, English poet and writer of fantasy, died aged 83.

1969 Judy Garland, American singer and film actress, died.

National day of Luxembourg.

1757 The Battle of Plassey took place in Bengal, with victory for the British, under Robert Clive, over the Indian forces—so laying the foundations of the British Empire in India.

1763 Empress Josephine, wife of Napoleon, born on the French island of Martinique as Marie Rose Josèphe Tascher de la Pagerie.

1894 King Edward VIII born at White Lodge, Richmond in Surrey, the eldest son of George V and Queen Mary.
A disaster took place at the Albion coal pit at Cilfynydd in South Wales, claiming the lives of 286 men.
1902 The award of the 'Order of Merit' was founded by King Edward VII—is limited in number to 24 at any one time.
1914 The Royal Naval Air Service was formed.
1916 Sir Leonard Hutton, England cricketer, born at Fulneck near Pudsey in Yorkshire.
1940 Adam Faith, British pop singer, born as Terence Nelhams.
1956 Nasser assumed office as the first President of Egypt, after an election at which voting was compulsory, and he was the only candidate.
1970 Brunel's 320-foot 'Great Britain', the world's first all-metal liner, returned to Bristol from the Falkland Islands where it had lain rusting since 1886.

24 JUNE (176)

Midsummer Day, a quarter day in England.

1314 The Battle of Bannockburn took place near Stirling Castle —Robert the Bruce inflicting a crushing defeat on King Edward II of England.
1509 The coronation of King Henry VIII took place.
1650 The Duke of Marlborough, British general and statesman, born as John Churchill at Ashe in Devon.
(Some sources quote 26th May).
1717 The first Freemason Lodge was inaugurated, in London.
1825 (William Henry) W. H. Smith, founder of the English bookselling chain, born in London.
1850 Lord Kitchener, British Army commander, administrator and statesman, born near Ballylongford, County Kerry in the Republic of Ireland.
1877 St John's Ambulance Brigade was formed, as the Ambulance Association, by the Red Cross.
1895 Jack Dempsey, American boxer and world heavyweight champion, born at Manassa in Colorado with the Christian names William Harrison.

1908 Grover Cleveland, American Democrat statesman and both 22nd and 24th President between 1885 and 1897, died at Princeton in New Jersey.

1911 Juan Fangio, 5 times world motor racing champion, born near Balcarce in Argentina.

1931 Billy Casper, American golf champion, born at San Diego in California.

1948 The Berlin air lift began, due to Russia stopping all land traffic between Berlin and the west.

1971 The first tube of the second Mersey road tunnel was opened.

1981 The bridge over the Humber estuary was opened to traffic, but its official opening by the Queen took place on 17th July.

25 JUNE (177)

1788 Virginia, the Old Dominion State, became the 10th state of the Union.

1876 In an attempt to drive the Indians out of the Black Hills, Colonel George Armstrong Custer and his 264 soldiers of the 7th Cavalry were killed in battle at Little Big Horn in Montana, by Sioux Indians led by Chiefs Gall and Crazy Horse.

1900 Earl Louis Mountbatten, British admiral and commander, born at Frogmore House, Windsor.

1903 George Orwell, English novelist, born at Motihari in Bengal as Eric Arthur Blair.

1906 Roger Livesey, British actor, born.

1920 The Hague was made the permanent seat of the International Court of Justice.

1932 The first England v India cricket Test match started, at Lord's in London—England ending winners by 158 runs.

1950 The Korean War began, when the Communist forces of the North crossed the 38th parallel and invaded the South.

1959 Eamon de Valera assumed office as President of the Republic of Ireland.

1975 Mozambique became fully independent after a 10-year war against Portuguese colonial domination.

26 JUNE (178)

1541 Francisco Pizarro, Spanish conquistador was assassinated in his palace at Lima by the followers of Diego Almagro.

1824 Lord Kelvin, British physicist and mathematician, born at Belfast as William Thomson.

1827 Samuel Crompton, English inventor of the 'spinning mule' in 1779 for spinning fine yarn, died at Bolton in Lancashire.

1830 Death of King George IV—was succeeded by his brother, as William IV.

1836 Rouget de Lisle, French Army officer and composer of 'La Marseillaise' in 1792, died.

1857 The first investiture ceremony of Victoria Crosses took place, at Hyde Park in London.

1892 Pearl Buck, American novelist, born at Hillsboro in West Virginia.

1898 Wilhelm Messerschmitt, German aviation engineer and designer, born at Frankfurt.

1904 Peter Lorre, Hungarian character actor in films, born at Rosenberg as Laszlo Loewenstein.

1905 The Automobile Association was established in Britain.

1906 The first motor racing Grand Prix was organised and run over 12 laps of a 65-mile triangular circuit at Le Mans in France.

1917 The first contingent of the American Expeditionary Force landed in France, with General John Pershing commander-in-chief.

1945 The United Nations Charter was adopted and signed at San Francisco, as a successor to the League of Nations.

1960 The Indian Ocean island of Madagascar became independent, having been a French colony since 1896.

27 JUNE (179)

1816 Samuel Hood, British admiral of distinction, died at Bath aged 91.

1829 James Smithson, English scientist whose bequest established the Smithsonian Institution at Washington to encourage scientific research, died at Genoa.

1844 Joseph Smith, American religious leader and founder of the Church of Jesus Christ of Latter-Day Saints (Mormons) in 1830, was killed in Carthage jail in Illinois, with his brother Hyrum.

1846 Charles Stewart Parnell, Irish politician and leader of the Home Rule movement, born at Avondale in County Wicklow.

1880 Helen Keller, American author and lecturer, born at Tuscumbia in Alabama.

1954 The world's first atomic power station at Obninsk near Moscow went into production.

1961 Dr Ramsey was enthroned as the 100th Archbishop of Canterbury in Canterbury Cathedral.

28 JUNE (180)

1461 The coronation of King Edward IV took place.

1491 King Henry VIII was born at Greenwich in London, the second son of Henry VII.

1712 Jean Jacques Rousseau, French writer and philosopher, born at Geneva.

1836 James Madison, American statesman and 4th President from 1809 to 1817, died at Montpelier in Virginia aged 85.

1838 The coronation of nineteen-year-old Queen Victoria took place at Westminster Abbey.

1855 Lord Raglan, British Army officer and commander of the Expeditionary Force in the Crimean War, died.

1861 Robert Burke, Irish traveller and one of the few to cross the Australian continent from south to north, died.

1883 Pierre Laval, French politician and Premier, born at Chateldon.

1902 Richard Rodgers, American composer, of the Rodgers and Hammerstein partnership, born in New York.

1910 'Deutschland', the first zeppelin airliner, crashed.

1914 Archduke Franz Ferdinand, heir to the Austrian throne, was assassinated with his wife at the Bosnian town of Sarajevo, by terrorist Gavrillo Princip.

1919 Peace Treaty between German representatives and Allied powers was signed in the Palace at Versailles in Northern France.

1928 Cyril Smith, British Liberal politician, born at Rochdale.

1976 Seychelles, the volcanic island group in the Indian Ocean, became an independent Republic within the Commonwealth —having been ceded to Britain in 1814.

29 JUNE

1577 Peter Paul Rubens, Flemish painter, born in Siegen in Westphalia, the son of a lawyer.

1801 The figures of Britain's first census were published.

1855 The 'Daily Telegraph' was published in London for the first time, with Alfred Bate Richards its first editor.

1861 William James Mayo, American surgeon and co-founder of the Mayo Clinic at Rochester, Minnesota, born at Le Sueur in that state.

1868 The Press Association, the News Agency, was founded in London.

1871 Labour Unions in Britain achieved guaranteed legal recognition, by Act of Parliament.

1886 Robert Schuman, French statesman and Prime Minister, born in Luxembourg.

1901 Nelson Eddy, American singer and film actor, born at Providence in the New England state of Rhode Island.

1911 Prince Bernhard, husband of Queen Juliana of the Netherlands, born at Jena in Germany.

1941 Paderewski, Polish pianist, composer, statesman and Prime Minister in 1919, died in Switzerland aged 80.

1967 Jayne Mansfield, American film actress, was killed in a car crash on the road to New Orleans.

1967 Primo Carnera, Italian heavyweight boxer and world champion 1933/34, died.

30 JUNE

1520 Montezuma, the last Mexican Emperor, was killed by his own subjects in Mexico City during the Spanish conquest of Mexico under Cortes.

1660 William Oughtred, English mathematician and inventor of the slide rule in 1622, died at Albury in Surrey.

1797 The Nore naval mutiny, led by Richard Parker against bad food and inadequate pay, was suppressed.

1859 Charles Blondin made the earliest crossing of the Niagara Falls on a tightrope—1100 feet long and 160 feet above the Falls.

1861 Elizabeth Barrett Browning, English poet and wife of Robert Browning, died at Florence in Italy.

1894 London's Tower Bridge, designed by Sir Horace Jones and Sir J. Wolfe Barry, was opened.

1919 Susan Hayward, American film actress and Oscar winner, born in Brooklyn, New York as Edythe Marriner.
Lord Rayleigh, English physicist, co-discoverer of the inert gas argon in 1894 and Nobel Prize winner, died at Witham in Essex aged 76.

1936 The German zeppelin 'Hindenburg' set out on its Atlantic crossing, reaching Lakehurst in New Jersey on 2nd July.

1939 The Mersey Ferry boat service between Liverpool and Rock Ferry was discontinued.

1957 The 'Lion' was stamped on British eggs for the first time—the practice ceased on 31st December 1968.

1963 Giovanni Battista Montini was crowned as Pope Paul VI.

1971 Soviet spacecraft Soyuz II crashed on its re-entry into the earth's atmosphere, killing the crew of 3.

1980 The British sixpence ceased to be legal tender after midnight.

National day of Canada.

1690 The Battle of the Boyne took place, fought at Oldbridge near Drogheda in Ireland, in which William III of England defeated the Jacobites under James II.

1804 George Sand, French woman novelist, born in Paris as Amandine Dupin.

1837 Registration of births, marriages and deaths came into effect in Great Britain.

1847 The first adhesive US stamps went on sale—Benjamin Franklin 5 cent and George Washington 10 cent.

1860 Charles Goodyear, American inventor of the vulcanised-rubber process, died a pauper.

1867 Canada became a Dominion by the British North America Act.

1872 Louis Blériot, French aviator and plane designer, born.
The Albert Memorial in Kensington Gardens was unveiled by Queen Victoria.

1884 Allan Pinkerton, Scottish-born American detective and founder of the agency that bears his name, died at Chicago.

1896 Harriet Beecher Stowe, American novelist, best known as the author of 'Uncle Tom's Cabin', died at Hartford in Connecticut.

1899 Charles Laughton, film actor and Oscar winner, born at Scarborough in Yorkshire.

1903 Amy Johnson, English record-breaking aviator, born at Hull in Yorkshire.

1912 The first Royal Command performance took place, at the Palace Theatre in London.

1916 Olivia de Havilland, American film actress, born at Tokyo in Japan, the older sister of Joan Fontaine.

1921 Sir Seretse Khama, Botswanan politician and later President of the Republic, born at Serowe.

1933 Speke aerodrome at Liverpool was declared open.

1937 The telephone 999 emergency service came into operation in Britain.

1960 Ghana was proclaimed a Republic, with Kwame Nkrumah its first President.

1961 Lady Diana Spencer, to become the Princess of Wales, born at Park House at Sandringham.

1967 Television in colour began on BBC2.

1969 Prince Charles was invested as Prince of Wales at Caernarvon Castle.

1974 Juan Peron, Argentinian political leader and President, died aged 78.

2 JULY (184)

1489 Thomas Cranmer, English clergyman and Archbishop of Canterbury, born at Aslockton in Nottinghamshire.

1644 The Battle of Marston Moor took place near York, in which the Cromwellian victory over the Royalist Cavaliers under Prince Rupert was the turning-point in the Civil War.

1778 Jean Jacques Rousseau, Geneva-born French political philosopher, died insane at Ermenonville.

1850 Sir Robert Peel, British statesman, twice Tory Prime Minister and founder of the Police Force in 1829, died in London as a result of a horse riding accident.

1865 The Salvation Army was originated by William Booth, with a revival meeting at London's Whitechapel.

1881 James Garfield, American Republican statesman and 20th President, was shot by Charles Guiteau in Washington, DC —died on 19th September at Elberon in New Jersey.

1892 Jack Hylton, British band leader and impresario, born.

1900 The 2nd Olympic Games opened in Paris.

1903 Sir Alec Douglas-Home, statesman and Conservative Prime Minister, born in London.
King Olav V of Norway, born at Sandringham in England, the only child of King Haakon VII.

1937 Amelia Earhart Putnam, American aviator, and co-pilot Fred Noonan, were lost near Howland Island in the Pacific during her attempt to fly round the world.

1940 The Vichy Government was formed after the collapse of France, with Henri Pétain as Head of State.

1961 Ernest Hemingway, American novelist and Nobel Prize winner in 1954, fearing ill-health, shot himself at Ketchum in Idaho.

1973 Betty Grable, American film actress and pin-up girl of World War II, died.

3 JULY (185)

1608 Quebec was founded by the French explorer Samuel de Champlain.

1728 Robert Adam, Scottish architect and house interior designer, born at Kirkcaldy in Fifeshire.

1863 General Meade's Union Army defeated the Confederacy under the command of Robert E. Lee at Gettysburg in Pennysylvania.

1866 The Battle of Sadowa took place in North Czechoslovakia, in which the Austrians were defeated by the Prussians.

1890 Idaho, the Gem State, became the 43rd state of the Union.

1898 Captain Joshua Slocum arrived back at Newport Harbour on Rhode Island in his 36¾ ft 'Spray', having sailed 46 000 miles to complete the first solo circumnavigation of the earth—started on 24th April 1895.

1904 Theodor Herzl, Hungarian-born journalist and founder of Zionism, died in Vienna.

1908 Joel Chandler Harris, American writer of the 'Uncle Remus' stories, died.

1920 The first RAF air display took place at Hendon.

1928 The world's first television transmission in colour was made by John Logie Baird, at the Baird Studios in London.

1938 'Mallard' of LNER achieved a speed of 126 mph, the world record for a steam locomotive.

1954 Food rationing ended in Britain.

1962 After a referendum President de Gaulle declared Algeria independent, with Ben Bella its first Prime Minister.

1976 Israeli commandos rescued 103 hostages held in the Entebbe Airport in Uganda by pro-Palestinian terrorists.

4 JULY (186)

1761 Samuel Richardson, English novelist, author of 'Pamela' and 'Clarissa', died at Parson's Green in Middlesex.

1776 The Declaration of Independence was adopted in Philadelphia—was actually signed on and after 2nd August 1776.

1804 Nathaniel Hawthorne, American novelist and short story writer, born at Salem in Massachusetts, the son of a Merchant Captain.

1807 Giuseppe Garibaldi, Italian military leader and patriot, born at Nice, the son of a sea captain.

1817 Work began on the construction of the Erie Canal—properly named the New York State Barge Canal—opened on 26th October 1825.

1826 Stephen Foster, American composer of minstrel songs and popular ballads, born at Pittsburgh in Pennsylvania.
John Adams, American Federalist statesman and 2nd President from 1797 to 1801, died at Quincy in Massachusetts aged 90.
Thomas Jefferson, American statesman and 3rd President from 1801 to 1809, died aged 83, and was buried near Charlottesville in Virginia.

1829 The first regular scheduled bus service was introduced in Britain, in London by George Shillibeer.

1831 James Monroe, American statesman and 5th President from 1817 to 1825, died in New York City.

1845 Thomas Barnardo, British founder of homes for destitute children, born in Dublin.

1872 Calvin Coolidge, American Republican statesman and 30th President, born at Plymouth in Vermont, the son of a storekeeper.

1900 Louis Armstrong, American jazz trumpeter, born at New Orleans.

1904 Work began on the construction of the 40-mile-long Panama Canal—was opened to traffic on 15th August 1914.

1928 Gina Lollobrigida, Italian film actress, born at Subiaco.

1934 Marie Curie, Polish-born French scientist and pioneer in the medicinal use of radioactivity, died.

1938 Suzanne Lenglen, French tennis champion, called the 'Pavlova of tennis', died aged 39.

1943 Wladyslaw Sikorski, Polish soldier, statesman and Prime Minister, was killed in an aircrash over Gibraltar.

1946 The Philippine Islands were given independence by USA, Manual Roxas being elected the first President of the new Republic.

5 JULY (187)

National day of Venezuela.

1791 George Hammond was appointed the first Ambassador to the United States.

1803 George Borrow, English writer of works on travel and gypsies, born at East Dereham in Norfolk, the son of an Army captain.

1810 (Phineas Taylor) P. T. Barnum, American showman extraordinary, born at Bethel in Connecticut.

1817 Sovereigns were first issued as coins in Britain.

1826 Sir Stamford Raffles, British colonial administrator and founder of Singapore in 1819, died in London.

1853 Cecil Rhodes, British colonial administrator and financier, born the 7th of 11 children at Bishop's Stortford in Hertfordshire, where his father was vicar.

1854 The Republican Party of American politics was formally established.

1865 The world's first speed limit was imposed in Britain, under the Locomotives and Highway Act, which became known as the 'Red Flag Act'.

1872 Edouard Herriot, French statesman and Prime Minister, born at Troyes.

1911 Georges Pompidou, French statesman, Prime Minister and President, born at Montboudif in the Auvergne.

1917 Joe Gormley, English mineworkers' union leader and President, born.

1924 The 8th Olympic Games opened in Paris.

1948 The National Health Service came into force in Britain.

1969 Tom Mboya, Kenyan politician influential in his country's independence movement, was assassinated in Nairobi.

1980 Bjorn Borg won the Wimbledon singles tennis championship for a record 5th consecutive time.

6 JULY (188)

National day of Malawi.

1189 Death of King Henry II at Chinon in France—accession of his third son as Richard I, called Coeur de Lion.

1483 The coronation of King Richard III took place.

1535 Sir Thomas More, English statesman and Lord Chancellor, was executed on London's Tower Hill for high treason.

1553 Death of King Edward VI at Greenwich, having developed tuberculosis—accession of his half-sister Mary Tudor as Mary I, known as 'Bloody Mary'.

1685 The Battle of Sedgemoor in Somerset took place—the last on English soil—with victory for James II's Royalist forces over the rebels under the Duke of Monmouth.

1747 John Paul Jones, American naval officer, born at Kirkbean in Scotland as John Paul, the son of a gardener.

1796 Nicholas I, Tsar of Russia, born the third son of Tsar Paul I.

1832 Emperor Maximilian, Austrian archduke and Emperor of Mexico, born in Vienna, the brother of Franz Joseph.

1886 Box numbers were first introduced in the classified advertisement columns of newspapers, by the 'Daily Telegraph'.

1893 King George V married Princess Mary of Teck, in St James' Chapel.

1907 Brooklands motor racing track near Weybridge in Surrey, was opened—closed in 1939.

1912 The 5th Olympic Games opened in Stockholm.

1919 The British airship R34, captained by Squadron Leader Scott, arrived at Mineola, New York from East Fortune in Scotland after 108 hours to become the first airship to cross the Atlantic.

1928 The first all-talking feature film, 'Lights of New York', was presented at the Strand Theatre in New York City.

1932 Kenneth Grahame, Scottish author of 'The Wind in the Willows', died.

1946 The Young Conservatives political organisation was founded in Britain.

1952 The last London tram ran.

1960 Aneurin Bevan, British Labour party politician and minister responsible for introducing the National Health Service in 1948, died.

1962 William Faulkner, American novelist and Nobel Prize winner in 1949, died.

1964 Malawi, formerly Nyasaland, became an independent State within the Commonwealth, having been a British Protectorate since 1891.

1966 Malawi became a Republic, with Dr Hastings Banda its President.

1971 Louis Armstrong, 'Satchmo', American jazz trumpeter and band leader, died.

1973 Otto Klemperer, German conductor, died aged 88.

7 JULY   (189)

1307 Death of King Edward I at Burgh-on-Sands near Carlisle on his march north—accession of his son as Edward II.

1816 (Richard Brinsley) R. B. Sheridan, Irish dramatist, who wrote 'School for Scandal' and 'The Rivals', died in great poverty in London.

1854 George Ohm, German physicist, noted for his work on electricity, died at Munich.

1860 Gustav Mahler, Austrian composer and musical director, born in Kalist in Bohemia.

1927 Christopher Stone became the first 'disc jockey' on British radio when he presented his 'Record round-up' from Savoy Hill.

1930 Sir Arthur Conan Doyle, British writer and creator of the crime detective character 'Sherlock Holmes', died.

1940 Ringo Starr, the drummer of the Beatles pop group, born in Liverpool as Richard Starkey.

1944 Tony Jacklin, English golf champion, born at Scunthorpe on Humberside.

1950 The first Farnborough Air Display took place.

1952 The American liner 'United States' on her maiden voyage made the fastest ever Atlantic crossing—doing the 2949 nautical miles from Ambrose Light Vessel to Bishop Rock Light in 3 days, 10 hours and 40 minutes.

1967 Francis Chichester was publicly dubbed Knight, at Greenwich, using Sir Francis Drake's sword.

1970 Sir Allen Lane, English publisher and founder of 'Penguin' paperback books in 1936, died.

8 JULY (190)

1822 (Percy Bysshe) P. B. Shelley, English poet, was accidentally drowned off Leghorn while sailing in his small schooner 'Ariel' to his home on the Gulf of Spezia.

1836 Joseph Chamberlain, British Liberal statesman, born in London.

1838 Count Zeppelin, German pioneer and builder of airships, born at Constance.

1839 John D. Rockefeller, American industrialist and philanthropist, born at Richford in the State of New York.

1882 Percy Grainger, Australian composer and pianist, born at Melbourne, capital of the State of Victoria.

1889 John L. Sullivan defeated Jake Kilrain at Richburg in Mississippi after 75 rounds, in the last bareknuckle heavyweight world title contest.

1908 Nelson Rockefeller, American statesman and vice-President to Gerald Ford, born at Bar Harbor in Maine—grandson of John D. above.

1918 National Savings stamps went on sale in Britain.

1965 Horse racing starting stalls were introduced in Britain, in the Chesterfield Stakes at Newmarket.

1967 Vivien Leigh, British film actress, best known for her Academy Award winning performance as Scarlett O'Hara in 'Gone with the Wind', died.

1979 Michael Wilding, English stage and film actor, died.

9 JULY (191)

National day of Argentina.

1441 Jan van Eyck, Flemish portrait and religious painter, died.

1797 Edmund Burke, British statesman, political writer and orator, died.

1816 Argentina declared independence from Spanish rule, by the Congress of Tucuman, after a long campaign conducted by José de San Martin.

1819 Elias Howe, American inventor of the first practical sewing machine, born at Spencer in Massachusetts.

1850 Zachary Taylor, American military General, Whig statesman and 12th President for only 16 months, died at Washington, DC—the remainder of his term of office was completed by Millard Fillmore.

1877 Wimbledon staged its first Lawn Tennis championship, at its original site in Worple Road.

1901 Barbara Cartland, British authoress of romantic novels, born.

1916 Edward Heath, British statesman and Conservative Prime Minister, born at Broadstairs in Kent.

1918 America suffered its worst train accident—101 killed at Nashville in Tennessee.

1932 King Camp Gillette, American inventor of the safety razor and blade, died.

10 JULY (192)

1509 John Calvin, French theologian who spread the Protestant Reformation, born at Noyon in Picardy.

1792 Frederick Marryat, English writer of novels on sea life, born in London, the son of a Member of Parliament.

1802 Robert Chambers, Scottish bookseller and publisher, born in Peebles.

1806 George Stubbs, English animal painter, especially of horses, died in London aged 81.

1834 James McNeill Whistler, American etcher and painter, born at Lowell in Massachusetts.

1890 Wyoming, the Equality State, became the 44th state of the Union.

1900 Métro, the Paris underground railway, the work of Fulgence Bienvenue, was opened.

1943 The US 7th Army under 'Old Blood and Guts' General Patton and the British-Canadian 8th Army began the invasion of Sicily.

Arthur Ashe, American tennis player and Wimbledon champion, born at Richmond in Virginia.

1945 Virginia Wade, British tennis champion, born at Bournemouth in Dorset, the daughter of a clergyman.

1954 Gordon Richards rode his last mount—at Sandown—the 21 834th of his near-34 year career.

1958 Parking meters came into operation for the first time in England, in London's Mayfair.

1962 Telstar I, the world's first television telecommunications satellite, was launched in America.

1970 At Baule in France, David Broome became the first Briton ever to win the World Show Jumping Championship.

1973 The Bahama Islands in north West Indies attained full independence within the Commonwealth, having been a British Colony since 1783.

11 JULY (193)

National day of Mongolia.

1274 Robert the Bruce, King of Scotland and the first man to unite his country into a nation, born at Turnberry in Ayrshire.

1708 The Battle of Oudenarde in west Belgium ended, with victory of the Duke of Marlborough's forces over the French, led by Louis Vendôme, in the War of the Spanish Succession.

1767 John Quincy Adams, American statesman and 6th President, born at Braintree in Massachusetts, the son of John Adams, the 2nd President.

1776 Captain Cook sailed from Plymouth in the 'Resolution', accompanied by the 'Discovery' on his third and last expedition.

1911 Liverpool's Gladstone Dock was opened by King George V.

1917 Yul Brynner, film actor in America, born at Sakhalin off Siberia.

1935 Alfred Dreyfus, French Army officer who was accused of selling military secrets to Germany, imprisoned and later pardoned, died aged 75.

1937 George Gershwin, American composer, including 'Rhapsody in Blue' and 'Porgy and Bess', died aged 38.

1950 BBC's children's television programme 'Andy Pandy' was first transmitted.

1962 American Fred Baldasare became the first to swim the English Channel underwater—from Cap Gris Nez to Sandwich in Kent—with 'scuba' (self-contained underwater breathing apparatus) equipment.

1979 America's Skylab I returned to earth after 34 981 orbits, since its launch on 14th May 1973.

12 JULY (194)

Orangeman's day in Northern Ireland.

1543 King Henry VIII married Catharine Parr—his sixth and last wife.

1730 Josiah Wedgwood, famous English potter, born at Burslem in Staffordshire.

1851 Louis Daguerre, French pioneer in photography, died.

1854 George Eastman, American pioneer in photography, born at Waterville in the State of New York.

1872 Lord Birkenhead, British Conservative statesman and law reformer, born as Frederick Edwin Smith.

1878 Cyprus was ceded by Turkey to Britain for administration.

1895 Kirsten Flagstad, Norwegian operatic soprano in Wagnerian roles, born in Hamar.

1895 Oscar Hammerstein, American librettist, famous for musicals created with composer Richard Rodgers, born in New York City.

1910 Charles Stewart Rolls, aviator and co-founder of the engineering firm of Rolls-Royce, was killed in an air crash at Bournemouth in Dorset.

1920 President Wilson officially opened the Panama Canal.

1932 Hedley Verity, Yorkshire bowler, took all 10 wickets for 10 runs in 118 deliveries for his county against Nottinghamshire.

13 JULY (195)

1705 Titus Oates, English Protestant conspirator who fabricated a supposed Catholic plot to assassinate King Charles II and restore Catholicism, died.

1793 Jean Paul Marat, French revolutionary leader, was stabbed to death in his bath by Charlotte Corday.

1837 Queen Victoria became the first Sovereign to move into Buckingham Palace.

1860 The last naval execution at the yard-arm took place, aboard HMS Leven in the River Yangtse—the victim was Marine Private John Dalliger.

1865 Englishman Edward Whymper became the first to climb the 14690 ft Matterhorn in the Alps, on the Swiss-Italian border.

1871 The first cat show was held, at Crystal Palace in London, organised by Harrison Weir.

1908 The 4th Olympic Games opened in London.

1919 The British airship R34, under the command of Squadron Leader Scott, arrived back at Pulham in Norfolk after making the first Atlantic aerial round trip—having set out from East Fortune in Scotland on 2nd July.

1930 The World Cup Football Competition was instituted—only 13 countries entered and the Cup was won by the hosts, Uruguay.

1980 Sir Seretse Khama, President of the African Republic of Botswana since 1966, died in a London hospital.

1982 Kenneth More, English film actor, died at his home at Fulham in London.

14 JULY

National day of both France and Iraq.

1789 The Bastille, a former State prison in Paris, was stormed by the citizens of Paris and razed to the ground, and so began the French Revolution.
1858 Emmeline Pankhurst, English suffragette, born at Manchester with the maiden name of Goulden.
1867 Alfred Nobel first demonstrated the use of dynamite, at Merstham Quarry, Redhill in Surrey.
1887 Alfred Krupp, German manufacturer of arms at Essen in the Ruhr, died.
1904 Paul Kruger, South African statesman and Boer Leader, called 'Oom Paul', died in Switzerland.
1913 Gerald Ford, American Republican statesman and 38th President, born at Omaha in Nebraska as Leslie King junior.
1958 King Faisal of Iraq was assassinated in a military coup led by General Kassem, and a Republic was established.
1959 Grock, world-famous Swiss clown, died.
1965 The Matterhorn was first climbed by a woman— Mme Vaucher.
Adlai Stevenson, American politician and diplomat, died in London.

15 JULY

St Swithin's Day.

1573 Inigo Jones, the first of the great English architects, born in London, the son of a clothmaker.
1606 Rembrandt, Dutch painter, born at Leyden as Rembrandt Harmensz van Rijn, the son of a prosperous miller.

1685 The Duke of Monmouth, the illegitimate son of King Charles II and Lucy Walter, was beheaded on London's Tower Hill for leading a Protestant rebellion on the accession of James II.

1795 'La Marseillaise' was officially adopted as the French national anthem—was composed and written in 1792 by Rouget de Lisle.

1857 The Massacre of Cawnpore took place, in which English women and children of the garrison were killed during the Indian Mutiny.

1865 Lord Northcliffe, English journalist and newspaper proprietor, born near Dublin as Alfred Harmsworth.

1869 Margarine was patented in France by Hippolyte Mège Mouriés of Paris.

1881 'Billy the Kid', the notorious American outlaw William H. Bonney, was shot by Sheriff Pat Garrett in New Mexico.

1904 Anton Chekhov, Russian dramatist and short story writer, died at Badenweiler.

1912 National insurance or Social payment, devised by Lloyd George, began in Britain.

1933 Julian Bream, British guitarist and lutenist, born in London.

1948 John Pershing, commander of the US Army in France in World War I, nicknamed 'Black Jack', died at Washington, DC. 'Alcoholics Anonymous' was founded in London, having been in existence in America since 1935.

1975 Apollo 18 was launched, with Vance Brand, Thomas Stafford and Donald Slayton.

16 JULY (198)

1377 The coronation of King Richard II of England took place.

1557 Anne of Cleves, the fourth wife of King Henry VIII, died.

1723 Sir Joshua Reynolds, English portrait painter, born near Plympton in Devon, the 7th son of a clergyman.

1821 Mary Baker Eddy, American religious leader and founder of the Christian Science movement, born at Bow in New Hampshire.

1827 Josiah Spode, English potter and creator of a type of bone china bearing his name, died.

1867 Reinforced concrete was patented by Joseph Monier of Paris.

1872 Roald Amundsen, Norwegian explorer and first to reach the South Pole, in 1911, born at Borge.

1896 Trygve Lie, Norwegian statesman and Secretary-General of the United Nations, born at Oslo.

1907 Barbara Stanwyck, American film actress, born in Brooklyn, New York as Ruby Stevens.

1911 Ginger Rogers, American dancer, film actress and Oscar winner, born at Independence in Missouri as Virginia Katherine McMath.

1918 The last Tsar, Nicholas II, was murdered at Ekaterinburg with his 5 children—daughters, Olga, Tatiana, Marie, Anastasia and son Alexis.

1935 Parking meters, devised by Carlton Magee, came into service in America—at Oklahoma City.

1945 The first atomic bomb, produced at Los Alamos under the direction of Robert Oppenheimer, was detonated at Alamogordo Air Base in New Mexico.

1950 199850 watched the Brazil v Uruguay World Cup final in Rio—a world record for a football match.

1953 Hilaire Belloc, Anglo-French writer and poet, died.

1965 The 7-mile Mont Blanc road tunnel was opened, linking France with Italy.

1969 Apollo 11 was launched, with Neil Armstrong, Edwin Aldrin and Michael Collins.

17 JULY (199)

1761 The Bridgewater Canal, from Worsley to Manchester, built by James Brindley, was opened.

1790 Adam Smith, Scottish economist and writer of 'Wealth of Nations', died in Edinburgh.

1841 The first issue of the English magazine 'Punch' was published in London.

1876 Maxim Litvinov, Soviet statesman, born a Polish Jew at Bielostok.

1889 Erle Stanley Gardner, American crime novelist and creator of the detective character 'Perry Mason', born at Malden in Massachusetts.

1899 James Cagney, American film actor, dancer and Oscar winner, born in New York City.

1903 James McNeill Whistler, expatriate American artist whose 'Mother' hangs in the Louvre, died in London.

1909 Hardy Amies, dressmaker to the Queen, born.

1917 The British Royal family adopted the name 'House of Windsor', in place of 'House of Saxe-Coburg-Gotha'.

1945 The Potsdam Conference of Allied leaders Truman, Stalin and Churchill (later replaced by Attlee) began.

1951 Baudouin became King of the Belgians, on the enforced abdication of his father, King Leopold III.

1964 Donald Campbell attained a world speed record of over 403 mph—by a wheel-driven car 'Bluebird'—on the salt flats at Lake Eyre in South Australia.

1981 The Queen formally opened the Humber Estuary Bridge— the longest single-span structure in the world—it having been opened to traffic on 24th June.

18 JULY (200)

National day of Spain.

1635 Robert Hooke, English physicist, born at Freshwater on the Isle of Wight.

1721 Antoine Watteau, French rococo painter, died.

1792 John Paul Jones, Scottish-born naval hero of the American Revolution, died in Paris.

1811 William Makepeace Thackeray, English novelist, born in Calcutta, where his father was in the service of the East India Company.

1817 Jane Austen, English novelist, author of 'Pride and Prejudice' and 'Emma', died in a lodging in College Street, Winchester in Hampshire.

1848 (William Gilbert) W. G. Grace, famous England cricketer, born at Downend near Bristol.

1864 Philip Snowden, British Labour statesman, born near Keighley in Yorkshire.

1887 Vidkun Quisling, Norwegian diplomat and later traitor, born in Fyresdal.

1892 Thomas Cook, English travel agent pioneer and founder of the agency bearing his name, died.

1904 Work began on Liverpool's Anglican Cathedral—the largest in the British Isles—was completed in October 1978.

1921 John Glenn, astronaut and first American to orbit the earth, born at Cambridge in Ohio.

1934 The 2.13 mile Mersey road tunnel was opened by King George V.

1936 The Spanish Civil War, between Fascists and Republican forces, began.

1955 Disneyland, the amusement resort at Anaheim in California, was opened.

1966 Spacecraft Gemini 10 was launched with John Young and Michael Collins.

1973 Jack Hawkins, British film actor, died.

1976 The 21st Olympic Games opened at Montreal in Quebec.

19 JULY (201)

1545 'Mary Rose', the pride of Henry VIII's battle fleet, suddenly heeled over and sank in the Solent—was raised on 11th October 1982, ready to be taken to Portsmouth dockyard.

1814 Matthew Flinders, English explorer who surveyed and charted the coasts of Australia, died aged 40.
Samuel Colt, American inventor and patentee in 1835 of a revolver that bears his name, born at Hartford in Connecticut.

1821 The coronation of King George IV took place in Westminster Abbey.

1834 Edgar Degas, French Impressionist painter and sculptor, born in Paris.

1837 Brunel's 236 ft 'Great Western' was launched at Patterson's Yard at Bristol.

1843 Brunel's 320 ft 'Great Britain', the first all-metal liner, was launched from London's Wapping Dock, by Prince Albert.

1860 Lizzie Borden, the alleged axe murderess, born at Fall River in Massachusetts.

1865 Charles Mayo, American surgeon who with his brother was founder of the Mayo Clinic, born at Rochester in Minnesota.

1877 The first men's Wimbledon tennis final took place, and was won by Spencer Gore.

1896 (Archibald Joseph) A. J. Cronin, British novelist, born at Cardross in Scotland.

1946 Ilie Nastasie, Romanian international tennis player, born at Bucharest.

1952 The 15th Olympic Games opened at Helsinki in Finland.

1969 John Fairfax arrived at Fort Lauderdale in Florida after 180 days, having rowed the Atlantic alone from Las Palmas in the 22-ft 'Britannia'—the first to make such a crossing.

20 JULY (202)

National day of Colombia.

1837 Euston Railway Station, the first in London, was opened.

1871 The English Football Association Challenge Cup competition was formed.

1885 Professional football was legalised in England.

1900 Maurice Leyland, Yorkshire and England cricketer, born at Harrogate.

1903 Leo XIII (Gioacchino Vincenzo Pecci), Pope since 1878, died aged 93.

1919 Sir Edmund Hillary, the first conquerer of Mount Everest in 1953 with Tenzing Norgay, born at Auckland on New Zealand's North Island.

1937 Guglielmo Marconi, Italian physicist and inventor who pioneered the use of wireless telegraphy, died in Rome.

1940 Singles-record charts were first published, in America, by 'Billboard'.

1969 'Eagle', the lunar module of Apollo 11, landed on the moon, on the Sea of Tranquillity.

1970 Ian MacLeod, British politician, died.

National day of Belgium.

1796 Robert Burns, Scottish national poet, died aged 37 at Dumfries, and there is buried.

1798 The Battle of the Pyramids took place, in which Napoleon, soon after his invasion of Egypt, defeated an army of some 60000 Mamelukes.

1816 Paul von Reuter, German founder of the world News Agency that bears his name, born at Kassel as Israel Beer Josaphat.

1831 Prince Leopold became Leopold I, King of Belgium on its separation from the Netherlands.

1890 Battersea Bridge over the Thames was opened by the Earl of Rosebery.

1897 The Tate Gallery in London was officially opened—built on the site of the Millbank Prison.

1899 Ernest Hemingway, American novelist, born at Oak Park in Illinois, the son of a country doctor.

1928 Ellen Terry, English Shakespearean stage actress, died at Hythe in Kent aged 81.

1959 The first nuclear merchant ship, US Savannah, was launched at Camden in New Jersey by Mrs Mamie Eisenhower.

1960 Mrs Sirimavo Bandaranaike took up office as Prime Minister of Ceylon, and became the world's first woman to hold such a position.

1961 Runcorn Bridge over the River Mersey—the longest steel arch bridge in the United Kingdom-was opened.

1969 Neil Armstrong, command pilot of Apollo 11, left the lunar module 'Eagle' and set foot on the moon, on the Sea of Tranquillity.

National day of Poland.

1812 The Battle of Salamanca took place in W Spain, the scene of the Duke of Wellington's victory over the French in the Peninsular War.

1822 Gregor Mendel, Augustine monk, botanist and pioneer of modern genetics, born at Heinzendorf, near Odrau in Austrian Silesia.

1844 Reverend William Spooner, British educationalist and originator of 'spoonerisms', born in London.

1932 Florenz Ziegfeld, American theatrical producer and impresario, died in Hollywood.

1933 Wiley Post became the first to fly solo round the world—with 10 stops from Floyd Bennett Field in New York City and back, via the Arctic Circle, in a Lockheed Vega monoplane 'Winnie Mae'—the journey took 7 days 18 hours and 49½ minutes.

1934 John Dillinger, American bank robber and public enemy, was gunned down by law officers in front of the Biograph Theatre in Chicago.

1946 Bread rationing began in Britain.

1950 Mackenzie King, Canadian statesman and Liberal Prime Minister on 3 occasions, died at Kingsmere in the Province of Quebec.

1976 Sir Mortimer Wheeler, British archaeologist and broadcaster, died.

National day of both Ethiopia and The United Arab Republic.

1759 Work commenced on the Royal Navy's 104-gun battleship HMS Victory, at Chatham in Kent—constructed from the wood of some 2200 oak trees.

1875 Isaac Singer, American inventor of the modern sewing machine, died at Torquay in Devon.

1885 Ulysses Grant, American commander of the Union Army, Republican statesman and 18th President from 1869 to 1877, died of cancer at Mount McGregor, near Saratoga in the State of New York.

1886 Sir Arthur Whitten Brown, British aviator and companion of Alcock on the first transatlantic flight, born at Glasgow.

1888 Raymond Chandler, American detective story writer, creator of the character 'Philip Marlowe', born at Chicago.

1891 Haile Selassie, Emperor of Ethiopia, born in the Harar Province as Tafari Makonnen.

1912 Michael Wilding, English actor, born at Westcliff-on-Sea in Essex.

1913 Michael Foot, British politician and Labour Party leader, born.

1916 Sir William Ramsay, Scottish chemist and Nobel Prize winner in 1904, who discovered 'inert' gases—argon, helium, neon, krypton and xenon—died at High Wycombe in Buckinghamshire.

1951 Marshal Pétain, Army marshal and Head of State of Vichy France from 1940 to 1944, died in prison at Île d'Yeu aged 95, serving a life sentence for collaboration.

1955 Cordell Hull, American statesman, diplomat and Nobel Peace Prize winner in 1945, died aged 83.

24 JULY (206)

1704 Admiral Sir George Rooke captured Gibraltar from the Spaniards—ceded to Britain by the 1713 Treaty of Utrecht.

1775 Eugène Francois Vidocq, the first police detective and founder of the Sûreté, born at Arras in Northern France, the son of a baker.

1783 Simon Bolivar, South American revolutionary leader and liberator of South America from Spanish Imperial control, born at Caracas, the capital city of Venezuela.

1802 Alexandre Dumas *père* (senior), French writer, notably 'The Count of Monte Cristo' and 'The Three Musketeers', born as Alexandre Dumas Davy de la Pailleterie.

1862 Martin van Buren, American Democrat statesman and 8th President from 1837 to 1841, known as 'The little magician', died at Kinderhook, New York.

1883 Matthew Webb, the first man to swim the English Channel, in 1875, was drowned attempting to swim the rapids above the Niagara Falls.

1898 Amelia Earhart, American aviator, born at Atchison in Kansas.

1926 Belle Vue, Manchester, was opened for greyhound racing, by Brigadier Critchley.

1927 The Menin Gate, a memorial at Ypres to the armies of the British Empire, was unveiled.

1936 The 'Speaking Clock' was introduced by the GPO at the suggestion of Eugene Wender of Hampstead—was known as 'TIM' from the dial letters.

1974 Sir James Chadwick, English physicist, discoverer of the neutron and Nobel Prize winner, died aged 82.

1980 Peter Sellers, English film actor and entertainer, died.

25 JULY (207)

1603 The coronation of King James I took place.

1834 (Samuel Taylor) S. T. Coleridge, English poet, who wrote 'Kubla Khan' and 'The Ancient Mariner', died.

1843 Charles Macintosh, Scottish chemist who developed and patented waterproof fabric in 1823, died near Glasgow.

1848 (Arthur James) A. J. Balfour, British statesman and Conservative Prime Minister, born in East Lothian in Scotland.

1909 Louis Blériot flew his Blériot XI monoplane across the English Channel, from Les Baraques near Calais to Northfall Meadow near Dover Castle, in 36½ minutes.

1934 Engelbert Dollfuss, Chancellor of Austria, was assassinated in Vienna by rebelling Austrian Nazis—Otto Planetta was convicted and hanged.

1943 Benito Mussolini resigned as Dictator of Italy, and the Fascist regime was abolished.

1957 Tunisia abolished the Monarchy and became a Republic, with Habib Bourguiba elected as President.

1959 The Hovercraft, the 'SRN 1' as it was called, made its first English Channel crossing—from Dover to Calais—in a little over 2 hours.

1978 The first test-tube baby in Britain was born—Louise Joy Brown, at Oldham General Hospital, in Lancashire.

26 JULY (208)

National day of Liberia.

1745 The first recorded women's cricket match took place, at Gosden Common, near Guildford in Surrey—when '11 maids from Hambledon' beat '11 maids from Bramley'.

1788 New York, the Empire State, became the 11th state of the Union.

1845 Brunel's 320-ft iron ship 'Great Britain' left Liverpool for New York on her maiden voyage.

1847 Liberia became the first African colony to secure independence.

1856 George Bernard Shaw, Irish dramatist and critic, born at Dublin.

1866 The Canoe Club was formed in England, by John MacGregor.

1875 Carl Jung, Swiss analytic psychologist, born at Kessevil.

1881 George Borrow, English writer of books of travel and gypsies, author of 'Lavengro', died.

1908 The Federal Bureau of Investigation was established at Washington, DC.

1952 King Farouk was forced to abdicate as a result of a coup d'état carried out by General Neguib.

1956 President Nasser took over and nationalised the Suez Canal.

1958 Her Majesty the Queen created her eldest son, Charles, Prince of Wales.

1963 Severe earthquakes occurred at Skopje in Yugoslavia, with 1100 deaths.

1965 The Maldive Islands in the Indian Ocean, SW of Sri Lanka, achieved independence, having been under British protection since 1887.

1971 Apollo 15 was launched, with David Scott, James Irwin and Alfred Worden—Scott and Irwin making the 4th moon landing.

27 JULY (209)

1689 The Battle of Killiecrankie took place near Pitlochry in Scotland, in which King William's forces, led by Mackay, were defeated by the Jacobites under John Graham of Claverhouse—who was killed.

1824 Alexandre Dumas *fils* (junior), French playwright, especially 'La Dame aux Camélias', born in Paris.

1844 John Dalton, English chemist and physicist who developed the modern atomic theory and pioneer in meteorology, died.

1870 Hilaire Belloc, English writer and poet, born at St Cloud, near Paris, the son of a French barrister.

1904 Anton Dolin, English ballet dancer and choreographer, born at Slinfold in Sussex as Patrick Healey-Kay.

1921 The first insulin was isolated by Canadians Sir Frederick Banting and his assistant Charles Best, at the University of Toronto, thus providing an effective treatment for diabetes.

1923 The BBC radio station 'Daventry' opened.

1949 The world's first jet-propelled airliner—the 'Comet'—first flew.

1953 The Korean Armistice was signed at Panmunjom.

1969 Irishman Tom McClean of the Parachute Regiment arrived at Blacksod Bay in County Mayo, after rowing solo across the Atlantic for 71 days, from St John's, in 20-foot 'Super Silver'.

1970 Antonio Salazar, Portuguese statesman and Prime Minister from 1932 to 1968, died at Lisbon aged 81.

1972 Work began on the Humber Estuary Bridge—the world's longest main span at 4626 ft. Was opened by the Queen on 17th July 1981.

1980 The Shah of Iran died in Egypt in exile.

National day of Peru.

1586 The first potatoes arrived in Britain, at Plymouth, brought from Colombia by Sir Thomas Harriot.

1655 Cyrano de Bergerac, French novelist and playwright, died.

1750 Johann Sebastian Bach, German composer, died, almost totally blind, of apoplexy.

1794 Maximilien Robespierre, French leader of the Jacobins during the Revolution, was guillotined in Paris.

1809 The Battle of Talavera in the Peninsular War ended, with the Duke of Wellington victorious over French Marshal Soult.

1821 San Martin and his forces liberated Peru, and proclaimed its independence from Spain.

1866 Beatrix Potter, English author and illustrator of children's books and creator of 'Peter Rabbit', born at South Kensington in London.

1904 Selwyn Lloyd, British Conservative politician, born at Liverpool.

1917 The formation of the Royal Tank Corps in the British army was authorised.

1928 The 9th Olympic Games opened in Amsterdam.

1929 Jacqueline Onassis, widow of President Kennedy, born at Southampton in New York as Jacqueline Lee Bouvier.

1936 Garfield Sobers, West Indian test cricketer, born at Bridgetown, capital of Barbados.

1938 The British liner 'Mauretania' was launched at Birkenhead on Merseyside.

1939 William James Mayo, American surgeon and co-founder of the Mayo Clinic Foundation, died aged 78.

1967 The steel industry was re-nationalised in Britain.

1976 Vic Feather, British trade union leader, created Baron Feather in 1974, died.

1565 Mary, Queen of Scots married her cousin Lord Darnley in the Old Abbey Chapel of the Palace of Holyroodhouse in Edinburgh.

1588 The Spanish Armada, a fleet of some 130 ships, sent by Philip II in an attempt to invade England, and led by Medina Sidonia, was defeated by the English fleet under Howard and Drake, off Plymouth.

1833 William Wilberforce, English philanthropist who played a large part in the abolition of the slave trade in 1807 and of slavery in the British empire in 1833, died.

1856 Robert Schumann, German composer and director of music, died in an asylum near Bonn.

1883 Benito Mussolini, Italian statesman and Fascist dictator, born at Predappio near Forli, the son of a blacksmith.

1887 Sigmund Romberg, Hungarian composer of musical comedies, notably 'The Student Prince', born at Szeged.

1890 Vincent van Gogh, famous Dutch painter, died after prolonged insanity—having shot himself in the chest 2 days earlier.

1900 Umberto I, King of Italy from 1878, was assassinated at Monza by anarchists.

1905 Dag Hammarskjöld, Swedish Secretary-General of the United Nations, born at Jönköping.

1907 The first Boy Scout movement originated with an experimental camp held on Brownsea Island, near Poole in Dorset by Robert Baden-Powell—ended on 9th August.

1913 Jo Grimond, British politician and a leader of the Liberal Party, born.

1945 The BBC 'Light Programme' began broadcasting.

1948 The 14th Olympic Games opened in London.
Bread rationing ended in Britain.

1949 BBC televised the first weather forecast.

1970 Sir John Barbirolli, English conductor and musical director, died.

1983 David Niven, British actor, died.

1718 William Penn, English Quaker leader and founder of the US state of Pennsylvania, died aged 73.

1771 Thomas Gray, English poet, noted for his 'Elegy written in a country churchyard', died in London.

1818 Emily Brontë, English novelist, author of 'Wuthering Heights', born at Thornton in Yorkshire.

1863 Henry Ford, American motor car engineer and manufacturer, born at Dearborn in Michigan, the son of a farmer.

1898 Otto von Bismarck, Prussian statesman, founder and Chancellor of the German empire, died at Friedrichsruh aged 83.
Henry Moore, English abstract sculptor, born at Castleford in Yorkshire, the son of a coal miner.

1932 The 10th Olympic Games opened at Los Angeles.

1935 'Penguin' paperback books, founded by Sir Allen Lane, went on sale in Britain.

1948 The world's first radar station was opened, to assist shipping at the port of Liverpool.

1966 England won the World Cup at football, beating West Germany 4-2 at Wembley Stadium in London.

1556 Ignatius Loyola, Spanish soldier, priest and founder of the Society of Jesus (Jesuits), died.

1875 Andrew Johnson, American Democrat statesman and 17th President from 1865 to 1869, died in Carter County in Tennessee.

1886 Franz Liszt, Hungarian pianist, composer and director of music, died at Bayreuth in West Germany aged 74.

1929 The World Boy Scouts' Jamboree at Arrowe Park, Birkenhead, was opened.

1943 Hedley Verity, Yorkshire and England cricketer, died when a prisoner of war in Italy, as a result of wounds received in action.

1956 At Old Trafford, Manchester, Jim Laker took all 10 Australian wickets in the second innings for 53 runs, after a first innings haul of 9 for 37.

1964 Jim Reeves, American 'country' singer, killed in an air crash.

1965 The advertising of cigarettes on British television was banned.

1971 Astronauts David Scott and James Irwin became the first to ride on the moon, in their Lunar Roving Vehicle.

1 AUGUST (214)

National day of Switzerland.

1714 Queen Anne, the last Stuart sovereign died—George I was proclaimed King of Great Britain under the Act of Settlement (1701), none of her children having survived her.

1779 Francis Scott Key, American poet who wrote 'The Star-Spangled Banner', which became the official US national anthem in 1931, born in Carroll County, Maryland.

1793 The kilogram was introduced in France as the first metric weight.

1798 Nelson, in the flagship 'Vanguard', was victorious in the Battle of the Nile at Aboukir Bay near Alexandria, against the French under Brueys aboard 'L'Orient', and thus isolated Napoleon and his army in Egypt.

1819 Herman Melville, American novelist, author of 'Moby Dick', born at New York City.

1831 New London Bridge, designed by John Rennie, was opened.

1876 Colorado, the Centennial State, became the 38th state of the Union.

1883 Parcel post was introduced in Britain.

1907 Eric Shipton, English mountaineer, born.

1930 Lionel Bart, British composer, lyricist and playwright, born as Lionel Begleiter.

1936 The 11th Olympic Games opened in Berlin, where the Olympic flame was carried from Greece for the first time.

1944 Post codes were first introduced, in Germany.

2 AUGUST

1100 King William II, called Rufus, was accidentally killed by an arrow while hunting in the New Forest—was succeeded by his brother as Henry I.

1784 The first specially constructed Royal Mail coach ran, from Bristol to London.

1788 Thomas Gainsborough, English painter of landscapes and portraits, including ''The Blue Boy', died.

1876 (James Butler) 'Wild Bill' Hickok was shot by Jack McCall while playing poker in a saloon in Deadwood in South Dakota.

1894 Death duties were introduced in Britain.

1905 Myrna Loy, American film actress, born at Helena in Montana as Myrna Williams.

1921 Enrico Caruso, internationally famous Italian operatic tenor, died at Naples.

1922 Alexander Graham Bell, Scottish-born inventor of the telephone in 1876, died at his home near Baddeck in Nova Scotia, aged 75.

1923 Warren Harding, American Republican statesman and 29th President from 1921, died in San Francisco on his return from a trip to Alaska—the remainder of his term of office was completed by Calvin Coolidge.

1934 Paul von Hindenburg, German military and political leader and President from 1925, died aged 86.

1936 Louis Blériot, French aviator and first to fly across the English Channel in 1909, died.

1945 Pietro Mascagni, Italian opera composer, best known for his 'Cavalleria Rusticana', died aged 81.

1492 Christopher Columbus left Palos de la Frontera in SW Spain on his famous westward voyage, in command of the small 'Santa Maria', attended by the 'Pinta' and the 'Nina'.

1721 Grinling Gibbons, English woodcarver, notably in St Paul's Cathedral, died.

1778 The famous Opera House La Scala in Milan, the work of Giuseppe Piermarini, was opened.

1792 Sir Richard Arkwright, English inventor who developed the mechanical cotton spinning process, died.

1801 Sir Joseph Paxton, English landscape gardener, architect and designer of the Crystal Palace, born at Milton Bryant, near Woburn in Bedfordshire.

1858 Lake Victoria, the source of the Nile, was discovered by the English explorer John Speke.

1867 Stanley Baldwin, British statesman and three times Conservative Prime Minister, born at Bewdley, a market town on the river Severn.

1872 King Haakon VII of Norway, born at Charlottenlund.

1881 William George Fargo, co-founder of the Wells-Fargo Express Traffic service in 1852, died.

1887 Rupert Brooke, English poet, born at Rugby, the son of a housemaster at the public school.

1916 Sir Roger Casement, Irish nationalist, was hanged in London for treason, because of his attempts to induce Germany to support the cause of Irish independence.

1924 Joseph Conrad, Polish-born novelist, author of 'Lord Jim', died.

1926 Tony Bennett, American singer and entertainer, born at Astoria, New York as Anthony Benedetto.

1934 The German cabinet joined the offices of President and Chancellor and made Hitler 'Der Führer'.

1977 Archbishop Makarios, religious leader and President of Cyprus, died.

4 AUGUST

1265 The Battle of Evesham took place, in which Simon de Montfort was defeated and killed by Royalist forces led by the future King Edward I, during the Barons' War.

1792 (Percy Bysshe) P. B. Shelley, English romantic poet, born at Warnham, near Horsham in Sussex.
John Burgoyne, British general in the War of American Independence, who was forced to surrender at Saratoga in 1777 to General Gates, died.

1870 The Red Cross Society was founded in Britain by Lord Wantage.
Sir Harry Lauder, Scottish comic singer and entertainer of the music hall, born at Portobello, near Edinburgh.

1875 Hans Christian Andersen, Danish writer of fairy tales, including 'The Ugly Duckling', died at Copenhagen.

1900 Queen Elizabeth, the Queen Mother, was born at St Paul's Waldenbury in Hertfordshire, as Elizabeth Angela Marguerite Bowes-Lyon, the ninth of 10 children.

1908 Osbert Lancaster, English artist and cartoonist, born.

1914 German troops invaded Belgium, in violation of the terms of the Treaty of London.
Britain declared war on Germany.

1917 Captain Noel Chavasse, of the Royal Army Medical Corps, the second of only 3 to be awarded a bar to the Victoria Cross, died from his wounds.

5 AUGUST

The oyster season opens.

1729 Thomas Newcomen, English inventor of the first atmospheric steam engine in 1705, died in London.

1754 James Gibbs, Scottish architect, especially responsible for St Martin's-in-the-Fields, died.

1792 Lord North, British Tory statesman and Prime Minister from 1770 to 1782, died.

1799 Richard Howe, British admiral and distinguished naval commander, died.

1858 The first transatlantic cable was completed by Cyrus Field, laid by USS Niagara and HMS Agamemnon, was opened by Queen Victoria and President Buchanan exchanging greetings.

1895 Friedrich Engels, German Socialist, political writer and co-founder with Karl Marx of modern Communism, died in London.

1906 John Huston, American film director, born at Nevada in Missouri.

1911 Robert Taylor, American film actor, born at Filley in Nebraska as Spangler Arlington Brugh.

1914 The first electric traffic lights were erected, in Cleveland, Ohio.

1930 Neil Armstrong, American astronaut and first man on the moon, born at Wapakoneta in Ohio.

1962 Marilyn Monroe, American film actress and sex symbol, tragically died in Los Angeles aged 36.

6 AUGUST (219)

National day of Bolivia.

1623 Anne Hathaway, wife of William Shakespeare, died.

1637 Ben Jonson, English dramatist and poet, died in London.

1660 Diego Velasquez, Spanish painter, died in Madrid.

1775 Daniel O'Connell, Irish nationalist leader, born in County Kerry in the Republic of Ireland.

1809 Alfred, Lord Tennyson, English poet and Poet Laureate, born at Somersby rectory in Lincolnshire.

1825 Bolivia was proclaimed an independent Republic, free from nearly 300 years of Spanish rule, with Antonio Sucre its first President.

1866 John Mason Neale, English hymn writer, notably 'Jerusalem the golden' and 'O happy band of pilgrims', died at East Grinstead in Sussex.

1881 Sir Alexander Fleming, Scottish bacteriologist and discoverer of penicillin, born at Loudon in Ayrshire.

1890 The electric chair was used for the first time in America, at Auburn Prison, New York—the victim was murderer William Kemmler.

1893 The 3½-mile Corinth Canal of Southern Greece was opened.

1911 Lucille Ball, American comedy film actress, born at Jamestown in New York.

1916 Dom Mintoff, Labour politician and Prime Minister of Malta, born.

1917 Robert Mitchum, American film actor, born at Bridgeport in Connecticut.

1922 Freddie Laker, British airline operator, born.

1926 Gertrude Ederle of America became the first woman to swim the English Channel, crossing from Cap Gris Nez to Deal in 14½ hours.

1945 An atom bomb was dropped on the Japanese city of Hiroshima, from a Boeing B29 bomber 'Enola Gay'.

1949 John Haigh, the 'acid bath' murderer, was executed.

1962 Jamaica became independent after being a British colony for over 300 years.

1978 Pope Paul VI (Giovanni Battista Montini), died aged 80.

7 AUGUST (220)

1657 Robert Blake, one of the greatest of Britain's naval commanders, died as his ship entered Plymouth harbour.

1711 The first Royal Ascot horse race meeting took place—attended by Queen Anne.

1831 Dean Farrar, English clergyman and writer of school stories, notably 'Eric, or Little by Little', born in Bombay.

1834 Joseph Jacquard, French silk weaver and inventor of the first loom to weave patterns, died.

1876 Mata Hari, Dutch dancer, courtesan and spy, born at Leeuwarden as Margarete Gertrude Zelle.

1925 Summer time or daylight saving, introduced in Britain on 21st May 1916 by William Willett, was made permanent.

1926 The first British Motor Racing Grand Prix was held, at the Brooklands track, over a distance of 110 laps and 287 miles.

1957 Oliver Hardy, of Laurel and Hardy fame, died.

1958 The Litter Act came into force in Britain.

1970 Syd Buller, one of the world's leading cricket umpires, collapsed and died during the break in play in the County championship at Edgbaston in Warwickshire.

8 AUGUST (221)

1827 George Canning, British Tory statesman, but Prime Minister for just over 3 months, died at Chiswick in London.

1870 The first America's Cup race, open to challenge by any nation's yachts, took place—'Magic' of the United States beating the British challenge of 'Cambria'.

1900 The Davis Cup for tennis, presented by Dwight Filley Davis, was contested for the first time, at Brookline in Massachusetts—won by USA on 10th.

1919 (Frank Winfield) F. W. Woolworth, American merchant and founder in 1879 of the store that bears his name, died.

1931 America's airship 'Akron' was launched by Mrs Hoover.

1937 Dustin Hoffman, American film actor, born at Los Angeles in California.

1963 The Great Train Robbery took place at Sears Crossing at Mentmore, near Cheddington in Buckinghamshire, on the Glasgow to London mail train. The haul was over 2½ million pounds in bank notes on their way for destruction.

1974 Richard Nixon announced his resignation as US President —the first to do so—because of his implication in the Watergate scandal.

1979 Nicholas Monsarrat, English novelist of the sea, notably 'The Cruel Sea', died.

9 AUGUST (222)

1593 Izaak Walton, English writer, author of 'The Compleat Angler' on the pleasures of fishing, born at Stafford.

1631 John Dryden, English poet and critic, born at the vicarage of Aldwinkle All Saints in Northamptonshire.

1757 Thomas Telford, Scottish engineer of roads, canals and bridges, born at Westerkirk, near Langholm, the son of a shepherd.

1848 Frederick Marryat, English writer of sea adventure novels, notably 'Mr Midshipman Easy', died at Langham in Norfolk.

1902 The coronation of King Edward VII took place—having been put back some 6 weeks because of the need of an emergency appendicitis operation.

1938 Rod Laver, Australian tennis champion, born at Rockhampton in the State of Queensland.

1945 The second atom bomb of the war was dropped on the Japanese city of Nagasaki.

1974 Gerald Ford was sworn in as the 38th President of America, on the resignation of Richard Nixon—the first to serve without being chosen by the people in a National Election.

1975 Dmitri Shostakovich, Soviet composer, died.

10 AUGUST (223)

National day of Ecuador.

1675 Greenwich Observatory was established by King Charles II, and its foundation stone laid.

1810 Count Cavour, Italian statesman, primarily responsible for the unification of his country, born at Turin.

1821 Missouri, the Show Me State, became the 24th state of the Union.

1846 The Smithsonian Institution was established at Washington, DC, by the bequest of British scientist James Smithson.

1874 Herbert Hoover, American Republican statesman and 31st President, born at West Branch in Iowa, the son of a blacksmith.

1885 The first electric street-railway in the United States was opened in Baltimore by Leo Daft.

1896 Otto Lilienthal, German engineer and gliding pioneer, died as a result of a glider crash the previous day.

1897 Britain's Royal Automobile Club was founded, under the name of 'The Automobile Club of Great Britain'.

1966 America's first moon satellite, Orbiter I, was launched.

11 AUGUST (224)

1890 Cardinal Newman, English churchman and leader of the Oxford Movement which intended to restore high-Church ideals, died at Edgbaston in Warwickshire aged 89.

1897 Enid Blyton, English writer of children's books, born at East Dulwich in South London.

1919 Andrew Carnegie, Scottish-born American steel industrialist and philanthropist, died at Lennox in Massachusetts aged 83.

1921 Alex Haley, American author of the best seller 'Roots', born at Ithaca, New York.

1942 The New Waterloo Bridge over the Thames opened to traffic.

1952 King Hussein succeeded as King of the Jordan on the deposition of his father, King Talal, because of mental illness.

1960 Chad, a member state of the French Community in Northern Africa, became an independent Republic.

12 AUGUST (225)

The grouse shooting season opens in Britain.

1762 King George IV born at St James's Palace in London's Pall Mall, the eldest son of George III.

1774 Robert Southey, English poet and Poet Laureate, born at Bristol.

1827 William Blake, English poet and artist, died in London.

1848 George Stephenson, English engineer who constructed the 'Rocket' and the first railway in 1825, from Stockton to Darlington, died at Tapton, near Chesterfield in Derbyshire.

1881 Cecil B. De Mille, American film producer, noted for his Biblical spectacles, born at Ashfield in Massachusetts.

1925 Norris and Ross McWhirter, editors and compilers of the Guinness Book of Records, born.

1944 'PLUTO'—'Pipe Line Under The Ocean'—supplying petrol across the English Channel to the allied forces in France, went into operation, from Shanklin on the Isle of Wight.

1955 Thomas Mann, German novelist and Nobel Prize winner, died at Zurich aged 80.

1960 The first communications satellite was launched— America's Echo I.

1964 Ian Fleming, English author and creator of the hero 'James Bond', died.

1982 Henry Fonda, American film actor, died aged 77.

13 AUGUST (226)

1704 The Battle of Blenheim took place in southern Germany, in which an Anglo-Austrian army under Marlborough and Prince Eugene decisively defeated the French and Bavarian armies in the War of the Spanish Succession.

1826 René Laennec, French physician who invented and named the stethoscope in 1819, died.

1860 Annie Oakley, American entertainer as a marksman with rifle and shotgun, born at Patterson in Ohio as Phoebe Anne Oakley Mozee.

1877 Birkenhead, on Merseyside, became a borough, with John Laird its first Lord Mayor.

1888 John Logie Baird, Scottish pioneer of television, born at Helensburgh, on the Firth of Clyde.

1896 Sir John Millais, English painter and a founder member of the Pre-Raphaelite Brotherhood, died, and was buried in St Paul's Cathedral.

1898 Jean Borotra, French tennis champion, born.

1899 Alfred Hitchcock, American film producer and master of suspense, born at Leytonstone in London, the son of a greengrocer.

1907 Sir Basil Spence, Scottish architect, designer of the new Coventry Cathedral, born in India.

1910 Florence Nightingale, English nurse in the Crimean War and founder of modern nursing, died in London aged 90.

1912 Ben Hogan, American golfing champion, born at Stephenville in Texas.

1913 Archbishop Makarios, President of Cyprus, born near Paphos, the son of a farmer.

1927 Fidel Castro, Cuban revolutionary and political leader, born near Biran, the son of a sugar planter.

1946 (Herbert George) H. G. Wells, English writer and pioneer in science fiction, died in London aged 79.

1961 The border between East and West Berlin was sealed off by East Germany with the closure of the Brandenburg Gate to stop the exodus to the West.

1964 The last hangings in Britain took place—Peter Allen at Walton Gaol, Liverpool and John Walby at Strangeways Gaol, Manchester.

1977 Henry Williamson, English author, notably 'Tarka the Otter' and 'Salar the Salmon', died.

14 AUGUST (227)

1778 Augustus Toplady, English clergyman and hymn writer, especially 'Rock of Ages', died.

1816 Tristan da Cunha, a group of 4 islands in the South Atlantic were annexed to and garrisoned by Britain.

1867 John Galsworthy, English novelist, playwright and Nobel Prize winner, born at Combe in Surrey.

1893 France became the first country to introduce motor vehicle registration plates.

1908 The first International Beauty Contest in Britain was held, at the Pier Hippodrome at Folkestone in Kent.

1920 The 7th Olympic Games opened in Antwerp.

1922 Lord Alfred Harmsworth, British newspaper publisher who launched the 'London Evening News', 'Daily Mail', 'Daily Mirror' and the 'Times', died.

1945 Japanese surrendered, ending World War II—the formal surrender took place aboard USS Missouri on 2nd September.

15 AUGUST (228)

1769 Napoleon Bonaparte, French military leader and Emperor, born at Ajaccio, capital of the Mediterranean island of Corsica, the son of a lawyer.

1771 Sir Walter Scott, Scottish novelist and poet, born at Edinburgh.

1856 Keir Hardie, Scottish Labour leader and one of the founders of the Labour Party, born near Holytown in Lanarkshire.

1879 Ethel Barrymore, American stage and screen actress, the first lady of the American theatre, born at Philadelphia as Ethel Blythe.

1888 (Thomas Edward) T. E. Lawrence, British soldier and writer who became known as 'Lawrence of Arabia', born at Tremadoc in Wales.

1914 The first ship, the SS Ancon, passed through the Panama Canal.

1930 Tom Mboya, Kenyan politician and leader in his country's struggle for independence, born.

1935 Wiley Post, American aviator, was killed in a plane crash in Alaska—with passenger, American humorist, Will Rogers.

1947 India became independent, with Pandit Nehru its first Prime Minister.

1950 Princess Anne (Anne Elizabeth Alice Louise) was born at Clarence House in London, the second child and only daughter of Queen Elizabeth II.

16 AUGUST (229)

1743 The earliest prize-ring code of boxing rules was formulated in England by the champion pugilist Jack Broughton.

1819 The Peterloo massacre took place in St Peter's Fields, Manchester. The large meeting held there, petitioning for Parliamentary reform, was dispersed by the Army—killing 11.

1899 Robert Bunsen, German chemist, physicist and inventor of the gas burner that bears his name, died aged 88.

1912 Ted Drake, Arsenal and England footballer, born.

1948 George Herman 'Babe' Ruth, the legendary American baseball player, died at New York City.

1950 Jeff Thomson, Australian cricketer and fast bowler, born.

1952 Severe thunderstorms in Somerset and North Devon caused rivers to flood, bringing devastation to the town of Lynmouth.

1956 Bela Lugosi, Hungarian-American film actor, best known for horror films especially 'Dracula', died.

1960 Cyprus became an independent Republic, with Archbishop Makarios its first President.

1977 Elvis Presley, American rock and roll singer and film actor, died at Memphis in Tennessee.

1979 John George Diefenbaker, Canadian Conservative politician and Prime Minister from 1957 to 1963, died aged 83.

17 AUGUST   (230)

National day of Indonesia.

1786 Frederick the Great, military leader and King of Prussia since 1740, died at Potsdam.
Davy Crockett, American frontiersman and later Congressman, born at Limestone in Tennessee.

1807 Robert Fulton made the first practical steamboat trip, 150 miles in 'Clermont' from New York City to Albany.

1892 Mae West, American film actress and sex symbol, born at Brooklyn in New York, the daughter of a boxer.

1897 The first gold was discovered in the Klondike.

1921 Maureen O'Hara, Irish-American film actress, born in Dublin as Maureen Fitzsimmons.

1938 Henry Armstrong won the lightweight boxing title, and so became the only man in the ring's history to hold 3 world titles at different weights, at the same time.

1945 Indonesia was proclaimed independent, following Japanese occupation.

1951 Alan Minter, British middleweight boxing champion, born at Penge in London.

1961 The construction of the Berlin Wall by the Russians began, separating East and West.

18 AUGUST (231)

1587 Virginia Dare became the first child born of English parents in the New World—on Roanoke Island in North Carolina —7 days after Sir Walter Raleigh's second expedition landed.

1809 Matthew Boulton, English engineer and partner of James Watt, died at Soho in London.

1850 Honoré de Balzac, French novelist, died in Paris.

1920 Godfrey Evans, Kent and England cricketer, born at Finchley.

1927 Rosalynn Carter, wife of America's 39th President, born at Plains in Georgia as Rosalynn Smith.

1932 Scottish aviator Jim Mollison made the first westbound trans-Atlantic solo flight, from Portmarnock in Ireland to Pennfield in New Brunswick.

19 AUGUST (232)

1646 John Flamsteed, English astronomer and first Astronomer Royal, born at Denby near Derby.

1662 Blaise Pascal, French philosopher and mathematician who invented the first digital calculator, died in Paris.

1743 Comtesse du Barry, the last mistress of Louis XV, born at Vaucouleurs as Marie Jeanne Bécu, the daughter of a dressmaker.

1745 After travelling from France to claim the throne of Britain, Bonnie Prince Charlie raised his father's standard at Glenfinnan.

1808 James Nasmyth, Scottish engineer who invented the first steam hammer, born at Edinburgh.

1819 James Watt, Scottish engineer and inventor of the modern steam engine under a patent of 1769, died at Heathfield Hall, near Birmingham aged 83.

1871 Orville Wright, American pioneer aviator, born at Dayton in Ohio, the younger of the two brothers.

1902 Ogden Nash, American poet known for his humorous verse, born in New York.

1928 Viscount Haldane, British statesman who re-organised the Army and founded the Territorials in 1908, died in London.

1929 Sergei Diaghilev, Russian ballet impresario and director, died.

1931 Willie Shoemaker, American champion jockey, the first to ride over 7000 winners, born near Fabens in Texas.

1942 Canadian and British Commandos raided the French port of Dieppe in Normandy—was called 'Operation Jubilee'.

1944 Sir Henry Wood, English conductor and co-founder of the Promenade Concerts in 1895, died at Hitchin in Hertfordshire.

1976 Alastair Sim, British comedy actor, died.

1981 Jessie Matthews, English stage and radio star, died in a London hospital.

20 AUGUST (233)

1833 Benjamin Harrison, American Republican statesman and 23rd President, born at North Bend in Ohio, the son of a member of Congress and grandson of the 9th President.

1912 William Booth, English social reformer, evangelist, founder and 'General' of the Salvation Army, died aged 83.

1924 Jim Reeves, American singer and entertainer, born in Panola County in Texas.

1940 Leon Trotsky, Russian revolutionary, was assassinated at Coyoacan near Mexico City—the killer was identified as Ramon Mercador del Rio.

1956 Calder Hall in Cumberland, the world's first large-scale atomic power station, began generating.

1965 Clive Inman, Leicestershire batsman, scored 50 in a record 8 minutes, at Trent Bridge cricket ground.

1968 Russian and troops of other Communist countries invaded Czechoslovakia.

1975 Viking I was launched, on its way to Mars.

1977 Julius or 'Groucho' Marx, American comedian of the famous Marx Brothers, died in Los Angeles.

21 AUGUST (234)

1754 William Murdock, Scottish engineer and inventor of coal-gas lighting in 1792, born at Auchinleck in Ayrshire.

1765 King William IV, the 'Sailor King', born at Buckingham Palace, the third son of King George III and Queen Charlotte.

1808 The Battle of Vimiero in the Peninsular War took place in Portugal, with Wellington defeating General Junot's French forces.

1904 Count Basie, American jazz pianist and band leader, born at Red Bank in New Jersey as William Basie.

1911 Leonardo da Vinci's painting of the 'Mona Lisa' was stolen from the Louvre in Paris by an Italian waiter Vicenzo Perruggia—was recovered in 1913.

1930 Princess Margaret born at Glamis Castle in Angus, Scotland, the younger sister of Queen Elizabeth II.

1944 Meetings started at Dumbarton Oaks at Washington, DC, building the foundations of the charter of the United Nations—ended on 7th October.

1959 Hawaii, the Aloha State, became the 50th state of the Union.
Sir Jacob Epstein, British sculptor, died.

1965 Spacecraft Gemini 5 was launched, with Gordon Cooper and Charles Conrad.
K. Peacock became the first substitute to be called on in a Football League match, for Charlton Athletic at Bolton.

22 AUGUST

1485 The Battle of Bosworth Field, the last of the Wars of the Roses, took place near Market Bosworth in Leicestershire, in which Richard III was defeated and killed by the forces of Henry VII.

1642 The Civil War in England began, between the supporters of Charles I (Royalists or Cavaliers) and of Parliament (Roundheads), when the King raised his standard at Nottingham.

1806 Jean Fragonard, French painter, died.

1818 Warren Hastings, British administrator and first Governor-General of British India, died in Worcestershire aged 85.

1862 Claude Debussy, French romantic composer, born at St Germain-en-Laye near Paris.

1892 Percy Fender, Surrey and England cricketer, born at Balham.

1922 Michael Collins, Irish politician and revolutionary, was assassinated by extremist Republicans in an ambush between Bandon and Macroom in Ireland.

1933 The first boxing match was televised in Britain, at Broadcasting House in London.

1940 Sir Oliver Lodge, English physicist and pioneer of wireless telegraphy, died.

1942 Michel Fokine, Russian dancer and choreographer, died.

1963 Viscount Nuffield, British motor car magnate and philanthropist, died.

1978 Jomo Kenyatta, Kenyan leader and his country's first President in 1964, died.

23 AUGUST

National day of Romania.

1305 William Wallace, Scottish patriot and leader against the English to obtain his country's independence, was hanged in London.

1628 The Duke of Buckingham, British statesman and favourite of King James I, was assassinated at Portsmouth by a subaltern, John Felton.

1754 Louis XVI, King of France, born at Versailles, the only son of Louis XV.

1866 The Treaty of Prague was signed, ending the war between Austria and Prussia.

1912 Gene Kelly, American film actor and dancer in Hollywood musicals, born at Pittsburgh in Pennsylvania.

1926 Rudolph Valentino, American film actor and romantic idol, died suddenly in a New York hospital at the age of 31.

1929 Peter Thomson, Australian golfing champion, born.

1938 Len Hutton completed an innings of 364, lasting 13 hours 17 minutes, for England against Australia in the fifth Test at the Oval, out of a record score of 903.

1944 Paris was liberated—having been captured and occupied by German forces since 14th June 1940.

24 AUGUST (237)

1572 The St Bartholomew's Day massacre took place in Paris— the massacre of thousands of French Huguenots, by order of the Catholic French Court.

1680 Captain Blood, Irish adventurer, noted for his attempt to steal the Crown jewels from the Tower of London in 1671, died.

1724 George Stubbs, English anatomist and painter of animals, especially horses, born at Liverpool.

1759 William Wilberforce, English philanthropist and anti-slavery campaigner, born at Hull on Humberside, the son of a merchant.

1814 The Capitol and the White House at Washington were burned by British troops under General Ross.

1872 Sir Max Beerbohm, English writer and caricaturist, born in London.

1892 Goodison Park, the home of Everton Football Club at Liverpool, was opened.

1903 Graham Sutherland, English artist, born in London.

1958 Johannes Strijdom, South African nationalist statesman and Prime Minister who enforced apartheid, died.

25 AUGUST (238)

National day of Uruguay.

1819 Allan Pinkerton, American founder of the national detective agency at Chicago that bears his name, born at Glasgow in Scotland.

1822 Sir William Herschel, German-born English astronomer who discovered the planet Uranus in 1781, died.

1825 Uruguay gained independence from Spain under José Artigas.

1867 Michael Faraday, English physicist and founder of the science of electro-magnetism, died at Hampton Court in London.

1875 Captain Matthew Webb became the first to swim the English Channel, swimming breaststroke from Admiralty Pier, Dover to Calais in just under 22 hours.

1918 Leonard Bernstein, American composer and conductor, born at Lawrence in Massachusetts.
Richard Greene, British film actor, born at Plymouth in Devon.

1919 George Wallace, American Democrat politician and Governor, born at Clio in Alabama.
Daily air service began between London (Hounslow) and Paris (Le Bourget).

1928 Anfield's famous Kop at Liverpool's football ground was opened.

1930 Sean Connery, British film actor, born at Edinburgh as Thomas Connery.

1940 The first air raid on Berlin took place, with 'Whitleys', 'Hampdens' and 'Wellingtons'.

1942 The Duke of Kent, the son of King George V, was killed on active service.

1960 The 17th Olympic Games opened in Rome.

1967 Paul Muni, Austrian-born American film actor and Academy Award (Oscar) winner in 1936 for his role in 'The Story of Louis Pasteur', died.

26 AUGUST

1346 The Battle of Crécy took place, 32 miles south of Boulogne, the scene of Edward III's victory over Philip VI of France in the Hundred Years War—the first use of the English longbow in continental warfare.

1676 Sir Robert Walpole, statesman regarded as the first British Prime Minister, born at Houghton Hall in Norfolk.

1743 Antoine Lavoisier, French founder of modern chemistry, born in Paris.

1819 Albert, German prince and Consort of Queen Victoria, born at Rosenau near Coburg in Bavaria.

1875 John Buchan, Scottish novelist and statesman, born at Perth.

1920 The right to vote was given to women in America, by the 19th amendment.
Percy Fender, Surrey cricketer, scored a century in a record 35 minutes, at Northampton.

1930 Lon Chaney, American silent-screen actor known as the 'man of a thousand faces', died.

1936 Leslie Mitchell became the first television announcer in Britain when he announced the BBC's programme to Olympia.

1958 Ralph Vaughan Williams, English composer, died in London aged 85.

1972 Sir Francis Chichester, English aviator and round-the-world yachtsman, died at Plymouth in Devon.
The 20th Olympic Games opened at Munich.

1974 Charles Lindbergh, American aviator noted for being the first to fly the Atlantic solo non-stop in 1927, died.

1978 Charles Boyer, French romantic actor, died 2 days before his 79th birthday.

1576 Titian, one of the greatest Venetian painters, died in Venice.

1859 The first commercially productive oil well was drilled, near Titusville in Pennsylvania, by Edwin Drake of Seneca Oil.

1879 Sir Rowland Hill, English pioneer in postal services and deviser of the Penny Post in 1840, died.

1882 Sam Goldwyn, American film producer and pioneer in the film industry, born of Jewish parents in Warsaw as Samuel Goldfish (Gelbfisch).

1883 Krakatoa, a volcanic island in the Sunda Strait between Sumatra and Java, erupted with thousands killed by the resulting tidal waves.

1899 (Cecil Scott) C. S. Forester, English novelist, creator of 'Captain Horatio Hornblower', born at Cairo in Egypt.

1908 Sir Donald Bradman, Australian cricketer of distinction, born at Cootamundra in New South Wales.
Lyndon Baines Johnson, American Democrat statesman and 36th President, born at Johnson City in Texas.

1919 Louis Botha, South African Boer general, statesman and first Prime Minister of the Union in 1910, died.

1928 The Kellogg-Briand Peace Pact, renouncing war, was signed in Paris.

1939 The world's first jet-propelled aeroplane, the Heinkel 178, with engine designed by Dr Von Ohain, made its first flight, at Marienehe in North Germany.

1966 Francis Chichester left Plymouth in 'Gipsy Moth IV' on his single-handed voyage around the world—arriving back at Plymouth on the following 28th May.

1975 Haile Selassie, the deposed Emperor of Ethiopia, nick-named 'The Lion of Judah', died in exile.

1979 Earl Mountbatten was murdered by members of the IRA, in a fishing boat off Mullaghmore in County Sligo.

28 AUGUST

1207 Liverpool was created a borough by King John.

1749 Johann Goethe, German poet and novelist, author of 'Faust', born at Frankfurt-am-Main, the son of a lawyer.

1828 Count Leo Tolstoy, Russian novelist and philosopher, born of noble family in Tula Province.

1840 Ira Sankey, American hymn writer and evangelist with Dwight Moody, born at Edinburgh in Pennsylvania.

1899 Charles Boyer, French romantic actor, born at Figeac.

1913 Lindsay Hassett, Australian Test cricketer, born at Geelong in the State of Victoria.

1933 The BBC made the first broadcast appeal on behalf of the police, for Stanley Hobday, wanted for murder.

1944 David Soul, American film actor, best known as star of 'Starsky and Hutch', born at Chicago as David Solberg.

1972 Prince William of Gloucester was killed in an air crash.

29 AUGUST

1782 The 100-ton battleship HMS Royal George sank while at anchor at Spithead, with the loss of more than 900 lives, including Admiral Kempenfelt.

1842 The Treaty of Nanking was signed, ending the Opium War (1839 to 1842) between China and Britain.

1877 Brigham Young, American Mormon leader and founder of Salt Lake City in Utah, died.

1885 The first motor cycle was patented, built by Gottlieb Daimler at Cannstatt in Germany.

1895 The Rugby League was formed at a meeting at the George Hotel in Huddersfield, with 21 representatives of the leading Lancashire and Yorkshire Rugby Union clubs—the present title of 'Rugby League' was adopted in 1922.

1898 Walter Lindrum, world billiards champion, born in Australia.

1904 The 3rd Olympic Games opened at St Louis in Missouri.

1915 Ingrid Bergman, American film actress and twice Oscar winner, born at Stockholm.

1923 Richard Attenborough, English film actor, producer and director, born at Cambridge.

1930 William Spooner, British scholar and originator of 'spoonerisms', died.

1947 James Hunt, British motor racing champion driver, born at Belmont in Surrey.

1975 Eamon de Valera, Irish statesman, 3 times Prime Minister and President from 1959 to 1973, died aged 92.

1982 Ingrid Bergman, Swedish-born American film actress and Oscar winner, died in London on her 67th birthday, after a long illness.

30 AUGUST   (243)

1797 Mary Shelley, English novelist, best known as the author of 'Frankenstein', born in London.

1860 The first tramway in Britain opened, at Birkenhead on Merseyside.

1871 Lord Rutherford, British physicist, eminent in the field of atomic research, born at Spring Grove, near Nelson on the southern island of New Zealand.

1896 Raymond Massey, American film actor, born at Toronto in Canada.

1908 Fred MacMurray, American film actor, born at Kankakee in Illinois.

1917 Denis Healey, British Labour politician and statesman, born.

1923 Victor Seixas, American lawn tennis champion, born.

1940 Sir J. J. Thomson, English physicist who discovered the electron in 1897, died at Cambridge, and was buried near Isaac Newton in the nave of Westminster Abbey.

1941 The siege of Leningrad by German forces began—ended in January 1943.

1945 Hong Kong was re-occupied by the British after 4 years of Japanese occupation.

31 AUGUST

National day of both Malaysia and Trinidad and Tobago.

1422 King Henry V of England died at Vincennes in France, struck down with dysentery—was succeeded by his 9-month-old infant son as Henry VI.

1688 John Bunyan, religious writer, author of 'Pilgrim's Progress', died at the house of a friend at Holborn in London.

1880 Wilhelmina, Queen of the Netherlands, born.

1889 'Bombardier' Billy Wells, British heavyweight boxer, born.

1897 Fredric March, American film actor and Oscar winner, born at Racine in Wisconsin as Frederick McIntyre Bickel.

1900 Roland Culver, British actor, born.

1913 Sir Bernard Lovell, English astronomer and a leader in the development of radio astronomy, born in Gloucestershire.

1918 Alan Jay Lerner, American lyric writer of musical comedies in collaboration with Frederick Loewe, born in New York City.

1944 Clive Lloyd, West Indian cricketer, born at Georgetown, the capital of Guyana.

1957 Malaya achieved independence.

1962 Trinidad and Tobago in the West Indies became independent, having been a British possession since 1802.

1968 Gary Sobers of Nottinghamshire became the first cricketer to score 6 sixes off an over, at Swansea against Glamorgan —bowled by Malcolm Nash.

1969 Rocky Marciano, American world heavyweight boxing champion from 1952 to 1956, who retired undefeated, was killed in an air crash in central Iowa.

1973 John Ford, American film director, best known for his westerns, including 'Stagecoach', died.

National day of Libya.
The partridge shooting season begins.

1159 Adrian IV, the only Englishman, Nicholas Breakspear, to be elected Pope, died.

1557 Jacques Cartier, French explorer of the North American coast and the St Lawrence river, died at St Malo.

1715 King Louis XIV of France, called the 'Sun King', died at Versailles, after reigning for just over 72 years—the longest in European history.

1834 Amilcare Ponchielli, Italian composer, notably 'La Gioconda', born near Cremona in Lombardy, the son of the town organist.

1854 Engelbert Humperdinck, German composer, born at Siegburg, near Bonn.

1864 Sir Roger Casement, British civil servant and Irish nationalist, born at Kingstown near Dublin.

1866 James Corbett, American heavyweight boxing champion known as 'Gentleman Jim', born in San Francisco.

1875 Edgar Rice Burroughs, American novelist best known for the series of 'Tarzan' books, born at Chicago.

1923 Rocky Marciano, American boxer and world heavyweight champion, born at Brockton in Massachusetts as Rocco Marchegiano.

An earthquake took place in Japan, leaving the cities of Tokyo and Yokohama in ruins and a total of nearly 100000 deaths.

1939 The BBC 'Home Service' on the radio began.

Hitler declared war on and invaded Poland, provoking World War II.

1969 Qaddhafi or Gadafy became Head of State of Libya, after leading a military coup overthrowing King Idris I.

2 SEPTEMBER (246)

1666 The Great Fire of London began at Pudding Lane, in the bakehouse of Thomas Farriner—burnt itself out on 6th.

1834 Thomas Telford, Scottish engineer, road, bridge and canal builder, died in London and was buried in Westminster Abbey.

1898 The Battle of Omdurman took place, with victory for Kitchener's Anglo-Egyptian forces over the Khalifa's forces —winning back the Sudan for Egypt.

1910 Henri Rousseau, French primitive painter known as 'Le Douanier' because of his job as a Customs official, died in Paris.

1916 The last of the famous Blaydon races in Northumberland were held.

1937 Pierre de Coubertin, reviver of the Olympic Games in 1896, died.

1945 The formal Japanese surrender to the Allies was signed on board the US battleship 'Missouri'.

1952 Jimmy Connors, American tennis champion, born at East St Louis in Illinois.

1973 J. R. R. Tolkien, South African-born English author, notably 'The Lord of the Rings', died at Bournemouth in Dorset.

3 SEPTEMBER (247)

1189 The coronation of King Richard I, the Lion Heart, took place at Westminster Abbey.

1658 Oliver Cromwell, statesman, Puritan leader and Lord Protector of England from 1653, died in Whitehall, London of pneumonia—was succeeded by his son Richard, as Protector.

1877 Adolphe Thiers, French statesman, Prime Minister and President, died of apoplexy at St Germain-en-Laye, near Paris.

1897 Cecil Parker, English film actor, born at Hastings in Kent as Cecil Schwabe.

1900 Urho Kekkonen, Finnish statesman, Prime Minister and President, born.

1913 Alan Ladd, American film actor, born at Hot Springs in Arkansas.

1939 Great Britain and France declared war on Germany.

1948 Eduard Benes, Czech statesman and President until the Communist takeover, died.

1966 Captain Ridgway and Sergeant Blyth became the first Britons to row across the Atlantic; the journey in 'English Rose III' took 91 days.

1967 Sweden switched to driving on the right of the road.

1969 Ho Chi Minh, Vietnamese leader and one of the most influential Communist leaders, died aged 79.

4 SEPTEMBER (248)

1870 Emperor Napoleon III, nephew of Bonaparte, deposed.

1886 Geronimo, Apache chief and leader of the last great American Red Indian rebellion, finally surrendered in Arizona to General Nelson Miles.

1907 Edvard Grieg, Norwegian composer, best known for his 'Peer Gynt Suite', died at Bergen.

1909 The first Boy Scout rally took place, at Crystal Palace in London.

1929 The German airship 'Graf Zeppelin' completed its 20-day round-the-world trip, from Friedrichshafen, on the shore of Lake Constance, via Tokyo, Los Angeles and Lakehurst.

1937 Dawn Fraser, Australian Olympic swimming champion, born at Sydney.

1939 The British liner 'Athenia' was sunk by a German submarine off the coast of Ireland.

1948 Wilhelmina abdicated as Queen of the Netherlands in favour of her daughter Juliana.

1949 Tom Watson, American golfing champion, born at Kansas City in Missouri.
Britain's largest-ever aircraft, the 130-ton 8-engined 'Bristol Brabazon', had its first flight.

1963 Robert Schuman, French statesman, Prime Minister and Foreign Minister, died.

1964 The Forth road bridge, 6156 ft long, and with a centre span of 3300 ft, was opened by Her Majesty the Queen.

1965 Albert Schweitzer, French medical missionary, noted organist and Nobel Prize winner in 1952, died aged 90 at Lambaréné in Gabon, where he set up a native hospital in 1913.

5 SEPTEMBER (249)

1174 Canterbury Cathedral was destroyed by fire.

1638 Louis XIV, King of France, known as the 'Sun King', born at St Germain-en-Laye, an outer suburb of Paris.

1781 The Battle of Chesapeake Bay took place off the east coast of America, between French and British fleets.

1826 John Wisden, Sussex cricketer and compiler of the record books that bear his name, born at Brighton in Sussex.

1847 Jesse James, American outlaw and robber, born near Excelsior Springs in Clay County in Missouri, the son of a Baptist minister.

1857 Auguste Comte, French philosopoher, sociologist and founder of Positivism, died.

1902 Darryl F. Zanuck, American film producer, born at Wahoo in Nebraska.

1905 The Treaty of Portsmouth was signed, ending the Russo-Japanese war.

1929 Bob Newhart, American comedian, born at Oak Park in Illinois.

1939 'Clay' Regazzoni, motor racing champion, born at Lugano in Switzerland.

1942 Raquel Welch, American film actress and sex symbol, born at Chicago in Illinois, with the maiden name of Jo-Raquel Tejada, of a Bolivian father.

1982 Douglas Bader, British pilot of distinction and leader of 'the few' in the Battle of Britain, died in the early hours of the morning.

6 SEPTEMBER (250)

1522 Ferdinand Magellan's ship the 'Vittoria', under the command of Del Cano, arrived at San Lucar in Spain after

completing the first circumnavigation of the world—
Magellan himself was killed on the island of Mactan in the
Philippines.

1666 The Great Fire of London came to an end—having started
at Pudding Lane on 2nd.

1757 Lafayette, French soldier, statesman and hero of the
American Revolution, born at Chavagnac.

1766 John Dalton, English chemist and physician, born at
Eaglesfield near Cockermouth in Cumberland, the son of a
Quaker weaver.

1880 England played Australia at the Oval in London, in the first
cricket test match in England.

1901 American President McKinley was shot by anarchist Leon
Czolgosz at a public reception in Buffalo—he died on 14th.

1939 The first air raid of the war on England took place.

1940 King Carol II of Romania abdicated in favour of his son
Michael.

1948 Queen Juliana became Queen of the Netherlands, on the
abdication of her mother, Queen Wilhelmina.

1966 Hendrik Verwoerd, South African statesman and Prime
Minister since 1958, was assassinated in Parliament at Cape
Town, by Dimitric Tsafondas.

1968 Swaziland became an independent Kingdom within the
Commonwealth.

7 SEPTEMBER (251)

National day of Brazil.

1533 Queen Elizabeth I, born at Greenwich Palace in London,
the daughter of Henry VIII and his second wife, Anne
Boleyn.

1548 Catharine Parr, the sixth wife of Henry VIII, died in
childbirth, by then the wife of Lord Seymour, at Sudeley
Castle near Cheltenham in Gloucestershire.

1812 The Battle of Borodino took place 70 miles west of
Moscow, in which Russian forces under Kutuzov failed to
stop Napoleon's march to the capital.

1822 Brazil proclaimed its independence from Portugal, with Pedro I acclaimed Emperor.

1836 Sir Henry Campbell-Bannerman, British statesman and Liberal Prime Minister, born at Glasgow.

1838 Grace Darling made the famous rescue of the crew of the 'Forfarshire', shipwrecked near the Farne Islands off the Northumberland coast.

1871 George Hirst, Yorkshire cricketer, born at Kirkheaton.

1892 'Gentleman' James J. Corbett beat John L. Sullivan in 21 rounds at New Orleans, and became the first world heavyweight boxing champion under Queensberry rules—with gloves and 3-minute rounds.

1895 The first Rugby League matches were played.

1910 Holman Hunt, English painter and co-founder of the Pre-Raphaelite Brotherhood, known for his religious works, died in London.

1913 Anthony Quayle, British Shakespearean actor, born in Lancashire.

1930 King Baudouin of the Belgians, born at Stuyenberg Castle, the elder son of King Leopold III and Queen Astrid.

1936 Buddy Holly, American singer and guitarist, born at Lubbock in Texas as Charles Harden Holley.

1943 Italy surrendered during World War II.

1956 C. B. Fry, English cricketer, footballer, Rugby player and athlete, died at Hampstead in London aged 84.

8 SEPTEMBER (252)

1157 King Richard I was born at Oxford, the third son of Henry II and Eleanor of Aquitaine—called Richard the Lion Heart (Coeur de lion).

1664 The Dutch settlement of New Amsterdam was seized by the English and re-named New York, in honour of James Duke of York, the future King James II.

1831 The coronation of King William IV took place.

1841 Antonin Dvorak, Czech composer, born near Prague, the son of a butcher.

1888 English Football League matches were played for the first time.

1901 Hendrik Verwoerd, Prime Minister of South Africa responsible for apartheid policy, born at Amsterdam in the Netherlands.

1921 Harry Secombe, British comedian, born in Wales.

1925 Peter Sellers, English comedian and film actor, born at Southsea in Hampshire.

1933 Faisal I or Feisal I, King of Iraq since 1921, died.

1944 The first German V2 flying bombs fell in Britain.

1946 Communists took power in Bulgaria, abolishing the monarchy.

1949 Richard Strauss, German composer, known for the opera 'Der Rosenkavalier', died.

1966 The Severn bridge over the Severn estuary, between Haysgate and Almondsbury, carrying the M4 motorway, was opened by Her Majesty the Queen.

1967 Uganda became a Republic, with Milton Obote its first President.

9 SEPTEMBER   (253)

1087 William the Conqueror died at Rouen in France, from injuries received when his horse stumbled.

1513 The Battle of Flodden Field took place near Branxton in Northumberland, in which James IV of Scotland was defeated and killed by English troops under Thomas Howard, the Earl of Surrey.

1583 Sir Humphrey Gilbert, English explorer who established a Newfoundland colony at St John's, was drowned when the 'Squirrel' went down off the Azores with all on board, during his voyage home.

1585 Cardinal Richelieu, French statesman and chief Minister of Louis XIII, born near Chinon.

1737 Luigi Galvani, Italian scientist and anatomist, born at Bologna.

1754 William Bligh, British captain of the 'Bounty' at the time of the mutiny, born at Plymouth in Devon.

1850 California, the Golden State, entered the Union as the 31st state.

1900 James Hilton, English novelist, author of 'Lost Horizon' and 'Goodbye, Mr Chips', born at Leigh in Lancashire.

1901 Toulouse-Lautrec, the stunted, bespectacled French painter, died at Malromé from a paralytic stroke.

1903 Emile Littler, British theatrical impresario, born at Ramsgate in Kent.

1943 Allied forces landed at Salerno in SW Italy.

1949 John Curry, English skating champion, born.

1950 Soap rationing ended in Britain.

1976 Mao Tse-Tung, Chinese revolutionary leader and founder of the Communist State, died aged 82.

10 SEPTEMBER (254)

1753 John Soane, English architect who designed the Bank of England, born at Goring in Oxfordshire, the son of a mason.

1771 Mungo Park, Scottish surgeon and explorer in West Africa, born at Foulshiels near Selkirk.

1897 London taxi-driver George Smith became the first motorist to be convicted of drunken driving.

1929 Arnold Palmer, American international golfing champion, born at Youngstown in Pennsylvania.

1945 Vidkun Quisling, the 'Puppet' Premier of Norway, was sentenced to death for collaboration—was executed on 24th October.

1960 The first English Football League match to be televised— Blackpool v Bolton Wanderers.

1966 Sir Seretse Khama became President of the new Republic of Botswana.

11 SEPTEMBER (255)

1709 The Battle of Malplaquet took place in Northern France near Mons, with the Duke of Marlborough and Prince Eugène in a costly victory over the French in the war of the Spanish Succession.

1777 The Battle of Brandywine Creek in the American war of Independence took place, in which the British under General Howe defeated George Washington.

1885 (David Herbert) D. H. Lawrence, English novelist, born at Victoria Street, Eastwood in Nottinghamshire, the son of a miner.

1915 The Women's Institute organisation was founded in Britain at Anglesey, Wales—founded originally in Canada in 1897.

1950 Barry Sheene, English motor cycle racing champion, born at Holborn in London.
Jan Smuts, South African Boer War guerilla leader, statesman and twice Prime Minister, died at Irene aged 80.

1971 Nikita Khruschev, Soviet Communist leader and Premier from 1958 to 1964, died near Moscow.

12 SEPTEMBER (256)

1818 Richard Gatling, American inventor of the revolving battery gun, born at Winton in North Carolina—his name is the origin of the slang 'gat', meaning a gun.

1819 Gebhard von Blücher, Prussian field marshal and contributor to the allied victories against Napoleon, died in Silesia.

1852 Herbert Henry Asquith, British statesman and Liberal Prime Minister, born at Morley in Yorkshire.

1878 'Cleopatra's Needle', an ancient Egyptian obelisk 68½ feet high in red granite presented to Britain, was erected on the Thames Embankment.

1888 Maurice Chevalier, French singer, musical comedy star and film actor, born in Paris.

1908 Winston Churchill married Clementine Hozier.

1910 The first policewoman was appointed, Alice Wells of the Los Angeles Police Department.

1913 Jesse Owens, American athlete, born at Danville in Alabama as John Cleveland Owens—the name Jesse was used because of its similarity to his initials J. C.

1953 John F. Kennedy married Jacqueline Lee Bouvier.

1960 MOT tests on motor vehicles were introduced in Britain.

1972 William Boyd, American film actor renowned as Hopalong Cassidy, died.

1974 Ethiopian Emperor Haile Selassie was deposed by leaders of the armed forces.

13 SEPTEMBER

1759 General Wolfe, British military commander, was killed in battle defeating Montcalm and the French forces on the Plains of Abraham, near Quebec—Montcalm died the following day from his wounds.

1806 Charles James Fox, British Liberal statesman, died at Chiswick in London.

1845 The first baseball club, the Knickerbockers Club, was formed in New York City.

1860 John Pershing, American commander-in-chief of the US Army in France in World War I, born in Linn County in Missouri.

1894 (John Boynton) J. B. Priestley, English author and playwright, born at Bradford in Yorkshire.

1902 The first conviction in Britain on the evidence of fingerprints was secured by the Metropolitan Police at the Old Bailey, in the case against Harry Jackson.

1905 Claudette Colbert, American film actress and Oscar winner, born in Paris as Lily Claudette Chauchoin.

1944 Heath Robinson, English artist known for his drawings of complex machinery which performed simple tasks, died.

1966 Johannes Vorster was sworn in as Prime Minister of the Republic of South Africa.

1977 Leopold Stokowski, London-born American conductor and musical director, died in Hampshire aged 95.

14 SEPTEMBER

1735 Robert Raikes, English founder of the Sunday School system in 1780, born at Gloucester, the son of a printer.

1752 The Gregorian calendar, a reformed version of the Julian calendar, was adopted in Britain—'losing' the 11 days from 3rd.

1812 Napoleon entered Moscow in his disastrous invasion of Russia.

1814 The US national anthem, 'The Star-Spangled Banner', was written by Francis Scott Key—set to the tune 'Anacreon in Heaven'.

1851 James Fenimore Cooper, American novelist, author of 'Last of the Mohicans', died.

1852 The Duke of Wellington, English military commander, victor at Waterloo, statesman and Tory Prime Minister, died aged 83 at Walmer Castle in Kent, as Lord Warden of the Cinque Ports.
Augustus Pugin, English architect and co-designer of the Houses of Parliament at Westminster with Sir Charles Barry, died at Ramsgate in Kent.

1886 Jan Masaryk, Czech statesman, born at Prague, the son of the country's President.

1891 The first penalty kick was awarded in an English Football League match, taken by Heath of Wolves against Accrington.

1901 William McKinley, America's 25th President, died of wounds inflicted by anarchist Leon Czolgosz, at Buffalo on 6th.
Theodore Roosevelt was elected as the 26th President of the US, and the youngest at 42.

1909 Peter Scott, English naturalist, born in London, the son of the famous Antarctic explorer.

1910 Jack Hawkins, British film actor, born in London.

1927 Isadora Duncan, American ballet dancer, was accidentally killed when her scarf caught in the wheel of her car.

1937 Thomas Masaryk, Czech statesman and his country's first President in 1918, died aged 87.

1938 The largest rigid airship ever built, the 803-ft German 'Graf Zeppelin II', made her maiden flight—was dismantled in April 1940.

1957 The last Liverpool tram ran—the 6A from the Pier Head to Bowring Park, full of civic dignitaries.

1959 The first direct hit on the moon was achieved by the Soviet space probe Lunik II, near the Mare Serenitatis.

1982 Princess Grace died at Monaco's hospital without regaining consciousness, after a car crash the previous day.

15 SEPTEMBER (259)

Battle of Britain day.
National day of Costa Rica.

1649 Titus Oates, English religious agitator against Roman Catholics, born at Oakham in Leicestershire.

1789 James Fenimore Cooper, American novelist of stories of the sea and Red Indians, born at Burlington in New Jersey.

1830 William Huskisson, British statesman, was run down by Stephenson's 'Rocket' at Parkside at the opening of the Liverpool and Manchester Railway—he died the same night.

1857 William Howard Taft, American Republican statesman and 27th President, born at Cincinnati in Ohio.

1859 Isambard Kingdom Brunel, British engineer of railways, steamships and docks, died at Westminster, London.

1864 John Speke, English explorer in Africa, who discovered Lake Victoria, accidentally shot himself while partridge shooting.

1877 Crazy Horse, Sioux chief and one of the leaders in the victory at Little Big Horn in 1876, died.

1891 Agatha Christie, English detective story writer, born at Torquay in Devon.

1916 Military tanks, originated by Sir Ernest Swinton, were first used by the British Army, at Flers in the Somme offensive.
Margaret Lockwood, British actress, born at Karachi in India as Margaret Day.

1960 Traffic wardens were first introduced in London.

1973 Gustavus VI, King of Sweden since 1950, died aged 90.

1978 Muhammad Ali regained the world heavyweight boxing title for the second time, beating Leon Spinks in New Orleans.
Wilhelm Messerschmitt, German aviation engineer and designer, died aged 80.

16 SEPTEMBER

National day of Mexico.

1387 King Henry V was born in Monmouth Castle in Wales, the eldest of 6 children of Henry IV.

1620 The 101 Pilgrim Fathers set sail from Plymouth in the 'Mayflower', captained by Myles Standish.

1736 Gabriel Fahrenheit, German physicist, who devised the scale of temperature that bears his name, died.

1812 Moscow was burnt by the French under Napoleon.

1824 Louis XVIII, King of France, died.

1858 Andrew Bonar Law, British statesman and Conservative Prime Minister, born at Kingston in New Brunswick in Canada.

1861 The Post Office Savings Bank was instituted in Britain.

1893 Sir Alexander Korda, British film producer and director, born at Turkeye in Hungary as Sandor Corda.

1924 Lauren Bacall, American film actress, born in New York City as Betty Joan Perske.

1927 Peter Falk, American TV actor who portrays detective 'Columbo', born in New York City.

1945 Count John McCormack, Irish-born American operatic tenor, died near Dublin.

1966 Britain's first Polaris submarine 'Resolution' was launched.

1968 'Two-tier' postal system began in Britain.

1977 Maria Callas, American prima donna operatic soprano, died in Paris.

17 SEPTEMBER

1701 King James II died after a stroke at St Germain in France.

1771 Tobias Smollett, Scottish novelist, author of 'Roderick Random', died at Leghorn in Italy.

1827 Wides in cricket were first scored as such in the Sussex v Kent game at Brighton.

1871 The 7½-mile Mont Cenis tunnel, carrying the main railway from Lyons to Turin, was opened.

1877 William Henry Fox Talbot, English pioneer of photography, died at Lacock Abbey in Wiltshire.

1901 Sir Francis Chichester, English yachtsman and aviator, born at Barnstaple in Devon.

1906 Sir Frederick Ashton, British ballet choreographer and director, born at Guayaquil in Ecuador.

1929 Stirling Moss, British motor racing champion, born at Paddington in London.

1931 33⅓ rpm long-playing records were first launched, with a demonstration held at the Savoy Plaza Hotel in New York City.

1934 Maureen Connolly, American international tennis champion, born at San Diego in California.

1944 The British air-borne invasion of Arnhem and Eindhoven in the Netherlands took place—was called 'Operation Market Garden'.

1948 Count Folke Bernadotte, Swedish diplomat and UN mediator for Palestine, was ambushed and killed in Jerusalem by Jewish terrorists.

18 SEPTEMBER (262)

National day of Chile.

1709 Samuel Johnson, English lexicographer and poet, born at Lichfield in Staffordshire, the son of a bookseller.

1819 Jean Foucault, French physicist, born in Paris.

1851 The 'New York Times', founded by Henry Jarvis Raymond, began publication.

1879 The Lancashire holiday resort of Blackpool held its first annual illuminations.

1895 John George Diefenbaker, Canadian statesman and Conservative Prime Minister, born at Normanby Township in Ontario.

1905 Greta Garbo, Swedish film actress, born at Stockholm as Greta Lovisa Gustafsson.

1909 Kwame Nkrumah, Ghanaian statesman and his country's first Prime Minister, born at Ankroful.

1931 Japan seized Manchuria and set up a puppet state called Manchukuo—was returned to China in 1945 after World War II.

1961 Dag Hammarskjöld, Swedish Secretary-General of the United Nations and Nobel Prize winner, was killed in a plane crash near Ndola in Northern Rhodesia when flying from Leopoldville.

1964 Sean O'Casey, Irish playwright, author of 'Juno and the Paycock', died at Torquay in Devon, aged 80.

1967 Sir John Cockcroft, English nuclear physicist who split the atom with Ernest Walton, died.

19 SEPTEMBER (263)

1356 The Battle of Poitiers in the Hundred Years War took place in west France, in which Edward the Black Prince defeated John II, King of France.

1839 George Cadbury, English chocolate manufacturer and social reformer, born at Birmingham.

1851 Viscount Leverhulme, English soapmaker and philanthropist, born, the son of a grocer, at Bolton in Lancashire as William Lever.

1876 The first practical carpet-sweeper was patented by Melville Bissell of Grand Rapids in Michigan.

1881 James Abram Garfield, American Republican statesman and 20th President since 4th March this year, died at Elberon in New Jersey, after being shot on 2nd July—the remainder of his term of office was completed by Chester Arthur.

1888 The first beauty contest was held, at Spa in Belgium.

1893 New Zealand became the first nation to grant its female citizens the right to vote—the first occasion on which they went to the polls was the General Election of 28th November.

1905 Thomas Barnardo, British social reformer and founder of homes for destitute children in 1867, died.

1922 Emil Zatopek, international long-distance runner known as the 'Bouncing Czech', born.

1949 'Twiggy', English model, actress and singer, born at Neasden in London as Lesley Hornby.

1963 Sir David Low, New Zealand-born political cartoonist, died in London.

20 SEPTEMBER (264)

1258 Salisbury Cathedral was consecrated.

1519 Ferdinand Magellan, with a fleet of 5 small ships ('Trinidad', 'San Antonio', 'Concepcion', 'Vittoria' and 'Santiago'), sailed from Seville on his expedition around the world. One ship only, the 'Vittoria', returned on 6th September 1522.

1746 To escape capture in Scotland Bonnie Prince Charlie sailed to safety in France aboard the French ship 'L'Heureux'.

1803 Robert Emmet, Irish patriot, was hanged for his part as a leader in the uprisings.

1842 Sir James Dewar, Scottish physicist and chemist and inventor of the vacuum flask, born at Kincardine-on-Forth, Fife.

1854 The Battle of Alma took place in the Crimean War, in which 6 Victoria Crosses were won.

1863 Jacob Grimm, German philologist and collector of folk tales with his younger brother Wilhelm, died in Berlin.

1914 Kenneth More, English film actor, born at Gerrards Cross in Buckinghamshire.

1927 Johnny Dankworth, British musician, born.

1931 British sterling currency was taken off the gold standard.

1934 Sophia Loren, Italian actress and Oscar winner, born as Sophia Scicoloni.

1957 Jean Sibelius, Finnish composer, principally national music, notably 'Finlandia', died aged 91.

1967 The British liner 'QE2' or 'Queen Elizabeth 2' was launched at Clydebank in Scotland.

National day of Malta.

1327 King Edward II was murdered in Berkeley Castle, to be succeeded by his son as Edward III.

1745 The Battle of Prestonpans took place in Scotland, in which Bonnie Prince Charlie's Jacobite army gained a victory over English Royal forces led by Sir John Cope.

1756 John McAdam, Scottish surveyor who introduced 'Macadam' system of roadmaking, born at Ayr.

1784 The first successful daily newspaper in America, 'The Pennsylvania Packet and General Advertiser', was published.

1792 France was declared a Republic.

1832 Sir Walter Scott, Scottish novelist and poet, died at Abbotsford on the banks of the river Tweed, and is buried at Dryburgh Abbey.

1866 H. G. Wells, English novelist and science fiction pioneer, born at Bromley in Kent, the son of a professional cricketer.

1874 Gustav Holst, English composer, notably 'The Planets', born at Cheltenham in Gloucestershire as Gustavus Theodore von Holst, of Swedish origin.

1902 Sir Learie Constantine, West Indian Test cricketer, born at Port of Spain in Trinidad.
Sir Allen Lane, English publisher and founder of Penguin books, born at Bristol as Allen Lane Williams.

1947 An American 'Skymaster' flew from Wilmington in Ohio to Brize Norton in England without crew, under automatic control, guided by radio impulses.

1957 Death of Norway's King Haakon VII, accession of his son as Olav V.

1964 Malta became independent, after 164 years of British rule.

22 SEPTEMBER (266)

1735 Sir Robert Walpole became the first Prime Minister to occupy 10 Downing Street.

1761 The coronation of King George III took place.

1776 Nathan Hale, American patriot, was hanged in New York City by the British for being a spy during the American Revolutionary War.

1791 Michael Faraday, English chemist and physicist, born at Newington Butts, near London, the son of a blacksmith.

1880 Christabel Pankhurst, English suffragette, born, the daughter of Emmeline.

1895 Paul Muni, film actor and Oscar winner, born at Lemberg in Austria as Muni Weisenfreund.

1934 The Gresford pit disaster took place in North Wales, in which 265 miners lost their lives.

1948 Captain Mark Phillips, husband of Princess Anne, born at Tewkesbury in Gloucestershire.

1955 Commercial television began in Britain—with 'Gibbs SR toothpaste' the first commercial.

23 SEPTEMBER (267)

National day of Saudi Arabia.

1779 John Paul Jones on the 'Bonhomme Richard' defeated the British ship 'Serapis' in an engagement in North Sea waters off Flamborough Head during the War of the American Revolution.

1846 The planet Neptune was discovered by the German astronomer Johann Galle, following predictions of Leverrier and Adams.

1870 Prosper Mérimée, French novelist, notably 'Carmen', died at Cannes.

1889 Wilkie Collins, English novelist and pioneer of detective fiction, died in London.

1920 Mickey Rooney, American film actor, born at Brooklyn in New York as Joe Yule.

1926 The famous Gene Tunney—Jack Dempsey fight took place at Philadelphia, with a record paid attendance of 120757 and a 10th-round victory for Tunney.

1939 Sigmund Freud, Austrian psychiatrist and founder of psychoanalysis and called the 'Copernicus of the mind', died at Hampstead in London aged 83.

1940 The George Cross, the highest British civilian award for acts of courage, was instituted.

24 SEPTEMBER (268)

1853 The 'Northern Daily Times' in Liverpool became the first provincial daily newspaper in England.
1869 An American financial disaster, called 'Black Friday', took place when Jay Gould, a shrewd and unscrupulous investor, attempted to corner gold.
1890 (Alan Patrick) A. P. Herbert, English writer and Member of Parliament, born.
1898 Sir Howard Florey, British pathologist and joint producer of penicillin with Sir Ernest Chain, born at Adelaide in Australia.
1953 The first film made in CinemaScope®, 'The Robe', was premièred in Hollywood.
1960 The first nuclear-powered aircraft carrier, USS Enterprise, was launched at Newport in Virginia.

25 SEPTEMBER (269)

1513 Vasco Balboa, Spanish explorer, became the first European to sight the Pacific Ocean after crossing the Darien isthmus.
1849 Johann Strauss the elder, Austrian conductor and composer of the 'Radetzky March', died in Vienna.
1872 (Charles Blake) C. B. Cochran, British theatrical producer and impresario, born at Lindfield in Sussex.
1897 William Faulkner, American novelist and Nobel Prize winner, born at New Albany in Mississippi.
1906 Dmitri Shostakovich, Russian composer, born at Leningrad.
1907 Raymond Glendenning, English journalist and sports commentator, born.
1929 Ronnie Barker, English comedy actor, born at Bedford, the county town on the river Ouse.

1942 Henri Pescarolo, motor racing champion, born at Paris.

1959 Solomon Bandaranaike, Prime Minister of Sri Lanka from 1956, was shot by a Buddhist monk in Colombo, and died the following day.

26 SEPTEMBER (270)

1087 The coronation of King William II of England took place.

1580 Francis Drake and crew arrived back in Plymouth in the 100-ton 'Golden Hind'—originally the 'Pelican'—after 33 months, to become the first Englishmen to circumnavigate the world.

1750 Lord Collingwood, British naval officer, Nelson's second-in-command at Trafalgar, born at Newcastle-upon-Tyne.

1820 Daniel Boone, American pioneer and frontiersman, died aged 85.

1861 The first British Golf Open was held, at Prestwick in Scotland, and won by Tom Morris.

1887 Barnes Wallis, English aircraft designer, noted for his work on airships and special bombs, born.

1888 T. S. Eliot, British poet and Nobel Prize winner, born at St Louis in Missouri.

1897 Pope Paul VI, born in Concessio as Giovanni Battista Montini.

1898 George Gershwin, American composer of musicals, born at Brooklyn, New York.

1907 New Zealand became a Dominion.

1915 James Keir Hardie, British Socialist and one of the founders of the Labour Party, died.

1934 The British liner 'Queen Mary' was launched at John Brown's Yard at Clydebank in Scotland.

1942 Wilson Carlile, English clergyman and founder of the Church Army in 1882, died aged 95.

1945 Bela Bartok, Hungarian composer and pianist, died.

1953 Sugar rationing ended in Britain.

1959 Solomon Bandaranaike, Prime Minister of Sri Lanka, died from wounds received at the hands of an assassin the previous day.

27 SEPTEMBER (271)

1722 Samuel Adams, American statesman, organiser of the Boston Tea Party and a signatory of the Declaration of Independence, born at Boston in Massachusetts.

1825 The steam locomotive 'Active' pulled the first public train— the 27 miles from Shildon through Darlington to Stockton. It was later re-named 'Locomotion No. 1'.

1862 Louis Botha, South African military commander, statesman and first Prime Minister of the Union in 1910, born near Greytown in Natal.

1895 George Raft, American film actor, best known for roles as gangsters, born in New York as George Ranft.

1907 Sir Bernard Miles, English character actor, born.

1917 Edgar Degas, French artist, died.

1919 Adelina Patti, Spanish-born Italian soprano, died.

1921 Engelbert Humperdinck, German composer whose chief work was the opera 'Hansel and Gretel', died of apoplexy at Neustrelitz.

1922 Constantine I abdicated as King of Greece.

1938 The British liner 'Queen Elizabeth', the largest passenger vessel ever built, was launched at Clydebank in Scotland by the Queen Mother.

1979 Dame Gracie Fields, English comedienne and music hall entertainer, died in retirement at her home on the Isle of Capri aged 81.

28 SEPTEMBER (272)

1745 The British national anthem, 'God Save the King', was first performed, at the Drury Lane Theatre.

1803 Prosper Mérimée, French novelist, author of 'Carmen', the basis of Bizet's opera, born in Paris, the son of a painter.

1841 Georges Clemenceau, French statesman and Premier, known as the 'Tiger', born in La Vendée.

1891 Herman Melville, American novelist, notably 'Moby Dick', died in New York City.

1894 The first Marks and Spencer's (Penny Bazaar) in Britain, opened at Cheetham Hill in Manchester.

1895 Louis Pasteur, French chemist and bacteriologist, died at Saint-Cloud near Paris.

1905 Max Schmeling, German heavyweight boxer and world champion, born at Brandenburg.

1916 Peter Finch, English film actor and Oscar winner, born at Kensington in London.

1923 The British magazine 'Radio Times' was instituted and first published.

1948 The first British motor racing Grand Prix at Silverstone took place.

1964 Arthur 'Harpo' Marx, the silent member of the Marx brothers, died aged 75.

1970 Gamal Abdel Nasser, Egyptian political leader and President since 1956, died.

29 SEPTEMBER   (273)

1399 Richard II became the first British monarch to abdicate— next day was deposed by Parliament, which chose Henry IV as his successor.

1518 Tintoretto, Venetian painter, born as Jacopo Robusti, the son of a dyer.

1725 Robert Clive, English soldier, statesman and administrator, born at Styche, near Market Drayton in Shropshire, the son of a lawyer and eldest of 13 children.

1758 Horatio Nelson, English naval commander, born at Burnham Thorpe rectory, one of 11 children of a Norfolk clergyman.

1810 Elizabeth Gaskell, English novelist, author of 'Cranford', born at Cheyne Row, Chelsea as Elizabeth Stevenson.

1899 Billy Butlin, holiday camp pioneer in Britain, born in South Africa.

1902 Emile Zola, French novelist, died in Paris, accidentally suffocated by charcoal fumes—received a State funeral and was buried in the Pantheon in Paris.

1907 Gene Autry, American singing cowboy in Westerns, born at Tioga in Texas, the son of a Baptist minister.

1908 Greer Garson, British film actress and Oscar winner, born in Co. Down in Northern Ireland.

1916 Trevor Howard, English film actor, born at Cliftonville in Kent.

(Carl Ronald) Giles, English cartoonist, born.

1931 Anita Ekberg, Swedish film actress, born at Malmo.

1934 Lance Gibbs, West Indian cricketer, born at Georgetown in Guyana.

1956 Sebastian Coe, British international athlete and world record holder, born at Chiswick in London.

1959 Bruce Bairnsfather, British cartoonist famous for his character 'Old Bill', died.

1962 Canada launched her first satellite—'The Alouette'.

1981 Bill Shankly, famous English soccer manager, died in a Liverpool hospital.

30 SEPTEMBER (274)

National day of Botswana.

1772 James Brindley, English engineer who constructed the Bridgewater, Grand Trunk and Manchester Ship canals, died at Turnhurst in Staffordshire.

1788 Lord Raglan, British army field marshal responsible for the disastrous 'Charge of the Light Brigade' at Balaklava, born at Badminton in Gloucestershire.

1832 Lord Roberts, British field marshal and commander, born at Cawnpore in India.

1913 Rudolf Diesel, German engineer and inventor of an internal combustion engine that bears his name, died—vanishing from an English Channel steamer.

1921 Deborah Kerr, British film actress, born at Helensburgh in Scotland.

1930 Lord Birkenhead, British Conservative statesman and law reformer, died.

1935 Johnny Mathis, American pop singer and entertainer, born in San Francisco.

1939 Identity cards were first issued in Britain.

1952 The first film in Cinerama® —'This is Cinerama'—was shown in New York.

1955 James Dean, American film actor and cult figure, died in a car crash in California aged 24.

1966 Bechuanaland became fully independent, changing its name to Botswana—with Sir Seretse Khama its first President.

1967 BBC's Radio 1 went on the air for the first time, with Tony Blackburn introducing 'The Breakfast Show'.

1 OCTOBER (275)

National day of Nigeria, China and Cyprus.

The pheasant shooting season begins in Britain.

1207 King Henry III was born at Winchester in Hampshire, the son of King John.

1792 Money orders were introduced in Britain.

1843 The English Sunday newspaper 'News of the World' began publication.

1865 Paul Dukas, French composer, best known for 'The Sorcerer's Apprentice', born in Paris.

1870 The first official issue of the postcard was made in Britain by the Post Office, together with the introduction of the halfpenny postage stamp.

1873 Sir Edwin Landseer, English animal painter noted for his 'Monarch of the Glen', died in London and was buried in St Paul's Cathedral.

1890 Stanley Holloway, English singer and comedy actor, born in London.

1920 Walter Matthau, American film actor, born in New York City as Walter Matuschanskayasky.

1924 James Earl (Jimmy) Carter, American Democrat statesman and 39th President, born at Plains in Georgia.

1933 Richard Harris, British actor, born in Co. Limerick in the Republic of Ireland.

1935 Julie Andrews, English film actress and singer, born at Walton-on-Thames in Surrey as Julie Wells.

1936 General Franco took office as Head of the Nationalist (Insurgent) Government.

1949 The People's Republic was founded in China, with Mao Tse-Tung its chairman.

1960 Nigeria achieved independence within the Commonwealth.

1963 Nigeria became a Republic.

1970 The funeral of President Nasser of Egypt took place at Cairo.

1971 'Disney World', the world's largest amusement resort, in central Florida, was opened.

2 OCTOBER (276)

1452 Richard III was born at Fotheringhay Castle in Northamptonshire, the youngest brother of Edward IV.

1608 The first telescope was demonstrated by the Dutch lens maker, Hans Lippershey.

1803 Samuel Adams, American patriot, statesman and one of the signatories of the Declaration of Independence, died aged 81.

1847 Paul von Hindenberg, German military leader and President of the Republic, born at Posen.

1851 Ferdinand Foch, French military commander, born at Tarbes.

1852 Sir William Ramsay, British chemist and discoverer of inert gases, born at Glasgow.

1869 Mohandas 'Mahatma' Gandhi, Indian political and religious leader, born at Porbander.

1871 Cordell Hull, American statesman and diplomat, born at Overton in Tennessee.

1890 'Groucho' Marx, American actor and comedian of the Marx Brothers, born in New York City as Julius Marx.

1901 The first Royal Navy submarine, built by Vickers, was launched at Barrow.

1904 Graham Greene, English novelist and short-story writer, born at Berkhamsted in Hertfordshire.

1909 The first Rugby match at Twickenham was played—Harlequins v Richmond.

1921 Robert Runcie, the 102nd Archbishop of Canterbury, born.

1942 The British cruiser 'Curacao' sank immediately off the coast of Donegal with the loss of 338 lives, after a collision with the Cunard liner 'Queen Mary'.

1948 Trevor Brooking, English international footballer, born.

1950 Legal aid became effective in Britain.

1958 The Republic of Guinea in West Africa opted for full independence, and France withdrew all aid.
Marie Stopes, English pioneer of birth control, died.

1973 Paavo Nurmi, Finnish distance running champion, died aged 76.

3 OCTOBER (277)

1811 The first women's County cricket match started, Hampshire v Surrey at Newington.

1867 Elias Howe, American inventor of the first practical sewing machine in 1846, died.

1906 SOS was established as an international distress signal at the Berlin Radio Conference—replacing the call sign CQD.

1914 The first national flag-day was held in England, in aid of the Belgian Relief Fund.

1921 Ray Lindwall, Australian fast bowler, born at Sydney.

1935 Italian forces invaded Abyssinia.

1941 Chubby Checker, American singer and entertainer, born at Philadelphia as Ernest Evans.

1952 Britain detonated her first atomic bomb, aboard a naval vessel in Monte Bello Islands off N W Australia.

1959 The post code, required in the addressing of mail for mechanical sorting, was first used in Britain, at Norwich.

1967 Sir Malcolm Sargent, English conductor, especially of Promenade Concerts, died.

National day of Lesotho.

1582 St Teresa (of Avila), Spanish nun and religious reformer, died—was canonised in 1622.

1626 Richard Cromwell, born the third son of Oliver Cromwell.

1669 Rembrandt, famous Dutch painter, died at Amsterdam.

1814 Jean Francois Millet, French painter of rural scenes, born at Grouchy near Gréville, the son of a farmer.

1821 John Rennie, Scottish civil engineer and designer of bridges, died in London.

1822 Rutherford Hayes, American Republican statesman and 19th President, born at Delaware in Ohio, the son of a farmer.

1878 The first Chinese Embassy to Washington was established.

1883 The Boys' Brigade organisation was founded in Glasgow, by Sir William Alexander Smith.

1892 Engelbert Dollfuss, Austrian statesman, Chancellor and dictator, born.

1895 'Buster' Keaton, American comedy actor of the silent film era, born at Piqua in Kansas as Joseph Francis Keaton.
The first official American Golf Open took place, at Newport, Rhode Island—won by Horace Rawlins.

1924 Charlton Heston, American film actor and Oscar winner, born at Evansville in Illinois.

1931 Basil D'Oliveira, Worcestershire and England cricketer, born at Cape Town.

1948 Sir Arthur Whitten Brown, British aviator of Alcock and Brown fame, died.

1962 'Patsy' Hendren, Middlesex and England cricketer, died.

1966 Basutoland became an independent Kingdom, having been a British Protectorate since 1868—now called Lesotho.

5 OCTOBER (279)

1830 Chester Arthur, American Republican statesman and 21st President, born at Fairfield in Vermont, the son of a Baptist minister.

1880 Jacques Offenbach, German-born French composer of operettas and the opera 'Tales of Hoffman', died in Paris.

1919 Donald Pleasence, English actor, born at Worksop.

1923 Glynis Johns, British film actress, born at Durban in South Africa.

1930 The 777-ft British airship R101, captained by Flight Lieutenant Irwin, crashed at the edge of a wood near Beauvais in France on its way from Cardington to India— killing 48 of the 54 passengers and crew.

1933 Diane Cilento, film actress, born in Queensland, Australia. English champion jockey Gordon Richards rode his 12th consecutive winner in 3 days—11 at Chepstow following 1 at Nottingham.

1936 The Jarrow March of unemployed shipyard workers to London started on its southward journey, led by Labour MP Ellen Wilkinson.

1967 The first majority verdict taken in Britain, by 10 to 2, at Brighton Quarter sessions.

6 OCTOBER (280)

1536 William Tyndale, English religious reformer and translator of the Bible, was burnt at the stake as a heretic, at Vilvarde near Brussels.

1820 Jenny Lind, Swedish international operatic soprano, born at Stockholm as Johanna Maria Lind.

1829 Trials began at Rainhill, near Liverpool, for a locomotive for use on the Liverpool and Manchester Railway— won by Stephenson's 'Rocket'. The other 4 entrants were 'Cycloped', 'Sans Pareil', 'Perseverance' and 'Novelty'.

1846 George Westinghouse, American engineer and inventor of the railway air brake, born at Central Bridge in the State of New York.

1891 Charles Stewart Parnell, Irish politician and leader for Home Rule, died at Brighton in Sussex.
W. H. Smith, English newsagent, bookseller and politician, died.

1892 Alfred, Lord Tennyson, English poet and Poet Laureate from 1850, died at Aldworth in Surrey.

1895 The Promenade Concerts were founded by Sir Henry Wood.

1905 Helen Wills-Moody, American tennis champion, born at Centerville in California.

1906 Janet Gaynor, American film actress, born at Philadelphia as Laura Gainer.

1911 Barbara Castle, British Labour politician, born.

1914 Thor Heyerdahl, Norwegian adventurer and leader of the Kon Tiki expedition, born at Larvik.

1919 Tommy Lawton, English international footballer, born.

1930 Richie Benaud, Australian cricketer and commentator, born at Penrith in New South Wales.

1969 Walter Hagen, American champion golfer, died aged 76.

1981 Anwar Sadat, Egyptian political leader and President since 1970, was assassinated during a military parade in Cairo.

7 OCTOBER (281)

1571 The naval Battle of Lepanto took place in the Gulf of Corinth, resulting in the destruction of the Turkish Fleet, commanded by Ali Pasha.

1769 Captain Cook reached New Zealand.

1799 The ship 'Lutine' sank off the island of Vlieland in Holland —its salvaged bell was presented to Lloyd's of London.

1806 A patent for the first carbon paper was secured by its inventor Ralph Wedgwood of London—'for producing duplicates of writings'.

1849 Edgar Allan Poe, American writer of mysterious and macabre stories, died at Baltimore in Maryland.

1900 Heinrich Himmler, German Nazi leader and notorious chief of police, born at Munich.

1919 KLM, the national airline of the Netherlands and the oldest existing, was established—opening its first scheduled service on the following 17th May.

1922 Marie Lloyd, English music hall entertainer, died after collapsing on the stage of the Alhambra theatre.

1923 June Allyson, American film actress, born at Lucerne in the State of New York as Ella Geisman.

1953 Liverpool's Liver clock first chimed at 2.30 pm.

1956 Clarence Birdseye, American inventor of a process for deep-freezing foodstuffs, died.

1959 Mario Lanza, American tenor singer and actor, died aged 38.

The first photograph of the far side of the moon was transmitted from Russia's Lunik III.

8 OCTOBER (282)

1754 Henry Fielding, English novelist, author of 'Tom Jones', died.

1869 Franklin Pierce, American Democrat statesman and 14th President from 1853 to 1857, died at Concord in New Hampshire.

1871 The Great Fire of Chicago broke out—ending on 11th— supposedly started in Mrs O'Leary's barn in DeKoven Street, by a cow upsetting a lantern.

1891 The first street collection for charity in Britain took place, in Manchester and Salford, for Lifeboat Day.

1895 Juan Peron, Argentinian general, statesman and nation- alist dictator, born at Lobos.

1928 Neil Harvey, Australian cricketer, born at Melbourne in the State of Victoria.

1944 Wendell Wilkie, American politician and Presidential candidate, died.

1953 Kathleen Ferrier, English international contralto singer, died.

1965 The 580-ft Post Office tower, in Maple Street, off Tottenham Court Road in London, was opened.

1967 Clement Attlee, British statesman and Labour Prime Minister from 1945 to 1951, died aged 84.

The first breathalyser test took place in Britain, admini- stered to a motorist at Flax Bourton in Somerset.

1973 London Broadcasting, the first commercial radio station on the British mainland, began transmitting.

9 OCTOBER (283)

National day of Uganda.

1835 Camille Saint-Saëns, French composer, pianist and music critic, born in Paris.

1874 The Universal Postal Union was established, with headquarters at Berne in Switzerland.

1888 The 555-foot white-marble Washington Monument, designed by Robert Mills, was opened.

1900 Alastair Sim, Scottish comedy film actor, born at Edinburgh.

1907 Lord Hailsham, British Conservative statesman and Attorney-General, born as Quintin Hogg.

1909 Donald Coggan, English prelate and 101st Archbishop of Canterbury, born.

1934 Alexander, King of Yugoslavia from 1921, was assassinated by Croatian terrorists at Marseilles.

1940 John Lennon, song writer and musician of the Beatles group, born in Liverpool, the son of a ship's steward.

1955 Steve Ovett, British international athlete, born.

1958 Pope Pius XII (Eugenio Pacell), died at the Castel Gandolfo, the Papal summer residence, some 27 kilometres SE of Rome, aged 82.

1962 Uganda became independent after nearly 70 years of British rule, with Milton Obote its first Prime Minister.

1967 Ernesto 'Che' Guevara, Argentinian-born guerilla leader and revolutionary, was murdered in Bolivia.

10 OCTOBER (284)

1684 Antoine Watteau, French rococo painter, born at Valenciennes.

1731 Henry Cavendish, English scientist and chemist who discovered what is now known as hydrogen, born at Nice in France.

1813 Giuseppe Verdi, Italian opera composer, born at Le Roncole near Busseto, the son of a tavern keeper.

1825 Paul Kruger, South African statesman and Boer leader, born at Colesberg in Cape Colony.

1861 Fridtjof Nansen, Norwegian Polar explorer, born near Oslo.

1877 Lord Nuffield, English car manufacturer and philanthropist, born in Worcestershire as William Morris.

1911 The Imperial Dynasty of China was forced to a 'voluntary' abdication, and a republic was proclaimed at Wuchang, under Sun Yat-Sen.

1930 The Tyne Bridge at Newcastle was opened.

1940 Sir William Grenfell, English medical missionary in Labrador, died.

1961 Volcanic eruption on the South Atlantic island of Tristan da Cunha—the whole population was evacuated to Britain.

1964 Eddie Cantor, American film actor and entertainer, died aged 72.
The 18th Olympic Games opened in Tokyo.

1970 Fiji became an independent member of the Commonwealth, having been a British colony since 1874.
Edouard Daladier, French statesman and Prime Minister, died aged 86.

1972 Sir John Betjeman was appointed Poet Laureate.

11 OCTOBER (285)

1727 The coronation of King George II took place.

1797 The naval Battle of Camperdown took place off the north Holland coast, with a British victory over a Dutch fleet which had threatened British naval supremacy.

1821 George Williams, English social reformer and founder of the YMCA in 1844, born at Dulverton, in Somerset.

1844 H. J. Heinz, American food-products manufacturer, born of German parents at Pittsburgh in Pennsylvania.

1884 Eleanor Roosevelt, wife and cousin of Franklin D. Roosevelt, born in New York City.

1889 James Joule, English physicist who established the first law of thermodynamics, died.

1899 The South African Boer War began, between the British Empire and the republics of the Orange Free State and the Transvaal.

1906 Bob Danvers-Walker, English newsreel commentator, born at Cheam in Surrey.

1927 James Prior, British Conservative politician, born.

1937 Bobby Charlton, English international footballer and scorer of a record 49 goals for his country, born at Ashington in Northumberland.

1957 The radio telescope at Jodrell Bank in Cheshire, planned by Sir Bernard Lovell, went into operation.

1961 'Chico' Marx, the piano-playing member of the Marx Brothers comedy team, died.

1968 Apollo 7 was launched with Walter Schirra, Don Eiselle and Walter Cunningham.

12 OCTOBER (286)

1492 Columbus sighted his first land in discovering the New World, calling it San Salvador.

1537 King Edward VI was born at the Palace of Hampton Court, the son of Henry VIII and his third wife Jane Seymour.

1845 Elizabeth Fry, English social worker and prison reformer, died.

1859 Robert Stephenson, English rail and civil engineer, died in London.

1860 Elmer Sperry, prolific American inventor, notably the gyroscopic compass, born at Cortland in the State of New York.

1866 Ramsay MacDonald, British statesman and Labour Prime Minister, born at Lossiemouth in Morayshire, Scotland.

1870 Robert E. Lee, American general and outstanding Confederate military leader during the Civil War, died at Lexington in Virginia.

1872 Ralph Vaughan Williams, English composer, born at Down Ampney in Gloucestershire.

1915 Edith Cavell, English nurse, was executed by a German firing squad in Brussels, for helping allied prisoners escape over the Dutch frontier.

1928 The first iron lung was used, at Boston Children's Hospital in Massachusetts.

1929 Magnus Magnusson, British writer and television presenter, born at Reykjavik in Iceland.

1940 Tom Mix, American film actor in over 400 Westerns, died.

1948 The first Morris Minor car, designed by Alex Issigonis, came off the production line at Cowley in Oxfordshire.

1965 Paul Müller, Swiss chemist who formulated the insecticide DDT in 1939, died at Basle.

1968 The 19th Olympic Games opened in Mexico City.

1969 Sonja Henie, former world skating champion and film actress, died.

1971 Dean Acheson, American politician and Secretary of State, died.

13 OCTOBER (287)

1399 The coronation of King Henry IV, the first King of the House of Lancaster, took place.

1792 The corner stone of the US President's official residence— The White House in Washington, DC, designed by James Hoban—was laid.

1853 Lillie Langtry, British actress, born in Jersey with the forenames Emilie Charlotte, the daughter of the Dean of the island.

1892 At the by-election at Cirencester in Gloucestershire the number of votes cast for Conservative and Liberal were found to have been equal—a new election was ordered.

1894 The first Merseyside 'derby' football match between Everton and Liverpool was played, at Goodison Park—Everton winning 3-0.

1905 Sir Henry Irving, English actor and first in the profession to receive a knighthood, in 1895, died at Bradford from a heart attack outside his hotel.

1925 Mrs Thatcher, Conservative politician and Britain's first woman Prime Minister, born as Margaret Roberts.

14 OCTOBER (288)

National day of Madagascar.

1066 The famous Battle of Hastings took place on Senlac Hill, near Pevensey (7 miles from Hastings), in which King Harold was slain and the English army routed.

1633 King James II was born at St James's Palace, the second son of Charles I and Henrietta Maria.

1644 William Penn, English Quaker leader and founder of Pennsylvania, born in London, the son of an admiral.

1830 Belgium was proclaimed an independent kingdom—having formed part of the 'Low Countries'.

1878 The first football match was played under floodlights, at Bramall Lane, Sheffield.

1882 Eamon de Valera, Irish statesman, Prime Minister and President, born at Manhattan, New York City.

1890 Dwight Eisenhower, American military commander, Republican statesman and 34th President, born at Denison in Texas.

1896 Lillian Gish, American film actress of the silent screen, born at Springfield in Ohio as Lillian de Guiche.

1913 Britain's worst pit disaster took place, at Universal Colliery at Senghenydd in Glamorgan—killing 439.

1928 Roger Moore, English film actor, born at Stockwell in London, the son of a policeman.

1929 Britain's largest airship, the 777-ft R101, built at Cardington, flew on its first trial.

1939 The Royal Navy battleship 'Royal Oak' was torpedoed and sunk in Scapa Flow, with the loss of 810 lives.

1940 Cliff Richard, English singer and entertainer, born at Lucknow in India as Harry Webb.

1947 The first supersonic flight was achieved, over Edwards Air Base at Muroc in California.

1959 Errol Flynn, Tasmanian-born actor in action-adventure films, died.

1968 New Euston station in London was opened.

1969 The 50p decimal coin was first issued in Britain.

1976 Dame Edith Evans, British actress, known principally for stage appearances, especially Shakespearean roles, died aged 88.

1977 Bing Crosby, American singer, actor and Academy Award (Oscar) winner in 1944 for his part in 'Going My Way', died on a golf course in Madrid.

15 OCTOBER (289)

1608 Evangelista Torricelli, Italian mathematician and scientist who devised the barometer, born at Faenza.

1851 The Great Exhibition at Crystal Palace in London's Hyde Park closed—having opened on 1st May.

1858 John L. Sullivan, American world heavyweight boxing champion, known as the 'Boston Strong Boy', born at Roxburgh in Massachusetts.

1881 (Pelham Grenville) P. G. Wodehouse, English novelist, born at Guildford in Surrey.

1895 The first motor show in Britain was held, at the Agricultural Show Ground at Tunbridge Wells in Kent.

1917 Mata Hari, Dutch spy, was shot in Paris, having been found guilty of espionage for the Germans.

1928 The German airship 'Graf Zeppelin', captained by Hugo Eckener, crossed the Atlantic from Friedrichshafen to Lakehurst in New Jersey.

1945 Pierre Laval, French leader of the Vichy Government's collaboration with the Germans, was executed for treason.

1946 Hermann Goering, Nazi war criminal, poisoned himself in Nuremberg Prison a few hours before he was scheduled to be hanged.

1951 The Liberals held the first BBC televised Party Political broadcast—given by Lord Samuel.

1964 Cole Porter, American prolific composer and lyricist, died.

1555 Hugh Latimer and Nicholas Ridley, the English Protestant reformers and Oxford martyrs, were burned at the stake for heresy.

1758 Noah Webster, American lexicographer and originator of the dictionary that bears his name, born at West Hartford in Connecticut.

1793 Marie Antoinette, Queen of France as wife of Louis XVI, was convicted of treason and guillotined in Paris.

1803 Robert Stephenson, English civil engineer, born at Willington Quay in Northumberland, the son of a famous father, George Stephenson.

1815 Napoleon was exiled to the Atlantic island of St Helena.

1834 The Palace of Westminster was burned down—firemen managed to save Westminster Hall and St Stephen's Chapel.

1854 Oscar Wilde, Irish playwright and dramatist, born at Dublin, the son of a surgeon.

1859 John Brown, American abolitionist, with 21 followers seized the US armoury at Harper's Ferry in Virginia—an action for which he was later hanged.

1863 Sir Austen Chamberlain, British statesman, born at Birmingham.

1886 David Ben-Gurion, statesman and first Prime Minister of Israel in 1948, born at Plonsk in Poland as David Green—he chose the name of 'Ben-Gurion' for its biblical flavour.

1888 Eugene O'Neill, American playwright, born in New York City, the son of an actor.

1902 The first Borstal Institution was opened, at the village of Borstal, near Rochester in Kent.

1908 The first aeroplane flight in England was made, at Farnborough in Hampshire, by American Samuel Franklin Cody.

1920 Gordon Richards rode the first of his 21 834 mounts, at Lingfield Park.

1922 The world's longest main-line tunnel, the Simplon II under the Alps, was completed, after 4 years work.

1946 The Nuremberg executions took place.

1959 George Marshall, American soldier and statesman who formulated the Marshall Aid Plan for postwar European relief, died at Washington, DC.

1978 Pope John Paul II was elected—the first non-Italian to be elevated to the Papacy since 1522.

1981 Moshe Dayan, Israeli military leader, died at Tel Aviv.

17 OCTOBER (291)

1727 John Wilkes, English political agitator and advocate of freedom of the Press, born at Clerkenwell, London, the son of a distiller.

1777 The Battle of Saratoga took place, with victory for the American colonists under General Horatio Gates, over John Burgoyne's British troops during the War of American Independence.

1849 Frédéric Chopin, Polish pianist and composer, died of tuberculosis in Paris, aged 39.

1860 The first professional golf tournament was held, at Prestwick in Scotland, and won by Willie Park.

1908 Jean Arthur, American film actress, born in New York City as Gladys Greene.

1915 Arthur Miller, American dramatist, notably 'Death of a Salesman', born in New York City.

1918 Rita Hayworth, American dancer and film actress, born in New York City as Margarita Carmen Cansino.

1938 Evel Knievel, American stunt motorcyclist, born at Butte in Montana.

1956 Calder Hall in Cumbria, Britain's first large-scale atomic energy station, was formally opened by the Queen, when power was first fed into the grid system.

1970 Anwar Sadat succeeded Nasser as President of Egypt.

18 OCTOBER (292)

1697 Canaletto, Italian painter of cityscapes, born at Venice as Giovanni Antonio Canal.

1865 Lord Palmerston, British Whig statesman and twice Prime Minister, died at Brocket Hall, Welwyn in Hertfordshire.

1873 Rules for American football were formulated in New York, by Columbia, Princeton, Rutgers and Yale delegates.

1884 Emanuel Shinwell, British Labour politician and Minister, born in Spitalfields, London.

1893 Charles Gounod, French composer of operas, including 'Faust', died at St Cloud, a suburb of Paris.

1898 America took formal possession of Puerto Rico from Spain.

1919 Pierre Trudeau, Canadian statesman and Liberal Prime Minister, born at Montreal in Quebec.

1926 Bing Crosby made his first commercial recording—'I've got the girl'.

1931 Thomas Alva Edison, American inventor of the phonograph and the electric lamp, died aged 84.

1958 Denis Law of Huddersfield Town became the youngest footballer to play for Scotland—being 18 years 7 months in the game against Wales at Cardiff.

1966 Elizabeth Arden, American cosmetics company founder, died.

1982 Elizabeth Truman, widow of Harry S. Truman, died.

19 OCTOBER (293)

1216 John, King of England from 1199, died of fever at Newark, and was buried in Worcester Cathedral.

1745 Jonathan Swift, Anglo-Irish satirist best known for his masterpiece 'Gulliver's Travels', died aged 77.

1781 Lord Cornwallis surrendered to General Washington at Yorktown in Virginia, and marked the end of fighting in the American War of Independence.

1859 Alfred Dreyfus, French army officer noted for the 'Dreyfus Treason Affair', born in Alsace of Jewish parents.

1864 The Battle of Cedar Creek took place during the American Civil War, with General Sheridan gaining victory over the Confederates.

1875 Sir Charles Wheatstone, English physicist and pioneer of telegraphy, died in Paris.

1897 George Pullman, American manufacturer of sleeping-cars and dining-cars that bear his name, died at Chicago in Illinois.

1937 Lord Rutherford, New Zealand-born atomic physicist, founder of modern atomic theory and Nobel Prize winner in 1908, died at Cambridge.

20 OCTOBER (294)

1524 Thomas Linacre, English physician to Henry VII and Henry VIII and founder of the Royal College of Physicians in 1518, died.

1632 Sir Christopher Wren, English astronomer, best known as the architect of St Paul's Cathedral, born at East Knoyle in Wiltshire, the son of a dean.

1714 The coronation of King George I took place.

1784 Lord Palmerston, British statesman and twice Prime Minister, born at 20 Queen Anne's Gate, Westminster, as Henry John Temple.

1818 The 49th parallel was established by USA and Britain as the boundary between Canada and USA.

1822 Thomas Hughes, English author of 'Tom Brown's Schooldays', born at Uffington in Berkshire.

1842 Grace Darling, English heroine renowned for saving the shipwrecked crew of the 'Forfarshire' in 1838, died.

1884 Bela Lugosi, actor best known for horror films, born in Hungary as Bela Lugosi Blasko.

1890 Sir Richard Burton, British explorer, writer and translator of the 'Arabian Nights' tales, died.

1891 Sir James Chadwick, English physicist who discovered the neutron in 1932, born in Manchester.

1904 Anna Neagle, English stage and film actress, born at Forest Gate as Marjorie Robertson.
George Woodcock, British trade unionist, born.

1941 Britain's largest ever and last battleship, HMS Vanguard, was laid at Clydebank—was launched on 30th November 1944.

1964 Herbert Hoover, American Republican statesman and 31st President from 1929 to 1933, died in New York City aged 90.

1968 Bud Flanagan, English comic and one of the Crazy Gang, died.

21 OCTOBER

1772 S. T. Coleridge, English poet whose works include 'The Ancient Mariner', born the son of a vicar of Ottery St Mary in Devon.

1805 Lord Nelson, English hero and victor in many naval battles, was killed, in one such battle off Cape Trafalgar in south-west Spain.

1824 Portland cement was patented by Joseph Aspdin of Wakefield in Yorkshire.

1833 Alfred Nobel, Swedish chemist and inventor of dynamite in 1867, born at Stockholm.

1868 Sir Ernest Swinton, British soldier and one of the originators of the military tank, born in Bangalore in India.

1940 Geoff Boycott, Yorkshire and England cricketer, born near Pontefract in Yorkshire.

1960 Britain's first nuclear-powered submarine, 'Dreadnought', was launched at Barrow in Lancashire.

1966 The Aberfan disaster occurred, when a coal tip slid down upon that mid-Glamorgan mining village, killing 144, including 116 children.

22 OCTOBER

1797 The first parachute descent was made, over the Parc Monceau in Paris, by André-Jacques Garnerin from a balloon.

1806 Thomas Sheraton, English furniture designer and cabinet-maker, died.

1811 Franz Liszt, Hungarian composer and piano virtuoso, born in the village of Raiding near Oedenburg.

1844 Sarah Bernhardt, French dramatic actress, born in Paris as Henriette Rosine Bernard.

1878 The first rugby match under floodlights took place, Broughton v Swinton, at Broughton in Lancashire.

1883 The Metropolitan Opera House in New York was opened.

1906 Paul Cézanne, French painter, died.

1910 American-born Dr Hawley Crippen was convicted at the Old Bailey of poisoning his wife Cora, and was subsequently hanged—23rd November—at Pentonville Prison in London.

1973 Pablo Casals, Spanish cellist, composer and conductor, died aged 96.

23 OCTOBER (297)

1642 The Battle of Edgehill, in the Cotswolds, took place—the first major conflict of the Civil War, between Charles I's Cavaliers and the Parliamentary Roundheads.

1844 Robert Bridges, English poet and Poet Laureate in 1913, born at Walmer in Kent.

1900 Douglas Jardine, Surrey and England cricketer, born in Bombay.

1915 W. G. Grace, the legendary English cricketer, died at Eltham in Kent.

1921 John Boyd Dunlop, Scottish veterinary surgeon and inventor of the pneumatic tyre, died.

1922 A. Bonar Law became British Prime Minister, to be replaced by Stanley Baldwin the following 22nd May, for the shortest term of office in the 20th century.

1931 Diana Dors, English film actress, born at Swindon in Wiltshire as Diana Fluck.

1939 Zane Grey, American writer of cowboy and western stories, notably 'Riders of the Purple Sage', died.

1940 Pelé, Brazilian footballer, born at Bauru as Edson Arantes do Nascimento.

1950 Al Jolson, American singer and entertainer, famous for his 'Mammy' and 'Sonny Boy', died in California.

1970 American Gary Gabelich achieved a world record speed of over 631 mph—for a rocket-engine car—on Bonneville Salt Flats in Utah.

24 OCTOBER (298)

National day of Zambia.

1601 Tycho Brahe, Danish royal astronomer, died at Benatky near Prague in Czechoslovakia.

1648 The Treaty of Westphalia was signed, ending the Thirty Years' War.

1857 A number of Cambridge University Old Boys formed the first football club, at Sheffield.

1861 The Pony Express Mail Service in America, running from St Joseph in Missouri to Sacramento in California, ended after operating for just over 18 months.

1882 Sybil Thorndike, English stage and film actress, born at Gainsborough in Lincolnshire.

1894 Jack Warner, English character actor, born as Jack Waters.

1915 Tito Gobbi, Italian international operatic baritone singer, born at Bassano del Grappa.

1945 The United Nations formally came into existence.
Vidkun Quisling, Norwegian Premier and Nazi collaborator, executed by a firing squad at Akershus Fortress at Oslo.

1948 Franz Lehar, Hungarian composer of operettas including 'The Merry Widow', died in Vienna.

1957 Christian Dior, French fashion designer and creator of the 'New Look', died.

1964 Northern Rhodesia became the Republic of Zambia, with Kenneth Kaunda its first President.

25 OCTOBER (299)

St Crispin's day.

1400 Geoffrey Chaucer, English poet and master storyteller, known for his unfinished 'The Canterbury Tales', died.

1415 The Battle of Agincourt took place, 20 miles inland from Boulogne, during the Hundred Years' War, with Henry V's longbowmen victorious over the French knights.

1647 Evangelista Torricelli, Italian mathematician and physicist who devised the barometer or 'Torricellian Tube', died in Florence.

1760 King George II died suddenly at Kensington in London—was succeeded by his grandson, as George III.

1825 Johann Strauss the younger, Austrian composer and 'waltz king', best known for 'The Blue Danube', born in Vienna.

1838 Georges Bizet, French composer, notably the opera 'Carmen', born in Paris.

1839 'Bradshaw's Railway Companion' became the first national railway timetable to be published.

1854 The infamous Charge of the Light Brigade took place at Balaklava during the Crimean War, led by Lord Cardigan.

1881 Pablo Picasso, Spanish painter and creator of Cubism, born at Malaga in Andalusia.

1888 Richard Byrd, American naval officer and Polar explorer, born at Winchester in Virginia.

1921 King Michael of Romania born, the son of King Carol II.

26 OCTOBER (300)

National day of both Iran and Austria.

1759 Georges Danton, French statesman and revolutionary leader, born at Arcis-sur-Aube.

1764 William Hogarth, English painter and engraver, died in London, and was buried in Chiswick churchyard.

1825 The Erie Canal—or properly named the New York State Barge Canal—linking Niagara river with the Hudson river, was opened to traffic.

1863 The English Football Association was formed at a meeting at Freeman's Tavern in Great Queen Street, London.

1879 Leon Trotsky, Russian Communist leader and one of the founders of the Soviet state, born at Yanovka in the Ukraine as Lev Davidovich Bronstein.

1907 The Territorial Army, a British volunteer force, was established by Richard Haldane, when Secretary of State for War.

1913 Hugh Scanlon, British trade unionist, born.

1914 Jackie Coogan, American film actor, born at Los Angeles in California as John Leslie.

1916 Francois Mitterrand, French statesman and President, born.

1972 Igor Sikorsky, Russian-born American aeronautical engineer who developed the first successful helicopter in 1939, died at Easton in Connecticut.

27 OCTOBER (301)

1728 Captain James Cook, English naval officer and explorer, born at Marton, in Cleveland, Yorkshire, the son of a farmer.

1782 Niccolo Paganini, Italian violin virtuoso and composer, born at Genoa, the son of a porter.

1811 Isaac Singer, American inventor and manufacturer of sewing machines, born at Pittsdown in the State of New York.

1854 Sir William Smith, Scottish founder of the Boys' Brigade movement in Glasgow in 1883, born.

1858 Theodore Roosevelt, American Republican statesman and 26th President, born in New York City, the son of a collector of the port.

1879 The 'Liverpool Echo' printed its first copy.

1904 The first section of the New York subway was opened.

1914 Dylan Thomas, Welsh poet, born at Swansea, the son of a schoolmaster.

1931 David Bryant, English bowls champion, born.

1939 John Cleese, English comedy actor, born at Weston-super-Mare.

1957 Glen Hoddle, Tottenham and England footballer, born at Hayes in Middlesex.

1971 The Republic of the Congo changed its name to the Republic of Zaire.

28 OCTOBER (302)

1636 Harvard University, America's oldest university, was founded at Cambridge in Massachusetts, and named after the English-born Puritan minister John Harvard.
1792 John Smeaton, English civil engineer, noted for his novel design for the third Eddystone lighthouse, died.
1846 Escoffier, the famous French chef known as the 'King of Cooks', born at Villeneuve-Loubet.
1886 The Statue of Liberty, presented by France to mark the 100th anniversary of the Declaration of Independence and designed by the French sculptor Auguste Bartholdi, was unveiled by President Grover Cleveland—having taken more than 9 years to complete.
1893 The Royal Navy's first destroyer, HMS Havock, went on trials.
1903 Evelyn Waugh, English novelist, born in London.
1914 Jonas Salk, American microbiologist and discoverer of the anti-poliomyelitis vaccine, born in New York City of Polish-Jewish immigrant parents.
1927 Cleo Laine, English singer and entertainer, born at Southall in London as Clementina Campbell.
1975 Georges Carpentier, French boxer and world light heavyweight champion from 1920 to 1922, died.

29 OCTOBER (303)

National day of Turkey.

1618 Sir Walter Raleigh, English navigator, courtier and favourite of Elizabeth I, was executed at Whitehall for treason.
1740 James Boswell, Scottish diarist and biographer, born at Edinburgh, the son of a judge.

1863 The International Red Cross was founded by Henri Dunant, as a result of his witnessing the tending of the wounded at the Battle of Solferino, near Mantua in Northern Italy.

1877 Wilfred Rhodes, Yorkshire and England cricketer, born at Kirkheaton.

1879 Franz von Papen, German politician and ambassador, born at Werl in Westphalia.

1886 Fred Archer rode 'Blanchland' at Newmarket—the last of his 2746 winners in his brief 16 years in the saddle.

1897 Joseph Goebbels, German political leader and Nazi propagandist, born at Rheydt, the son of a factory foreman.

1923 The Turkish Republic was proclaimed, with Mustafa Kemal (or Kemal Ataturk) becoming its first President.

1927 Frank Sedgman, Australian tennis champion, born in the state of Victoria.

1929 The New York Stock Exchange in Wall Street 'crashed'— was known as 'Black Tuesday'.

1932 The French passenger liner 'Normandie' was launched at St Nazaire, at the mouth of the river Loire.

1950 Gustav V, King of Sweden from 1907, died aged 92.

30 OCTOBER (304)

1735 John Adams, American Federalist statesman and 2nd President, born at Braintree in Massachusetts, the son of a farmer.

1751 R. B. Sheridan, Irish playwright and dramatist, born in Dublin, the son of a teacher of elocution.

1823 Edmund Cartwright, English inventor of the power loom in 1785 and wool-combing machines, died at Hastings in Sussex aged 80.

1910 Henri Dunant, Swiss philanthropist who inspired the foundation of the International Red Cross in 1863, died.

1918 Czechoslovakia was proclaimed a republic, under the leadership of Jan Masaryk and Eduard Benes.

1923 Andrew Bonar Law, Canadian-born British Conservative statesman and Prime Minister, died.

1932 Ralph Reader presented the first Gang Show, at the Scala Theatre in London.

1959 Jim Mollison, Scottish aviator and holder of many flying records, died.

1974 Muhammad Ali knocked out George Foreman in round 8 at Kinchasa in Zaire, to regain the world heavyweight title.

31 OCTOBER (305)

1485 The coronation of King Henry VII took place.

1620 John Evelyn, English diarist and author, born at Wotton, near Dorking in Surrey.

1632 Jan Vermeer, Dutch painter, born at Delft, the son of an art dealer.

1795 John Keats, one of the foremost English romantic poets, born in London, the son of an innkeeper.

1828 Sir Joseph Swan, English chemist and inventor of an electric lamp independently of Edison, born at Sunderland.

1864 Nevada, the Sagebrush or Battle Born State, became the 36th state of the Union.

1887 Chiang Kai-Shek, Chinese military and political leader, born at Fenghwa in Chekiang Province.

1903 Hampden Park in Glasgow was opened.

1922 Benito Mussolini became Prime Minister and dictator of Italy.

1926 Harry Houdini, the famous American escape artist, whose real name was Erich Weiss, died in a Detroit hospital.
Jimmy Saville, British television and radio broadcaster, born at Leeds in Yorkshire.

1951 Zebra crossings came into effect in Britain.

1952 United States detonated her first hydrogen bomb, at Eniwetok Atoll in the Marshall Islands in mid-Pacific.

1961 Augustus John, Welsh portrait painter of many leading personalities of his day, died at Fordingbridge in Hampshire aged 83.

National day of Algeria.

Fox-hunting begins in Britain.

1695 The Bank of Scotland was founded.
1755 A great earthquake occurred in Lisbon, resulting in an estimated 60000 deaths.
1793 Lord George Gordon, British anti-Catholic agitator and leader of the 'Gordon Riots' in 1780, died in Newgate Prison in London.
1848 W. H. Smith's first railway bookstall was opened, at London's Euston Station.
1887 (Laurence Stephen) L. S. Lowry, English artist of the Lancashire industrial scene, born at Rusholme in Manchester.
1895 The first motoring association, the 'American Motor League', was founded at Chicago in Illinois.
1922 Licences for radios were introduced in Britain, at ten shillings (50p) per annum.
1929 The Pony Club movement was founded in Britain.
1935 Gary Player, South African golfer, born at Johannesburg in the Transvaal.
1956 Premium Bonds first went on sale in Britain.

1734 Daniel Boone, American frontiersman and hunter, born in Pennsylvania.
1755 Marie Antoinette, Austrian Princess and Queen Consort of Louis XVI of France, born in Vienna.
1766 Joseph Radetsky, Austrian field marshal and national hero, born at Trebnitz near Tabor.
1795 James Polk, American Democrat statesman and 11th President, born in Mecklenburg County in North Carolina.

1865 Warren Harding, American Republican statesman and 29th President, born near Corsica (now called Blooming Grove) in Ohio, the son of a country physician.

1871 All prisoners in Great Britain were photographed, thereby starting the 'Rogues Gallery'.

1887 Jenny Lind, Swedish international operatic soprano, known as the 'Swedish nightingale', died.

1889 North Dakota, the Sioux or Flickertail State, became the 39th state of the Union.
South Dakota, the Sunshine or Coyote State, became the 40th state of the Union.

1899 Ladysmith in Natal was besieged by the Boers—until relieved by Sir Redvers Buller the following 28th February.

1903 The British newspaper 'Daily Mirror' was first published in London.

1913 Burt Lancaster, American film actor and Oscar winner, born in New York City.

1924 The first crossword appeared in a British newspaper—sold to the Sunday Express by C. W. Shepherd.

1930 Haile Selassie was crowned as Emperor of Ethiopia.

1936 The first British high definition TV broadcast took place, from the BBC studios at Alexandra Palace in North London.

1944 Erwin Rommel, German military commander in North Africa, known as the 'Desert Fox', died by self-administered poison at Herringen.

1950 George Bernard Shaw, British playwright and Nobel Prize winner in 1925, died at Ayot St Lawrence in Hertfordshire aged 94.

1961 James Thurber, American cartoonist, humorous writer and creator of 'Walter Mitty', died in New York City.

1964 King Faisal ascended the throne of Saudi Arabia, succeeding his brother.

3 NOVEMBER (308)

National day of Panama.

1706 A violent earthquake occurred at Abruzzi in Italy, destroying the town and killing some 15000 inhabitants.

1843 The 17-foot 16-ton statue of Lord Nelson was hauled up to the top of the column in Trafalgar Square—in 2 pieces—the top half was hoisted the following day.

1901 Leopold III, King of the Belgians from 1934, born the son of King Albert I.

1903 After a revolt Panama declared its independence from Colombia.

1926 Annie Oakley, American entertainer as a markswoman with rifle and shotgun in Buffalo Bill's Wild West Show, died.

1945 Gerd Müller, West German international footballer, born.

1954 Henri Matisse, French painter and sculptor, died at Nice aged 84.

1957 The dog 'Laika' was launched into space in Russia's Sputnik II.

1961 Viscount Linley, son of Princess Margaret, sister of the Queen, and the Earl of Snowdon, born.

4 NOVEMBER (309)

1650 William III, King of England, Scotland and Ireland, born at The Hague in Holland, the posthumous son of William II of Orange.

1677 King William III married his cousin Princess Mary, the eldest daughter of King James II and Anne Hyde.

1740 Augustus Toplady, English writer of hymns, the best known of which is 'Rock of Ages', born at Farnham in Surrey.

1841 The first emigrant wagon train for California reached Stanislaus River—having left Independence in Missouri on 1st May.

1847 Felix Mendelssohn, German composer and pianist, died at Leipzig.

1862 Richard Gatling patented his revolving battery gun with 10 parallel barrels, firing some 1200 shots a minute.
Eden Phillpotts, English novelist, born at Mount Aboo in India.

1879 The first cash register was patented, by saloon owner James Ritty of Dayton in Ohio.

1946 The United Nations Educational, Scientific and Cultural Organisation (UNESCO) was established, with headquarters in Paris.

5 NOVEMBER (310)

1605 The Gunpowder Plot of Guy Fawkes to blow up King James I and Parliament was foiled when 36 barrels of gunpowder were found in Parliament's cellar.

1854 The Battle of Inkerman in the Crimean War took place, with a French and British victory over the Russians.

1905 Joel McCrea, American film actor, born at Los Angeles in California.

1909 The first Woolworth's store in Britain was opened, in Liverpool's Lord Street.

1912 Roy Rogers, American singing cowboy film actor, born at Cincinnati in Ohio as Leonard Slye.

1913 Vivien Leigh, British film actress and Oscar winner, born at Darjeeling in India, as Vivien Hartley.

1914 Cyprus was annexed to Britain on the outbreak of war with Turkey.

1927 The first automatic traffic lights in Britain began functioning, at Prince Square crossroads in Wolverhampton.

1935 Lester Piggott, English champion jockey, born at Wantage in Berkshire.

1960 Mack Sennet, American film producer and creator of the 'Keystone Kops', died at Richmond in Canada.

1963 Tatum O'Neal, American film actress, born at Los Angeles in California, the daughter of Ryan O'Neal.

6 NOVEMBER (311)

1429 The coronation of King Henry VI of England took place.

1632 Gustavus II, King of Sweden from 1611, was killed in victory in the battle at Lutzen near Leipzig.

1796 Catharine the Great, German-born Empress of Russia from 1762, died.

1814 Adolphe Sax, Belgian musical instrument maker and designer of the saxophone and the saxhorn, born.

1854 John Philip Sousa, American bandmaster and composer of many marches, including 'Stars and Stripes Forever', born in Washington, DC.

1892 Sir John Alcock, English aviator of Alcock and Brown fame as the first to make the Atlantic crossing, born at Manchester.

1893 Tchaikovsky, famous Russian composer, died of cholera at St Petersburg.

1901 Kate Greenaway, English artist and illustrator of children's books, died.

1956 Work began on the Kariba High Dam on the river Zambesi, between Zambia and Zimbabwe.

7 NOVEMBER (312)

National day of Russia.

1867 Marie Curie, Polish-French scientist, born in Warsaw as Marie Sklodowska.

1885 The last spikes were driven in at Craigellachie in British Columbia to complete the Canadian Pacific Railway, after 4½ years work.

1910 Leo Tolstoy, Russian novelist, notably 'War and Peace' and 'Anna Karenina', died in a siding of Astapovo railway station.

1917 The Bolshevik Revolution, led by Lenin, overthrew Prime Minister Alexander Kerensky's government.

1918 Billy Graham, American Baptist evangelist, born at Charlotte in North Carolina, the son of a dairy farmer.

1926 Joan Sutherland, Australian operatic soprano singer, born at Sydney.

1944 Franklin D. Roosevelt was re-elected American President, for a record fourth time.

1959 Victor McLaglen, English-born film actor and Academy Award (Oscar) Winner in 1935 for his part in 'The Informer', died.

1962 Eleanor Roosevelt, niece of Theodore and wife of Franklin Delano, called 'The First Lady of the World', died aged 78.

1975 Cardinal Heenan, English Roman Catholic Archbishop of Westminster, died.

1978 Gene Tunney, the legendary American heavyweight boxing champion, died aged 80.

8 NOVEMBER (313)

1656 Edmond Halley, English astronomer and mathematician, born in London.

1674 John Milton, English poet, blind since 1652 and author of 'Paradise Lost', died at Chalfont St Giles in Buckinghamshire.

1868 Viscount Lee of Fareham, who gave the Buckinghamshire country-house Chequers to the nation in 1921, born.

1886 Fred Archer, English champion jockey, shot himself at his house in Newmarket, aged 29.

1889 Montana, the Treasure State, became the 41st state of the Union.

1895 At Würzburg, Wilhelm Röntgen discovered electro-magnetic rays which he called X-rays.

1922 Dr Christiaan Barnard, South African surgeon and heart-transplant pioneer, born at Beaufort West in Cape Province.

1927 Ken Dodd, English comedian, born in Liverpool.

1942 British and American troops invaded North Africa—in French Algeria, with Eisenhower in command—called 'Operation Torch'.

1967 Radio Leicester, the first local radio station, was opened by the Postmaster General, Edward Short.

1974 After 300 years in central London Covent Garden market moved to its new site at Nine Elms.

1976 Gottfried von Cramm, German tennis star of the thirties, died in Egypt.

National day of Cambodia.

1841 King Edward VII, second child and eldest son of Queen Victoria, born at St James's Palace in London.

1908 Britain's first woman Mayor, Elizabeth Garrett Anderson, was elected at Aldeburgh in Suffolk.

1909 Katharine Hepburn, American film actress and Oscar winner on 2 occasions, born at Hartford in Connecticut.

1915 Hedy Lamarr, American film actress, born at Vienna in Austria as Hedwig Kiesler.

1918 Spiro Agnew, American politician and vice-President to Richard Nixon, born at Baltimore in Maryland.
Kaiser William, Emperor of Germany, abdicated and fled to Holland.

1937 Ramsay MacDonald, British statesman and the first Labour Prime Minister in 1924, died at sea while on a cruise for his health.

1940 Neville Chamberlain, British statesman and Prime Minister from 1937 to 1940, died.

1942 Tom Weiskopf, American golfer, born.

1951 Sigmund Romberg, Hungarian-born composer of operettas, notably 'The Student Prince', died.

1953 Dylan Thomas, Welsh poet, notably 'Under Milk Wood', died in New York City aged 39.

1970 Charles de Gaulle, French general, statesman and President from 1958 to 1969, died of a heart attack at Colombey-les-deux-Eglises.

1483 Martin Luther, German religious reformer, leader of the Protestant reformation, born at Eisleben, the son of a miner.

1683 George II, King of England, born at Hanover in Germany, the only son of George I.

1697 William Hogarth, English painter and engraver, born at Smithfield, London, the son of a teacher.

1728 Oliver Goldsmith, Irish poet and novelist, notably 'The Vicar of Wakefield', born the son of a curate.

1775 The United States Marine Corps was formed.

1871 Stanley met Livingstone at Ujiji, on the eastern shore of Lake Tanganyika—now in Tanzania.

1880 Jacob Epstein, British sculptor of Russo-Polish descent, born in New York City.

1889 Claude Rains, stage and film character actor, born in London.

1925 Richard Burton, British dramatic actor, born as Richard Jenkins at Pontrhydfen in South Wales.

1938 Kemel Ataturk, statesman, founder and first President of the Turkish Republic in 1923, died.

1944 Tim Rice, English songwriter, born in Amersham in Buckinghamshire.

1982 Leonid Brezhnev, Soviet politician and President since 1964, died aged 75.

11 NOVEMBER (316)

1821 Dostoyevsky, Russian novelist, born in Moscow, the son of a surgeon.

1880 Ned Kelly, Australian bushranger and notorious bank robber, was hanged in Old Melbourne Gaol in Russell Street in his mid-twenties.

1882 Gustaf VI, King of Sweden, born the elder son of Gustaf V.

1885 George Patton, American military commander in World War II, born at San Gabriel in California.

1889 Washington, the Evergreen State, became the 42nd state of the Union.

1918 The Armistice was signed in Marshal Foch's railway coach, near Compiègne.

1920 Roy Jenkins, British politician and Labour Member of Parliament, born at Abersychan in Wales.

The 35-foot Cenotaph War Memorial in Whitehall, London, designed by Sir Edwin Lutyens, was unveiled by King George V.

1921 The British Legion held its first Poppy Day.

1936 Sir Edward German, English composer, notably 'Merrie England', died.

1945 Jerome Kern, American composer of Broadway shows and numerous songs, died.

1946 Stevenage in Hertfordshire became the first 'new town' to be designated in Britain.

1947 Rodney Marsh, Australian cricketer, born.

1953 BBC's television programme 'Panorama' was first transmitted by Patrick Murphy.

1965 Ian Smith, Prime Minister of Rhodesia, announced his country's unilateral declaration of independence (UDI).

1971 Sir Alan P. Herbert, created CH in 1970, died.

1975 Angola gained independence from Portugal.

12 NOVEMBER (317)

1671 Thomas Fairfax, British general and leader of the Parliamentary Army in the Civil War, died at Nunappleton in Yorkshire.

1840 Auguste Rodin, French sculptor, born in Paris, the son of a clerk.

1842 Lord Rayleigh, English physicist and Nobel Prize winner, born at Witham near Maldon in Essex.

1865 Elizabeth Gaskell, English novelist, notably 'Cranford', died near Alton in Hampshire.

1866 Sun Yat-Sen, Chinese nationalist and revolutionary leader, born at Tsuiheng near Canton.

1916 Percival Lowell, American astronomer who predicted the existence of the planet Pluto prior to its 1930 discovery, died at Flagstaff in Arizona.

1919 British pilots Smith and Ross set out from Hounslow on the first aeroplane flight to Australia—reaching Darwin in their Vickers Vimy on 13th December.

1927 The first veteran car rally from London to Brighton, sponsored by the 'Daily Sketch', took place, and was won by John Bryce from an entry of 51.

1929 Princess Grace of Monaco was born at Philadelphia in Pennsylvania as Grace Patricia Kelly.

1944 The German battleship 'Tirpitz' was sunk in Tromso Fjord, by Lancaster bombers of the RAF.
1951 The BBC television programme 'Come Dancing' was first transmitted.
1961 Nadia Comaneci, Romanian international gymnast, born at Onesti.

13 NOVEMBER (318)

1312 King Edward III was born at Windsor Castle, the son of Edward II.
1687 Nell Gwyn or Gwynne, British actress and principally remembered as the mistress of Charles II by whom she had 2 sons, died in London aged 37.
1850 Robert Louis Stevenson, Scottish author, notably 'Treasure Island' and 'Kidnapped', born at 8 Howard Place in Edinburgh, the son and grandson of famous light-house builders.
1851 The telegraph service between London and Paris was opened.
1854 John Peel, English squire, the subject of the old hunting song, died at Caldbeck in the Lake District.
1868 Gioacchino Rossini, Italian composer of operas, notably 'The Barber of Seville' and 'William Tell', died at Passy in France aged 76.
1906 Hermione Baddeley, English character actress of stage and films, born at Broseley in Shropshire.
1922 Charles Bronson, American film actor, born at Ehrenfield in Pennsylvania as Charles Buchinsky.
1969 Quins were born to Mrs Irene Hanson of Rayleigh in Essex.
1982 Chesney Allen, co-founder and last surviving member of the 'Crazy Gang', died aged 88.

14 NOVEMBER (319)

1765 Robert Fulton, American engineer and inventor of the first steamboat, born of Irish parents in Pennsylvania.

1770 The source of the Blue Nile—Lake Tana in NW Ethiopia—was discovered by the British explorer James Bruce.

1840 Claude Monet, French Impressionist painter, born in Paris.

1863 Leo Baekeland, American chemist and inventor of 'Bakelite® ', one of the first plastics, born at Ghent in Belgium.

1889 Pandit Nehru, statesman and first Prime Minister of India on its independence, born at Allahabad.

1891 Sir Frederick Banting, Canadian co-discover of insulin with Macleod and Best in 1922, born at Alliston in Ontario.

1896 Mamie Eisenhower, wife of America's 34th President, born at Boone in Iowa as Mamie Doud.

1904 Harold Larwood, English cricketer and fast bowler, born at Nurcargate in Nottinghamshire.

1905 Robert Whitehead, English engineer who invented the naval torpedo in 1866, died in Berkshire.

1908 Joe McCarthy, American politician and lawyer noted for his purge against Communism, born at Grand Chute in Wisconsin.

1914 Lord Roberts, British soldier and Boer War commander, died while visiting troops in the field in France.

1922 The BBC transmitted its first regular radio programme—a news bulletin from 2LO in London's Strand.

1935 King Hussein of Jordan was born at Amman, the son of King Talal.

1940 Coventry Cathedral was destroyed by enemy action.

1941 Britain's aircraft carrier 'Ark Royal' was sunk.

1946 Manuel de Falla, Spanish composer of the ballet 'The Three-Cornered Hat', died.

1948 Prince Charles (Charles Philip Arthur George), Prince of Wales, born at Buckingham Palace.

1952 Charts for single records were first published in Britain, by 'New Musical Express'.

1963 The island of Surtsey off Iceland was 'born' by the eruption of an under-water volcano.

1969 Apollo 12 was launched, with Charles Conrad, Richard Gordon and Alan Bean—Conrad and Bean making the 2nd moon landing.

Colour programmes began on British TV.

1973 Princess Anne married Captain Mark Phillips at Westminster Abbey.

Bobby Moore made his record 108th football international appearance for England, against Italy at Wembley Stadium.

15 NOVEMBER (320)

1708 William Pitt the Elder, British statesman and orator, born at Westminster in London.

1738 Sir William Herschel, English astronomer who discovered the planet Uranus in 1781, born at Hanover in Germany.

1802 George Romney, English portrait painter, died at Kendal in Cumbria.

1837 Pitman's system of shorthand was published, under the title 'Stenographic Sound-Hand'.

1889 Dom Pedro was dethroned as Emperor, and a republic was proclaimed in Brazil.

1891 Averell Harriman, American administrator and ambassador, born in New York City.

Erwin Rommel, German Army Field Marshal and commander of the Afrika Korps, born at Heidenheim.

1897 Aneurin Bevan, British politician and Labour Party leader, born at Tredegar in Monmouth, one of 13 children of a miner.

1905 Mantovani, Italian conductor, born in Venice.

1908 The State of the Congo, founded in 1885, became a Belgian colony.

1934 Petula Clark, British singer and actress, born at Ewell in Surrey.

1954 Lionel Barrymore, American film actor and Academy Award (Oscar) winner in 1931 for his part in 'A Free Soul', died aged 76.

1958 Tyrone Power, American film actor and leading man, died.

1965 American Norman Breedlove achieved a world record speed of almost 614 mph for a jet-engined car—on Bonneville Salt Flats in Utah.

1968 The British liner 'Queen Elizabeth' ended her last passenger voyage.

16 NOVEMBER

1272 Death of King Henry III at Westminster, resulting in the accession of his elder son as Edward I.

1665 The 'London Gazette', originally called the 'Oxford Gazette', was first published.

1724 Jack Sheppard, English highwayman, hanged at Tyburn.

1811 John Bright, British Radical statesman and orator, born at Rochdale in Lancashire, the son of a Quaker cotton spinner.

1824 Hamilton Hume discovered the Murray River in Australia.

1896 Sir Oswald Mosley, British politician and Fascist leader, born in London.

1907 Oklahoma, the Sooner State, became the 46th state of the Union.

1942 Willie Carson, English champion jockey, born at Stirling in Scotland.

1960 Gilbert Harding, British television personality, collapsed and died on the steps of the BBC studios in London.
Clark Gable, American film actor and Academy Award (Oscar) winner in 1934 for his part in 'It Happened One Night', died.

1982 Arthur Askey, Liverpool-born comedian, died in London aged 82.

17 NOVEMBER

1558 Mary I, Queen of England, called Mary Tudor and 'Bloody Mary', died at St James's Palace in London—accession of her half-sister as Queen Elizabeth I.

1755 Louis XVIII, King of France after the fall of Napoleon, born at Versailles.

1858 Robert Owen, social reformer and early trade unionist, died aged 87.

1869 The 100-mile Suez Canal from Port Said to Port Tewfik, the work of Ferdinand de Lesseps, was opened at Port Said —work having begun on 25th April 1859.

1887 Viscount Montgomery, British soldier and commander of distinction in World War II, born the son of a vicar in Kennington in South London.

1917 Auguste Rodin, French sculptor whose works include 'The Thinker' and 'The Kiss', died at Meudon near Paris aged 77.

1925 Rock Hudson, American film actor, born at Winnetka in Illinois as Roy Scherer.

18 NOVEMBER (323)

1626 St Peter's Church in Rome was consecrated.

1786 Carl von Weber, German composer, born at Eutin near Lübeck of an Austrian family.

1789 Louis Daguerre, French artist and pioneer in photography, born near Paris.

1836 Sir W. S. Gilbert, English writer of comic operas, of Gilbert and Sullivan fame, born in London's Strand.

1852 The funeral of the Duke of Wellington took place in St Paul's Cathedral.

1860 Paderewski, Polish pianist, statesman and his country's first Prime Minister, born at Kurylowka.

1880 The Irish Football Association was formed.

1886 Chester Alan Arthur, American Republican statesman and 21st President from 1881 to 1885, died in New York City.

1901 George Gallup, American public opinion statistician who evolved the Gallup Polls, born at Jefferson in Iowa.

1918 Latvia was proclaimed an independent republic.

1935 Economic sanctions against Italy went into effect by members of the League of Nations, because of her invasion of Ethiopia—ended on 15th July 1936.

1963 The Dartford-Purfleet tunnel, linking Kent and Essex under the Thames, was opened.

1600 King Charles I, born in Dunfermline Palace in Scotland, the second son of James I and Anne of Denmark.

1805 Ferdinand de Lesseps, French diplomat and engineer, best known as the builder of the Suez Canal, born at Versailles.

1828 Franz Schubert, Austrian composer, died in Vienna of typhus.

1831 James Garfield, American Republican statesman and 20th President, born near Orange in Ohio.

1850 Alfred, Lord Tennyson was appointed Poet Laureate—an appointment he held until his death in 1892.

1863 Abraham Lincoln delivered his famous address at the dedication of the military cemetery at Gettysburg in Pennsylvania.

1900 Anton Walbrook, actor in British films, born in Vienna as Adolf Wohlbruck.

1905 Tommy Dorsey, American trombonist, band leader and younger of the musical brothers, born at Shenandoah in Pennsylvania.

1917 Indira Gandhi, Indian stateswoman and first woman Prime Minister of her country, born at Allahabad, the daughter of Jawaharlal Nehru.

1969 Pelé, Brazilian footballer, scored the 1000th goal of his brilliant career.

1759 The naval battle of Quiberon Bay took place—British Admiral Hawke destroying the French invasion fleet under Admiral Conflans, during the Seven Years War.

1894 Anton Rubinstein, Russian pianist, composer and musical director, died at Peterhof.

1908 Alistair Cooke, English-American journalist and broadcaster, born at Salford in Manchester.

1917 Bobby Locke, South African golfing champion, born at Germiston in the Transvaal.

1920 Gene Tierney, American film actress, born at Brooklyn in New York.

Dulcie Gray, British actress, born as Dulcie Bailey.

1925 Robert Kennedy, American politician and younger brother of the 35th President, born at Brookline in Massachusetts.

Queen Alexandra, wife of King Edward VII, died.

1945 The Nuremberg war crimes tribunal began, with the trials of 24 Nazi leaders.

1947 Queen Elizabeth II, as Princess Elizabeth, married Prince Philip in Westminster Abbey.

1970 The Bank of England ten-shilling note went out of circulation.

1975 General Franco, Spanish statesman and Head of State from 1936, died.

21 NOVEMBER (326)

1695 Henry Purcell, English composer, died in London from tuberculosis.

1789 North Carolina, the Tar Heel or Old North State, became the 12th state of the Union.

1843 Vulcanised rubber was patented in England by Thomas Hancock.

1918 The mighty German High Seas Fleet was handed over to the British Fleet for internment, at Scapa Flow in the Orkneys.

1936 The first television gardening programme was broadcast by the BBC—'In Your Garden' with Mr Middleton.

1942 James Hertzog, South African soldier, statesman and anti-British Premier, died.

1953 The Piltdown skull, 'discovered' by Charles Dawson in Sussex in 1912, was found by anthropologists to be a hoax.

1958 Work began on the construction of the Forth Road Bridge in Scotland—to be the longest suspension bridge in Europe.

1964 The Verrazano-Narrows Bridge (until the Humber Bridge the world's longest single span) across the entrance to New York City harbour was opened to traffic.

National day of Lebanon.

1497 Vasco da Gama became the first to round the Cape of Good Hope—his fleet comprised the 'St Gabriel', the 'St Raphael', the 'Berrio' and a store ship.

1718 Edward Teach, English pirate known as 'Blackbeard', was killed off the coast of North Carolina.

1774 Robert Clive, English soldier and British administrator in India, died from an overdose of opium.

1808 Thomas Cook, English travel agent pioneer, born at Melbourne in Derbyshire.

1819 George Eliot, English novelist, author of the 'Mill on the Floss', born near Nuneaton in Warwickshire as Mary Ann or Marian Evans, the daughter of an estate agent.

1890 Charles de Gaulle, French soldier, statesman and President, born at Lille.

1899 'Hoagy' Carmichael, American pianist and composer, born at Bloomington in Indiana.
Wiley Post, American aviator, born at Grand Saline in Texas.

1900 Sir Arthur Sullivan, English composer of comic operas in conjunction with W. S. Gilbert, died in London.

1913 Benjamin Britten, English composer, born at Lowestoft in Suffolk.

1916 Jack London, American novelist, notably 'Call of the Wild' and 'White Fang', died in California.

1930 The first Irish Sweep was held, on the Manchester November Handicap horse race.

1943 Billie-Jean King, American tennis champion, born at Long Beach in California.

1954 Andrei Vyshinsky, Soviet politician and Foreign Minister, died in New York City.

1956 The 16th Olympic Games opened in Melbourne.

1963 John F. Kennedy, American Democrat statesman and 35th President from 1961, was assassinated at Dallas allegedly by Lee Harvey Oswald—the remainder of his term of office was completed by Lyndon Johnson.

1975 King Juan Carlos II became Head of State in Spain—2 days after the death of General Franco.

1980 Mae West, American film actress and sex symbol, died aged 88.

23 NOVEMBER

1499 Perkin Warbeck, Flemish impostor claiming to be Richard of York, son of Edward IV, was executed in the Tower of London.

1804 Franklin Pierce, American Democrat statesman and 14th President, born at Hillsborough in New Hampshire.

1859 Billy the Kid, American outlaw and gunman, born in New York City as William H. Bonney.

1876 Manuel de Falla, Spanish composer of the ballet 'The Three-Cornered Hat', born at Cadiz.

1887 Boris Karloff, film actor best known for horror roles, born at Dulwich in London as William Henry Pratt.

1888 'Harpo' Marx, of the Marx brothers comedy team, born in New York City.

1889 The first jukebox was installed, in the Palais Royal Saloon in San Francisco.

1910 American Dr Hawley Crippen was executed in London's Pentonville prison for the murder of his wife, Cora.

1964 The first British commercial radio station—Manx—was opened.

24 NOVEMBER

1572 John Knox, Scottish religious leader and founder of Scottish Presbyterianism, died.

1642 Abel Tasman, Dutch navigator, discovered Van Diemen's Land, which was renamed Tasmania in 1853.

1713 Laurence Sterne, Irish clergyman and novelist, author of 'Tristram Shandy', born at Clonmel in the county of Tipperary, the son of an Army officer.

1784 Zachary Taylor, American soldier, Whig statesman and 12th President, born in Orange County in the state of Virginia.

1815 Grace Darling, heroine of a rescue in the North Sea in 1838, born at Bamburgh in Northumberland, the daughter of the lighthouse keeper.

1848 Lord Melbourne, British statesman and Whig Prime Minister on 2 occasions, died near Welwyn in Hertfordshire.

1864 Toulouse-Lautrec, French painter, born at Albi.

1868 London's Smithfield meat market was opened by the Lord Mayor.

1894 Herbert Sutcliffe, Yorkshire and England cricketer, born at Pudsey, near Leeds.

1916 Sir Hiram Maxim, English-born American inventor of the machine gun in 1883 that bears his name, died in London.

1929 Georges Clemenceau, French statesman and twice Premier, known as the 'Tiger', died.

1955 Ian Botham, Somerset and England all-round cricketer, born in Cheshire.

25 NOVEMBER (330)

1748 Isaac Watts, English hymn writer, notably 'O God, our help in ages past' and 'When I survey the wondrous cross', died.

1823 The chain pier at Brighton was opened.

1835 Andrew Carnegie, American industrialist and philanthropist, born at Dunfermline in Scotland, the son of a weaver.

1844 Karl Benz, German engineer and pioneer of early motor cars, born in Karlsruhe.

1881 Pope John XXIII, born at Sotto il Monte, near Bergamo, Italy, as Angelo Giuseppe Roncalli, the son of a peasant.

1903 British-born boxer Bob Fitzsimmons won the world light-heavyweight title, and so became the only boxer to have won the 3 heaviest titles.

1912 Francis Durbridge, English writer of mystery novels, born.

1941 The Royal Navy battleship HMS Barham was sunk.

1952 The long-running play 'The Mousetrap' by Agatha Christie opened in London, at the Ambassador's Theatre.

1965 Dame Myra Hess, British concert pianist, died in London aged 75.

1974 U Thant, Burmese diplomat and Secretary-General of the United Nations from 1962 to 1971, died.

1975 Surinam, a republic of NE South America—previously called Dutch Guiana—became fully independent.

26 NOVEMBER (331)

1731 William Cowper, English poet, born at Berkhamsted in Hertfordshire, the son of a rector.

1832 Trams were first introduced by John Mason in New York City, between Prince Street and 14th Street.

1836 John McAdam, Scottish engineer who introduced the 'macadamising' system of road-making, died.

1851 Nicolas Soult, French general under Napoleon, died at Soultberg aged 82.

1905 Emlyn Williams, British playwright and actor, born at Mostyn in North Wales.

1917 Sir Leander Jameson, British colonial administrator and leader of the 'Jameson' raid into the Transvaal, died.

1922 The tomb of the king Tutankhamun was discovered by Howard Carter and his patron, Lord Carnarvon.

1956 Tommy Dorsey, American trombonist and key figure in the big band era, died.

1966 The world's first major tidal power station, at the Rance estuary in the Golfe de St Malo in Brittany, was officially opened by President de Gaulle.

27 NOVEMBER (332)

1582 William Shakespeare, at 18, married Anne Hathaway.

1701 Anders Celsius, Swedish astronomer who devised the centigrade temperature scale in 1742, born at Uppsala.

1811 Andrew Meikle, Scottish agricultural engineer, inventor of the threshing machine in 1786, died at Dunbar in East Lothian.

1895 Alexandre Dumas *(fils),* French playwright, author of 'La Dame aux Camélias', died.

1921 Alexander Dubcek, Czechoslovakian statesman and political leader, born in Uhrovek.

1925 Ernie Wise, of Morecambe and Wise comedy team, born at Leeds in Yorkshire as Ernest Wiseman.

1942 The French fleet in the harbour was scuttled when German forces entered Toulon.

1953 Eugene O'Neill, American playwright and Nobel Prize winner in 1936, died at Boston in Massachusetts.

1975 Ross McWhirter, co-editor and compiler of the Guinness Book of Records, killed.

28 NOVEMBER (333)

1820 Friedrich Engels, German Socialist and associate of Karl Marx, born at Barmen.

1829 Anton Rubinstein, Russian pianist and composer, born at Wechwotynetz.

1837 John Wesley Hyatt, American inventor of celluloid, born at Starkey in the State of New York.

1859 Washington Irving, American author, notably 'Rip Van Winkle' and 'The Legend of Sleepy Hollow', died.

1883 Andrei Vyshinsky, Soviet politician, born at Odessa of Polish origin.

1905 Sinn Fein Irish political party was founded in Dublin by Arthur Griffith.

1919 Keith Miller, Australian Test cricketer, born at Melbourne, the capital of Victoria.

1920 Cecilia Colledge, British ice skating champion, born.

1935 The Miles quads (Ann, Ernest, Paul, and Michael) were born at St Neots in Cambridgeshire.

1945 Dwight Davis, American donor of the Davis Cup for international tennis, died.

1959 The dockyard at Hong Kong closed, after 80 years.

1962 Wilhelmina, Queen of the Netherlands from 1890 to 1948, died.

1968 Enid Blyton, English writer of children's books, died.

1976 Len Harvey, British boxing champion, died in London.

29 NOVEMBER (334)

National day of Yugoslavia.

1530 Cardinal Wolsey, English churchman, statesman and Lord Chancellor, died on his way from his York diocese to London.

1780 Maria Theresa, Empress of Austria and Queen of Hungary and Bohemia, died in Vienna.

1832 Louisa M. Alcott, American novelist, author of 'Little Women', born at Germanstown in Philadelphia.

1864 The Sand Creek massacre took place—the tribes were waiting to surrender—of Cheyenne and Arapahoe Indians by soldiers under the command of Colonel Chivington.

1872 Horace Greeley, American newspaper editor and founder of the 'New York Tribune', died.

1924 Giacomo Puccini, Italian opera composer, notably 'La Bohème' and 'Madame Butterfly', died in a hospital in Brussels of cancer of the throat.

1929 Richard Byrd, American admiral, explorer and aviator, made the first flight over the South Pole, with Pilot Bernt Balchen.

1945 Yugoslavia was proclaimed a communistic Republic.

1954 Sir George Robey, English comedian, dubbed the 'Prime Minister of mirth', died.

1975 Graham Hill, British racing driver and Grand Prix winner, was killed in a plane crash at Arkley in Hertfordshire.

30 NOVEMBER (335)

St Andrew's Day—national day of Scotland.

1667 Jonathan Swift, Irish clergyman and writer, author of 'Gulliver's Travels', born in Dublin.

273

1835 Mark Twain, American author and humorist, born near Florida in Missouri as Samuel Langhorne Clemens.

1872 The first football international took place, Scotland and England drawing 0-0 at Partick, Glasgow.

1874 Sir Winston Churchill, British statesman and Prime Minister, born at Blenheim Palace, Woodstock in Oxfordshire.

1900 Oscar Wilde, Irish poet and dramatist, died in poverty and exile in Paris, having adopted the name of Sebastian Melmoth.

1920 Virginia Mayo, American film actress, born at St Louis in Missouri as Virginia Jones.

1936 Crystal Palace, a building of glass and iron, designed by Joseph Paxton to house the Great Exhibition of 1851, was burned down on its new site at Sydenham.

1944 Britain's largest ever and last battleship, HMS Vanguard, was launched at Clydebank in Scotland—having been laid down on 20th October 1941.

1956 Floyd Patterson became the youngest boxer ever to win the world heavyweight title when he knocked out Archie Moore in Round 5 in Chicago for the title left vacant by Rocky Marciano.

1957 Beniamino Gigli, Italian operatic tenor, died.

1966 Full independence was proclaimed in Barbados.

1977 Terence Rattigan, English playwright, notably 'French without Tears' and 'The Winslow Boy', died.

1979 'Zeppo' Marx, the agent of the Marx Brothers, died.

1 DECEMBER   (336)

1135 Death of King Henry I of England near Rouen—accession of his nephew Stephen.

1655 Samuel Pepys married Elizabeth St Michel in St Margaret's, Westminster.

1822 Dom Pedro was crowned Emperor of recently independent Brazil.

1844 Queen Alexandra, wife of Edward VII, born, the eldest daughter of King Christian of Denmark.

1895 Henry Williamson, English novelist and nature writer, notably 'Tarka the Otter', born in Bedfordshire.

1910 Alicia Markova, English prima ballerina, born in London as Lilian Alicia Marks.

1919 Nancy, Viscountess Astor, Member of Parliament for the Sutton division of Plymouth, became the first woman Member to take her seat in the House of Commons.

1925 The Locarno Pact was signed in London, guaranteeing peace and frontiers in Europe.

1935 Woody Allen, American comedian, born at Brooklyn, New York, as Allen Stewart Königsberg.

1939 Lee Trevino, American international golf champion, born near Horizon City in Texas.

1966 Britain's post offices issued the first special Christmas stamps.

1973 David Ben-Gurion, Israeli statesman, his country's first Prime Minister, often called the 'Father of the Nation', died.

2 DECEMBER (337)

1547 Hernando Cortez, Spanish conqueror of Mexico in 1521, died near Seville.

1697 The re-built St Paul's Cathedral was formally opened.

1804 Napoleon Bonaparte was crowned Emperor in Paris, by Pope Pius VII.

1805 The Battle of Austerlitz took place near Brunn in Moravia, in which Napoleon defeated the Austro-Russian force under the command of Kutuzov—is sometimes called the 'Battle of the Three Emperors'.

1823 The Monroe Doctrine was declared, opposing European attempts to interfere.

1849 Queen Adelaide, wife of William IV, died.

1859 John Brown, American anti-slavery campaigner, was hanged for treason, at Charlestown in West Virginia.

1899 Sir John Barbirolli, English conductor and musical director, born in London of Italian parents.

1901 King Camp Gillette patented the first safety razor.

1903 Jim Sullivan, Wigan's international Rugby League footballer, born.

1942 The world's first nuclear chain reaction took place at Stagg Field at the University of Chicago, under physicists Enrico Fermi and Arthur Compton.

3 DECEMBER (338)

1753 Samuel Crompton, English inventor of the spinning-mule, which substituted machinery for hand work in the cotton industry, born at Firwood near Bolton in Lancashire, the son of a farmer.

1795 Sir Rowland Hill, English educator and pioneer in postal services, born at Kidderminster in Worcestershire.

1818 Illinois, the Prairie State, became the 21st state of the Union.

1857 Joseph Conrad, English novelist, born in Berdichev of Polish parents as Teodor Jozef Konrad Korzeniowski.

1894 Robert Louis Stevenson, Scottish novelist, author of 'Treasure Island' and 'Kidnapped', died on the island of Samoa in the Pacific.

1905 Leslie Ames, Kent and England cricketer, born at Elham.

1910 Mary Baker Eddy, American religious leader and founder of the Christian Science movement, died.

1917 The Quebec Bridge, the world's longest cantilever, over the St Lawrence river, was opened to traffic—87 lives were lost during its construction.

1919 Pierre Auguste Renoir, French Impressionist painter, died at Cagnes-sur-Mer.

1930 Andy Williams, American singer and entertainer, born at Wall Lake in Iowa.

1967 Christiaan Barnard performed the first heart transplant operation—Louis Washansky received the heart of traffic victim Denise Darvali, at Groote Schuur Hospital at Cape Town, but died 18 days later.

1969 Marshal Voroshilov, Soviet political leader and army marshal, died.

1980 Sir Oswald Mosley, English politician and leader of the British Union of Fascists, died in exile at his home near Paris.

4 DECEMBER (339)

1154 Nicolas Breakspear became the only English Pope—as Adrian IV.
1642 Cardinal Richelieu, French statesman and chief minister to Louis XIII from 1624, died in Paris.
1732 John Gay, English poet and playwright, notably 'The Beggar's Opera', died in London.
1791 'The Observer', the oldest Sunday newspaper in the United Kingdom, was first published.
1795 Thomas Carlyle, Scottish historian and writer, born at Ecclefechan, Dumfriesshire, the son of a master mason.
1798 Luigi Galvani, Italian scientist and anatomist who researched into animal electricity, or galvanism, died.
1835 Samuel Butler, English novelist and satirist, known especially for his Utopian satire, 'Erewhon', born at Langar rectory, near Bingham in Nottinghamshire.
1850 William Sturgeon, English physicist who built the first electromagnet, died at Prestwich in Lancashire.
1865 Edith Cavell, English nurse and patriot, born the daughter of the rector of Swardeston in Norfolk.
1875 Edgar Wallace, English writer of detective thrillers and playwright, born.
1892 General Franco, Spanish dictator and Head of State, born at El Ferrol.
1922 Deanna Durbin, singer and film actress, born at Winnipeg in Manitoba, Canada.
1965 Gemini 7 was launched, with Frank Borman and James Lovell.
1969 Jack Payne, British dance band leader, died.
1976 Benjamin Britten, English composer, died at Aldeburgh in Suffolk.

National day of Thailand.

1594 Gerard Mercator, Flemish geographer and cartographer, died at Duisberg.

1697 The first Sunday service was held in the new St Paul's Cathedral.

1766 Christie's, famous auctioneers of London, held their first sale.

1782 Martin van Buren, American Democrat statesman and 8th President, born at Kinderhook in the State of New York, the son of a Dutch farmer.

1791 Wolfgang Amadeus Mozart, Austrian composer, died of typhus in Vienna, and was buried in the common ground of St Mark's churchyard.

1839 George Armstrong Custer, American cavalry commander in the West, born in Harrison County in Ohio.

1870 Alexandre Dumas the elder, French novelist, best known for 'The Three Musketeers' and 'The Count of Monte Cristo', died at Dieppe.

1872 'Marie Celeste', an American brig, captained by Benjamin Briggs, was found by the 'Dei Gratia' abandoned in the Atlantic on its way to Genoa with a cargo of alcohol.

1899 Sir Henry Tate, English businessman, philanthropist and founder of the Tate Gallery in London, died aged 80.

1901 Walt Disney, American cartoon film producer, born at Chicago in Illinois.

1926 Claude Monet, French painter and one of the founders of the Impressionist movement, died as a recluse at Giverny.

1933 Prohibition in America was repealed by the 21st Amendment—having come into effect on 16th January 1920.

1958 The first STD telephone service in Britain was inaugurated at Bristol, by the Queen calling up the Lord Provost of Edinburgh.
The first motorway in Britain, the 8½-mile Preston by-pass section of the M6, was opened by the then Prime Minister Harold MacMillan.

National day of Finland.

1421 Henry VI, born at Windsor Castle, the only child of Henry V.

1492 Haiti, a republic of the West Indies, was discovered by Columbus—was then named Hispaniola.

1732 Warren Hastings, British administrator and first Governor-General of India, born at Churchill in Oxfordshire.

1778 Joseph Gay-Lussac, French physicist and chemist, born at St Léonard.

1882 Anthony Trollope, English novelist, best known for his 'Barchester Chronicles' of Victorian life, died in London, and was buried at Kensal Green in London.

1889 Jefferson Davis, American political leader and President of the Confederate States, died aged 81.

1905 James J. Braddock, American heavyweight boxing champion, known as the 'Cinderella Man', born at North Bergen in New Jersey.

1907 America suffered its worst mine disaster, with 361 deaths at Monongah in West Virginia.

1914 Cyril Washbrook, Lancashire and England cricketer, born.

1917 Finland proclaimed independence from Russian rule.

1921 The Irish Free State was established after independence from the United Kingdom.

1732 The original Covent Garden Opera House in London, designed by Edward Shepherd, was opened.

1783 William Pitt the Younger became the youngest of Britain's Prime Ministers—aged 24.

1787 Delaware, the Diamond or First State, achieved statehood.

1815 Marshal Ney, French soldier, the most famous of Napoleon's marshals, was shot in Paris for high treason.

1817 Captain Bligh, captain of the 'Bounty', died in London.

1863 Pietro Mascagni, Italian composer, famous for his 'Cavalleria Rusticana', born at Leghorn, the son of a baker.

1894 Ferdinand de Lesseps, French diplomat, engineer and promoter of the Suez Canal, died aged 89.

1915 Eli Wallach, American film actor, born at Brooklyn in New York.

1916 David Lloyd George became head of the wartime coalition Government.

1941 Some 360 Japanese planes attacked the US Pacific Fleet anchored at Pearl Harbor in Hawaii.

1962 Kirsten Flagstad, Norwegian operatic soprano, died.

1972 Apollo 17 was launched, with Eugene Cernan, Ronald Evans and Dr Harrison Schmitt—Cernan and Schmitt making the 6th moon landing.

1975 Thornton Wilder, American novelist, especially 'The Bridge of San Luis Rey', died.

8 DECEMBER (343)

1542 Mary, Queen of Scots, cousin of Queen Elizabeth I, born at Linlithgow Palace, the daughter of James V of Scotland.

1765 Eli Whitney, American inventor who perfected the cotton-gin, which made cotton growing highly profitable, born at Westborough in Massachusetts.

1841 Prince Albert Edward was created Prince of Wales—later became King Edward VII.

1863 The first heavyweight boxing championship of the world took place, at Wodhurst in Kent—Tom King of England beating American John Heenan.

1864 Brunel's Clifton Suspension Bridge over the river Avon at Bristol was opened.

1865 Jean Sibelius, Finland's leading composer, noted for 'Finlandia', born at Hameenlinna, the son of a surgeon.

1894 James Thurber, American humorous artist, writer and creator of 'Walter Mitty', born at Columbus in Ohio.

1925 Sammy Davis junior, American singer and entertainer, born in New York City.

1939 James Galway, British international flautist, born in Belfast.

1941 Britain and the United States declared war on Japan.

1978 Golda Meir, Israeli stateswoman and Prime Minister from 1969 to 1974, died.

1980 John Lennon, British composer, of Beatles fame, was murdered outside his Manhattan home, by Mark David Chapman.

9 DECEMBER (344)

National day of Tanzania.

1608 John Milton, English poet, notably 'Paradise Lost', born at Cheapside in London, the son of a scrivener.

1641 Sir Anthony van Dyck, Flemish court painter to Charles I, died in his studio in Blackfriars, London, and was buried in Old St Paul's.

1837 Émile Waldteufel, French composer, notably of the 'Skaters Waltz', born at Strasbourg.

1848 Joel Chandler Harris, American writer and creator of 'Uncle Remus', born at Eatonton in Georgia.

1868 W. E. Gladstone became Prime Minister on the first of his four terms of office.

1886 Clarence Birdseye, American inventor of a process for deep-freezing foodstuffs, born in New York City.

1902 R. A. Butler, British Conservative politician, born at Attock Serai in India.

1909 Douglas Fairbanks junior, American film actor, born in New York City.

1918 Kirk Douglas, American film actor, born at Amsterdam in New York to Russian-Jewish parents as Issur Danielovitch Demsky.

1921 Sir Arthur Pearson, English newspaper owner and founder of 'Pearson's Weekly' in 1890, died.

1933 The London to Singapore airline service was inaugurated.

1957 Donny Osmond, American entertainer, born at Ogden in Utah.

1960 The first episode of British television's 'Coronation Street' was screened.

1961 Tanganyika became independent.

1962 Tanganyika became a republic within the Commonwealth, with Julius Nyerere its first President.

Grouse shooting ends.

1768 The Royal Academy of Arts was founded, with Joshua Reynolds its first President.

1817 Mississippi, the Magnolia State, became the 20th state of the Union.

1819 Felice Orsini, Italian nationalist and conspirator, born at Meldola.

1845 The first pneumatic tyres were patented by the Scottish civil engineer Robert Thomson.

1851 Melvil Dewey, American librarian who devised the system of classification for library cataloguing, born at Adams Centre in the State of New York.

1865 Leopold I, King of the Belgians, the first sovereign on its separation from the Netherlands, died.

1868 The first edition of 'Whitaker's Almanack' was published.

1891 Earl Alexander, British army commander in North Africa and Italy in World War II, born in County Tyrone in Ireland.

1896 Alfred Nobel, Swedish chemist and philanthropist, inventor of dynamite and founder of the Nobel Prizes, died at San Remo in Italy.

1898 Cuba became an independent State—Spain giving up all claims after the short Spanish-American War.

1901 Nobel Prizes were first awarded.

1902 The Aswan Dam, built to control the Nile flood, was opened.

1941 The British battleships 'Repulse' and 'Prince of Wales' were sunk off Malaya by Japanese aircraft.

1963 Zanzibar became independent, after being a British Protectorate since 1890.

11 DECEMBER (346)

1803 Hector Berlioz, French composer, born at La Côte Saint André, near Grenoble, the son of a doctor.

1816 Indiana, the Hoosier State, became the 19th state of the Union.

1843 Robert Koch, German bacteriologist, born at Klausthal.

1883 Victor McLaglen, English-American film actor and Oscar winner, born in London.

1894 The first Motor Show opened in the Champs-Elysées, Paris, with 9 exhibitors—closed on 25th.

1903 The first wildlife preservation society in Britain was founded, under the name of 'The Society for the Preservation of the Wild Fauna of the Empire'.

1914 The Royal Flying Corps (later the Royal Air Force) adopted the roundel for aircraft identification.

1918 Alexander Solzhenitsyn, Russian novelist, born at Rostov.

1931 The Statute of Westminster, recognising independence of the British Commonwealth, became law.

1936 Edward VIII abdicated as King, in favour of his brother, the Duke of York, who became George VI.

1965 Ed Murrow, American journalist, broadcaster and director of the US Information Agency, died in New York.

12 DECEMBER (347)

National day of Kenya.

1724 Samuel Hood, British admiral of distinction, born at Thorncombe in Dorset.

1787 Pennsylvania, the Keystone State, became the 2nd state of the Union.

1849 Sir Marc Isambard Brunel, French-born English engineer, builder of the Thames tunnel from Wapping to Rotherhithe, died in London aged 80.

1889 Robert Browning, English poet, died.

1893 Edward G. Robinson, American film actor, born at Bucharest in Hungary as Emanuel Goldenburg.

1901 The first transatlantic wireless signal, the letter 'S', was sent from Poldhu in Cornwall and received by Marconi at Signal Hill, St John's, in Newfoundland.

1912 Henry Armstrong, American boxer, known as 'Homicide Hank', who held titles at 3 weights simultaneously, born at Columbus in Mississippi as Henry Jackson.

1915 Frank Sinatra, American entertainer, born at Hoboken in New Jersey.

1917 The world's worst train accident occurred at Modane in France, with 543 killed.

1925 The first motel opened, at San Luis Obispo in California.

1929 John Osborne, English playwright and actor, born in London.

1939 Douglas Fairbanks senior, American film actor famous for his swashbuckling hero parts, died.

1946 Emerson Fittipaldi, motor racing champion, born at Sao Paulo in Brazil.

1955 The hovercraft or air-cushion vehicle was patented by the British engineer Christopher Cockerell.

1963 Kenya attained independence, with Jomo Kenyatta its first Prime Minister.

1964 Kenya became a republic, with Jomo Kenyatta its President.

1968 Tallulah Bankhead, American actress renowned for her gravel voice, died in New York City.

13 DECEMBER (348)

1577 Francis Drake began his famous voyage from Plymouth in the 'Golden Hind' that was to take him around the world—returning on 26th September 1580.

1642 New Zealand was discovered by the Dutch navigator Abel Tasman.

1784 Dr Samuel Johnson, English writer and lexicographer known for his dictionary, died in London and was buried in Westminster Abbey.

1915 Johannes Vorster, South African Nationalist statesman and Prime Minister, born at Jamestown in Cape Province.

1939 The Battle of the River Plate took place—a naval action between British cruisers 'Exeter', 'Ajax' and 'Achilles' and the German battleship 'Graf Spee', off the SE coast of South America.

1973 A 3-day work week was ordered by the British Government because of the Arab oil embargo and the coalminers' slowdown.

1546 Tycho Brahe, Danish astronomer and mathematician, born at Knudstrup.

1799 George Washington, American soldier, Federalist statesman and first President from 1789 to 1797, died in Mount Vernon on the south bank of the Potomac in Virginia.

1819 Alabama, the Heart of Dixie or Cotton State, entered the Union as the 22nd state.

1861 Albert, German Prince, consort and husband of Queen Victoria, died of typhoid at Windsor Castle.

1871 George Hudson, English 'Railway King', died.

1895 King George VI, the second son of George V and Mary, born at Sandringham, a Royal residence in Norfolk.

1911 Roald Amundsen, Norwegian explorer, in his ship 'The Fram', became the first to reach the South Pole—35 days ahead of Captain Scott.

1918 Women voted in a British General Election for the first time.

1932 The first Rugby League match was played under floodlights, Leeds v Wigan at the White City Stadium in London.

1947 Stanley Baldwin, British Conservative statesman and three-times Prime Minister, who became Earl Baldwin of Bewdley, died.

1959 Archbishop Makarios was elected first President of Cyprus.

1675 Jan Vermeer, Dutch painter, died.

1683 Izaak Walton, English writer, best known as the author of 'The Compleat Angler' on pleasures of fishing, died at Winchester aged 90.

1832 Gustave Eiffel, French engineer, best known for his design of the tower built for the Paris exhibition of 1889 and which bears his name, born at Dijon.

1859 Ludwig Zamenof, Polish linguist and creator of the artificial language of Esperanto, born at Bielostock (Bialystok).

1890 Sitting Bull, Red Indian chief of the Sioux, was killed by police in South Dakota while resisting arrest.

1892 Paul Getty, American oil magnate, born at Minneapolis in Minnesota.

1906 The Piccadilly branch of the London Underground Railway system was opened.

1939 Nylon was first produced commercially, at Seaford in Delaware, and made up into stockings by various manufacturers.

1961 Adolph Eichmann, Nazi official responsible for the execution of millions of Jews, was sentenced to death after a 4-month trial in Jerusalem.

1962 Charles Laughton, English-born film actor and Academy Award (Oscar) winner in 1933 for his part in 'The Private Lives of Henry VIII', died.

1966 Walt Disney, American film producer and leader in movie animation, died.

1968 Jesse Willard, American heavyweight boxing champion, died at Pacoimo in California, aged almost 87.

1969 City status was conferred on Swansea.

16 DECEMBER (351)

1485 Catharine of Aragon, the first wife of King Henry VIII, born the fourth daughter of Ferdinand and Isabella.

1653 Oliver Cromwell became Lord Protector of England—ruling for over 4 years.

1742 Gebhard von Blucher, Prussian field marshal, born at the seaport of Rostock.

1770 Beethoven, German composer, born at Bonn, the son of an undistinguished tenor.

1773 The 'Boston Tea Party', promoted by Samuel Adams, took place off Griffin's Wharf in Boston harbour, as a protest against British taxation.

1775 Jane Austen, English novelist, born at Steventon, a remote hamlet in Hampshire, the 7th of 8 children of the rector.

1859 Wilhelm Grimm, the younger of the two brother philologists who made a great collection of fairy tales, died in Berlin.

1882 Jack Hobbs, Surrey and England cricketer, born at Cambridge.

1899 Noel Coward, English actor, composer and playwright, born at Teddington near London.

1921 Camille Saint-Saens, French composer, best known for 'The Carnival of the Animals', died in Algiers.

1925 Construction began on the building of the Mersey Road Tunnel—was opened on 18th July 1934.

1929 The British airship R100, designed by Barnes Wallis, first flew on trials.

1944 Glenn Miller, American dance band leader and trombonist, was tragically killed in an aircraft accident.

1965 W. Somerset Maugham, English novelist and short-story writer, died at Nice in the south of France, aged 91.

17 DECEMBER (352)

1778 Sir Humphry Davy, English chemist and inventor of the miners' safety lamp, born at Penzance in Cornwall, the son of a woodcarver.

1830 Simon Bolivar, South American statesman and Revolutionary leader, called 'The Liberator', died from tuberculosis.

1874 Mackenzie King, Canadian statesman and Prime Minister, born at Kitchener in Ontario.

1891 Robertson Hare, British actor, born.

1903 Orville Wright made the first successful controlled flight in a powered aircraft, at Kill Devil Hill, near Kitty Hawk in North Carolina.

1907 Lord Kelvin, Irish-born physicist and inventor, died.

1933 For this day only the public was allowed to walk through the new Mersey Road Tunnel.

1936 Tommy Steele, British pop singer and entertainer, born at Bermondsey in London as Thomas Hicks.

1939 The German battleship 'Graf Spee', captained by Langsdorf, was scuttled in the entrance of Montevideo harbour.

1707 Charles Wesley, English evangelist and hymn writer, born at Epworth in Lincolnshire, the son of the rector.

1737 Antonio Stradivari, famous Italian violin-maker, died at Cremona in Lombardy.

1787 New Jersey, the Garden State, became the 3rd state of the Union.

1856 Sir J. J. Thomson, English physicist and discoverer of the electron, born at Cheetham Hill near Manchester, the son of a bookseller.

1865 Slavery was abolished throughout the United States of America, ratified by the 13th Amendment.

1912 The Piltdown man 'discovery' in East Sussex by Charles Dawson was announced—was proved in 1953 to have been a hoax.

1913 Willy Brandt, German statesman and Chancellor, born at Lübeck as Karl Herbert Frahm.

1916 Betty Grable, American film actress and pin-up girl, born at St Louis in Missouri.

1919 Sir John Alcock, English aviator who first flew the Atlantic with Arthur Brown, died of injuries received in an aeroplane accident.

1957 Dorothy L. Sayers, English author of detective novels featuring hero 'Lord Peter Wimsey', died.

1969 The death penalty for murder was formally abolished in Britain.

1971 Stan Mellor, English National Hunt champion jockey, rode his 1000th winner—'Ouzo'—at Nottingham.
Bobby Jones, American golfer and winner of many international championships, died.

19 DECEMBER (354)

1154 Henry II acceded as King of England on the death of Stephen on 24th October.

1741 Vitus Bering, Danish-born explorer for Russia, who gave his name to the Bering Strait and Bering Sea, died on Bering Island leading an expedition.

1848 Emily Brontë, English novelist, died aged 30.

1851 Joseph Turner, English painter of landscapes and sea pictures, notably 'The Fighting Téméraire', died in a lodging at Chelsea, under the assumed name of Booth.

1902 Sir Ralph Richardson, English stage and film actor, born at Cheltenham in Gloucestershire, the son of an art teacher.

1906 Leonid Brezhnev, Soviet political leader and President, born at Kamenskoye (now Dneprodzerzhinsk) in the Ukraine.

1957 Air service between London and Moscow was inaugurated.

1980 Alexei Kosygin, Soviet Communist leader, died aged 77.

1981 The Penlee lifeboat, 'Solomon Browne', was lost with all of her crew of 8 attempting to rescue the crew of the coaster 'Union Star'.

20 DECEMBER (355)

1894 Sir Robert Menzies, Australian Liberal statesman and Prime Minister, born at Jeparit in the state of Victoria.

1904 Irene Dunne, American film actress, born at Louisville in Kentucky.

1937 Erich Ludendorff, German general who helped to formulate World War I strategy, died.

1946 Uri Geller, Israeli known for his claims to psychic powers, born at Tel Aviv.

1954 James Hilton, English novelist, known for 'Lost Horizon' and 'Goodbye Mr Chips', died in California.

1968 John Steinbeck, American author, notably 'The Grapes of Wrath', 'Of Mice and Men' and Nobel Prize winner in 1962, died in New York City.

1982 Artur Rubinstein, Polish-born American concert pianist, died at his home in Geneva aged 95.

21 DECEMBER (356)

1375 Giovanni Boccaccio, Italian writer, best known for his 'Decameron', died at Certaldo.

1620 The Pilgrim Fathers landed at Plymouth in Massachusetts from the 'Mayflower'—the family had increased to 103 with 2 births on the voyage.

1804 Benjamin Disraeli, British statesman and Tory Prime Minister, born at 22 Theobald's Road in London.

1844 The Rochdale Pioneers opened the first co-operative store, at Toad Lane.

1879 Joseph Stalin, Soviet political leader, born at Gori in Georgia as Joseph Vissarionovich Dzhugashvili, the son of a shoemaker.

1892 Walter Hagen, American golf champion, born at Rochester in the State of New York.

1913 The first crossword puzzle was published in the week-end supplement of the 'New York World', compiled by Liverpool-born Arthur Wynne.

1937 Jane Fonda, American film actress, born in New York City, the daughter of Henry Fonda.

1945 George Patton, American general and military commander in Europe, nicknamed 'Old Blood and Guts', died at Heidelberg in Germany.

1954 Christine Evert, American tennis champion, born at Fort Lauderdale in Florida.

1963 Sir Jack Hobbs, Surrey and England cricketer—the first in his sport to be knighted—died aged 81.

1968 Apollo 8 was launched, with Frank Borman, James Lovell and William Anders.

1971 Kurt Waldheim succeeded U Thant as Secretary-General of the United Nations.

22 DECEMBER (357)

1135 The coronation of King Stephen took place.

1552 St Francis Xavier, Basque Jesuit missionary, called the 'Apostle of the Indies', died near Canton in China.

1715 James Stuart, the 'Old Pretender', landed at Peterhead after his exile in France.

1768 John Crome, English landscape painter, born at Norwich, the son of a poor weaver.

1858 Giacomo Puccini, Italian operatic composer of 'Tosca', 'La Bohème' etc., born at Lucca in Tuscany.

1880 George Eliot, English novelist, author of 'The Mill on the Floss', died at Chelsea and was buried in Highgate Cemetery.

1894 Alfred Dreyfus, French artillery officer, found guilty of selling army secrets to Germany—was imprisoned on Devil's Island, but was later pardoned and completely exonerated.

1912 'Ladybird' Johnson, wife of America's 36th President, born at Karnack in Texas.

1943 Beatrix Potter, English writer of children's books and creator of 'Peter Rabbit', died.

1965 A 70 mph speed limit was introduced in Britain.
Richard Dimbleby, British television commentator, died.

1979 Darryl F. Zanuck, American film producer and executive, died.

23 DECEMBER (358)

1732 Sir Richard Arkwright, English inventor of mechanical spinning processes in the cotton industry, born at Preston in Lancashire, the youngest of 13 children.

1805 Joseph Smith, American religious leader and founder of The Church of Jesus Christ of Latter-day Saints (Mormons), born at Sharon in Vermont.

1834 Hansom cabs were patented by the English architect Joseph Hansom.

1888 J. Arthur Rank, British film magnate, born at Hull on Humberside.

1905 The final of the earliest recorded beauty contest in Britain took place, at Newcastle upon Tyne.

1913 The Federal Reserve, the Central banking system of the United States, was established.

1922 The BBC began daily news broadcasts.

1948 Hideki Tojo, Japanese Premier who provoked the

American entry into the war by the bombing of Pearl Harbor, was hanged as a war criminal.

1959 Earl of Halifax, British Conservative statesman and Viceroy of India from 1926 to 1931, died.

24 DECEMBER (359)

1167 King John, the sixth and youngest son of Henry II and Eleanor of Aquitaine, born at Oxford.

1491 Ignatius Loyola, Spanish priest and founder of the Society of Jesus (Jesuits), born at Azpeitia.

1524 Vasco da Gama, Portuguese explorer and navigator, died at Cochin on the Malabar coast of India.

1809 Christopher 'Kit' Carson, American frontiersman and guide, born in Madison County in Kentucky.

1814 The Treaty of Ghent was signed, ending the war of 1812 between America and Britain.

1818 James Joule, English physicist famous for his experiments in heat, born at Salford, Manchester.

1822 Matthew Arnold, English poet and critic, born at Laleham near Staines in Surrey.

1863 W. M. Thackeray, English novelist, best known for 'Vanity Fair', died in London.

1905 Howard Hughes, American industrialist and film producer, born at Houston in Texas.

1914 The first air raid on British soil took place—a single bomb on Dover, in the grounds of St James's Rectory.

1922 Ava Gardner, American film actress, born at Smithfield in North Carolina as Lucy Johnson.

1932 Colin Cowdrey, English Test cricketer, born at Bangalore in India.

1951 Libya became an independent monarchy, with Idris I as King.

25 DECEMBER (360)

1066 The coronation of William the Conqueror took place at Westminster Abbey.

1497 The South African province of Natal was discovered and named by the Portuguese explorer and navigator Vasco da Gama.

1642 Sir Isaac Newton, English mathematician and scientist, born at Woolsthorpe near Grantham in Lincolnshire, the son of a farmer.

1864 The Christmas-day dip in the Serpentine in London's Hyde Park was inagurated.

1899 Humphrey Bogart, American film actor, born in New York City, the son of a doctor.

1906 Lew Grade, English impressario, born in Russia as Lewis Winogradsky.

1918 Anwar Sadat, Egyptian statesman and President, born at Talah Minufiya.

1926 Hirohito became Emperor of Japan.

1941 Hong Kong surrendered to the Japanese forces.

1946 W. C. Fields, American vaudeville and film comedian, died.

1950 The Stone of Scone or Stone of Destiny. the Scottish Coronation Stone, was stolen from Westminster Abbey by nationalists—was returned the following 13th April.

1974 Darwin, capital of Northern Territory in Australia, was devastated by cyclone 'Tracy'.

1977 Charlie Chaplin, American film actor and director, died.

26 DECEMBER (361)

1716 Thomas Gray, English poet, author of 'Elegy in a country churchyard', born in London, the son of a money broker.

1797 John Wilkes, British radical politician and champion of freedom of the Press, died in London.

1891 Henry Miller, American novelist, born in New York City.

1893 Mao Tse-Tung, Chinese statesman and one of the founders of the Communist Party, born in Hunan the son of a peasant farmer..

1898 Radium was discovered and isolated by Pierre and Marie Curie and G. Bémont.

1908 Jack Johnson became the first coloured boxer to win the world heavyweight title, knocking out Tommy Burns in round 14 in Sydney in Australia.

1914 Richard Widmark, American film actor, born at Sunrise in Minnesota.

1931 Melvil Dewey, American librarian and pioneer in book classification, died.

1943 The German battleship 'Scharnhorst' was sunk off North Cape.

1957 Charles Pathe, French film pioneer who inaugurated newsreels, died in Monte Carlo.

1972 Harry S. Truman, American Democrat statesman and 3rd President from 1945 to 1953, died at Independence in Missouri ahed 88.

1974 Jack Benny, American comedian famed for his deadpan delivery, died aged 80.

27 DECEMBER (362)

1703 The Methuen Treaty was signed between Portugal and England, giving preference to the import of Portuguese wines into England.

1822 Louis Pasteur, French chemist and bacteriologist, born at Dôle.

1831 The Admiralty survey ship 'HMS Beagle', with Charles Darwin aboard, set out from Plymouth on its famous scientific voyage round the world, which was to last 5 years.

1834 Charles Lamb, English essayist, died.

1879 Sydney Greenstreet, English actor, notably in the film 'The Maltese Falcon', born in Kent.

1901 Marlene Dietrich, film actress, born in Berlin as Maria Magdalena von Losch.

1927 Leon Trotsky was expelled from the Communist Party.

1931 John Charles, Welsh international footballer, born at Swansea.

1945 The International Monetary Fund was established, with headquarters at Washington.

1965 The North Sea oil rig 'Sea Gem' collapsed.

1972 Lester Pearson, Canadian statesman, Prime Minister from 1963 to 1968 and Nobel Prize winner in 1947, died.

1975 The Sex Discrimination and Equal Pay Acts came into force in Britain.

28 DECEMBER (363)

1694 Queen Mary II died of smallpox, after which William III reigned alone.

1846 Iowa, the Hawkeye State, became the 29th state of the Union.

1856 Woodrow Wilson, American Democrat statesman and 28th President, born at Staunton in Virginia, the son of a Presbyterian minister.

1879 The Tay railway bridge, from Fife to Angus, designed by Thomas Bouch, collapsed, carrying the Edinburgh to Dundee train and its passengers into the water below—killing about 90.

1908 Messina, on the island of Sicily, was severely damaged by an earthquake.

1923 Alexandre Gustave Eiffel, French engineer and designer of the 300 metre tower in Paris that bears his name, died aged 91.

1926 Victoria scored the highest recorded cricket innings total of 1107 runs, against New South Wales, at Melbourne.

1934 The first women's Test match at cricket took place at Brisbane, Australia v England.

1937 Maurice Ravel, French composer of 'Bolero', died in a Paris hospital.

1947 Victor Emmanuel III, King of Italy from 1900 until he abdicated in 1946, died.

1950 The Peak District was designated as the first National Park in Britain.

1981 Hoagy Carmichael, American pianist and song writer, died of a heart attack in Palm Springs, California.

29 DECEMBER (364)

1170 Thomas à Becket, the 40th Archbishop of Canterbury, was murdered in his own cathedral by 4 knights—Reginald

Fitzurse, William de Tracy, Hugh de Merville and Richard le Breton—acting on Henry II's orders.

1721 Madame de Pompadour, French mistress of King Louis XV of France, born in Paris as Jeanne Antoinette Poisson.

1766 Charles Macintosh, Scottish chemist and inventor of waterproof fabrics, born at Glasgow.

1800 Charles Goodyear, American inventor who developed the art of vulcanising rubber, born at New Haven in Connecticut.

1808 Andrew Johnson, American Democrat statesman and 17th President, born at Raleigh in North Carolina, the son of an inn porter.

1809 William Ewart Gladstone, British Liberal statesman and four times Prime Minister, born at Liverpool, the son of a wealthy Scottish merchant.

1813 Alexander Parkes, English chemist who invented celluloid, born at Birmingham.

1845 Texas, the Lone Star state, became the 28th state of the Union.

1860 Britain's first seagoing iron-clad warship, HMS Warrior, was launched.

1881 Jesse Willard, American heavyweight boxing champion, born at St Clere in Kansas.

1890 The Battle of Wounded Knee in South Dakota, the last major conflict between Red Indians and US troops, took place.

1895 The Jameson Raid into the Boer colony of Transvaal to support the Uitlanders—the European settlers—to overthrow Kruger's government, started.

1914 The first zeppelin appeared over the British coast.

1931 The discovery of heavy water (deuterium) was publicly announced by the American chemist H. C. Urey.

1938 Harvey Smith, British international show jumper, born in Yorkshire.

1972 'Life' ended publication after 36 years as the leading weekly pictorial magazine.

30 DECEMBER (365)

1691 Robert Boyle, British physicist and chemist who formulated Boyle's Law on gases, died.

1865 Rudyard Kipling, English story writer and poet, born in Bombay.
1876 Pablo Casals, Spanish cellist and conductor, born at Vendrell.
1894 Amelia Bloomer, American social reformer who campaigned for temperance and women's rights, died.
1906 Carol Reed, English film director, born at Putney in London.
1932 The London-Brighton line became electrified, and the 'Southern Belle' was renamed the 'Brighton Belle'.
1934 Barry Briggs, speedway champion rider, born at Christchurch in New Zealand.
1947 King Michael of Romania abdicated in favour of a Communist Republic.
1956 The last passenger train ran on the Liverpool Overhead Railway.
1968 Trygve Lie, Norwegian statesman and first Secretary-General of the United Nations from 1946 to 1952, died.
1970 'Sonny' Liston, American heavyweight boxer and world champion from 1962 to 1964, died.
1979 Richard Rodgers, American composer in collaboration with Lorenz Hart and Oscar Hammerstein, died.

31 DECEMBER (366)

1491 Jacques Cartier, French navigator and explorer of the North American coast and the St Lawrence River, born at St Malo on the Normandy coast.
1719 John Flamsteed, English astronomer, the first Astronomer Royal, for whom King Charles II built the Greenwich Observatory, died.
1720 Bonnie Prince Charlie was born in Rome, the elder son of James, the 'Old Pretender'.
1763 Villeneuve, French naval officer, born at Valensoles.
1869 Henri Matisse, French painter and sculptor, born at Le Cateau.
1880 George Marshall, American general and statesman who originated the Marshall Aid Plan for the post-war

reconstruction of Europe, born at Uniontown in Pennsylvania.

1890 Ellis Island, in upper New York Bay, opened as the Immigration Depot on the closure of Castle Garden.

1923 The chimes of Big Ben were first broadcast.

1938 The first breath tests for drunken drivers were officially introduced by the Indianapolis Police Department—using a 'Drunkometer', a type of breathalyser.

1943 John Denver, American singer and composer, born at Roswell in New Mexico as Henry John Deutschendorf.

1948 Sir Malcolm Campbell, English racing driver and holder of world land and water speed records, died.

1960 After midnight British farthings ceased to be legal tender.

1968 Russia's TU144 flew, thus becoming the first supersonic airliner.

Aberfan disaster 295
Abruzzi earthquake 308
Abyssinia 277
Acheson, Dean 102-286
Adam, Robert 63-185
Adams, John 186-304
Adams, John Couch 157
Adams, John Quincy 54-193
Adams, Samuel 271-276
Addinsell, Richard 13
Addison, Joseph 122-169
Addled Parliament 96-159
Adelaide, Queen 337
Adenauer, Konrad 5-110
Adler, Alfred 38-149
Adler, Larry 41
Adrian IV, Pope 245-339
'Aeroflot' 40
Aeroplane flight, first GB 290
Aeroplane registration numbers 140
'Affray', submarine 107
Agadir earthquake 60
Agincourt, Battle of 299
Agnew, Spiro 314
Agostini, Giacomo 168
Aircraft, largest GB 248
Aircraft carrier, nuclear 268
Aircraft disaster, worst 87
Airline services:—
  London to Australia 104
  London to Cape Town 118
  London to Hong Kong 74
  London to Moscow 354
  London to Paris 238
  London to Singapore 344
Airliner, first jet 209
Air raids 152-250-359
Airy, Sir George 2
'Akron', airship 95-221
Alabama 349
Alamo, Siege of the 54-66
Alaska 3-90
Albania 11-98
Albert I, King 48-99
Albert Memorial 183
Albert, Prince 239-349
Albuera, Battle of 137
Alcock, John 167-311-353
'Alcoholics Anonymous' 133-197
Alcott, Louisa M. 66-334
Alda, Alan 28
Aldrin, Edwin 'Buzz' 20
Alexander, Earl 168-345
Alexander II; Tsar 73-120

Alexandra, Queen 325-336
Alfonso XIII, King 59-105
Algeria 185
Algoa Bay, settlers 101
Allen, Chesney 96-318
Allen, Woody 336
Allenby, Viscount 114-135
Allyson, June 281
Alma, Battle of 264
Alpert, Herb 61
'Altmark' 47
Amati, Niccolo 103
Ameche, Don 152
America, 49th parallel 294
American Civil War 103-147
American Expeditionary Force 178
American football 292
American Legion 75
America's Cup, first 221
Ames, Leslie 338
Amies, Hardy 199
Amin, Idi 25
Amis, Kingsley 107
'Amoco Cadiz' 77
Ampère, André 22-162
Amritsar massacre 104
Amundsen, Roald 170-198-349
Andersen, Hans Christian 93-217
Andretti, Mario 59
Andrew, Prince 50
Andrews, Julie 275
'Andy Pandy', TV programme 193
Angola 316
Anne of Cleves 198
Anne, Princess 80-228-319
Anne, Queen 37-68-114-214
Annigoni, Pietro 159
Anzac day 116
Anzio landing 22
Apollo 1, accident 27
Apollo 7 285
Apollo 8 356
Apollo 9 63
Apollo 10 139
Apollo 11 198-202-203
Apollo 12 319
Apollo 13 102
Apollo 14 31
Apollo 15 208
Apollo 16 107
Apollo 17 342
Apollo 18 197
Archer, Fred 11-303-313
'Archers, The' 159

Arden, Elizabeth 292
Argentina 191
Arizona 45
Arkansas 167
'Arkle', steeplechaser 152
Ark Royal, HMS 56-148-319
Arkwright, Sir Richard 216-358
Arliss, George 36-101
Arlott, John 56
Armistice 316
Armstrong, Henry 230-347
Armstrong, Louis 186-188
Armstrong, Neil 203-218
Arne, Thomas 65-72
Arness, James 147
Arnhem invasion 261
Arnold, Benedict 14-166
Arnold, Matthew 106-359
Arnold, Thomas 164-165
Arthur, Chester 279-323
Arthur, Jean 291
Ashe, Arthur 192
Ashmolean Museum 158
Ashton, Sir Frederick 261
Askey, Arthur 158-321
Asquith, Herbert 46-99-256
Astaire, Fred 131
Astor, Mary 126
Astor, Viscountess 55-123-140-336
Aswan Dam 345
Aswan High dam 9-15
Ataturk, Kemal 72-303-315
'Athenia', liner 248
Atomic bombs 198-219-222-277
Atomic power stations 179-233-291
Attenborough, David 129
Attenborough, Richard 242
Attlee, Clement 3-282
Auber, Daniel 29-133
Auckland Harbour bridge 151
Austen, Jane 200-351
Austerlitz, Battle of 337
Australia 1-26
Australia, first flight to 317
Autogyro 9
Automatic control flight 265
Automatic ticket barrier 5
Automobile Association 178
Autry, Gene 273

Baby, first test-tube 207
Bacall, Lauren 260
Bach, J. S. 81-210

Bacharach, Burt 133
Bacon, Francis 22-100
Baddeley, Hermione 318
Baden-Powell, Robert 8-53
Bader, Douglas 52-249
Badminton horse trials 111
Baekeland, Leo 54-319
Baez, Joan 9
Bahamas 192
Baird, John Logie 27-166-226
Bairnsfather, Bruce 273
Baker, Richard 167
Bakerloo Line 70
Balaklava, Battle of 299
Balchin, Nigel 138
Baldwin, Stanley 143-216-349
Balfour, A. J. 79-207
Ball, Lucille 219
Ball-point pens 162
Balzac, Honoré de 141-231
Bandaranaike, Sirimavo 108-203
Bandaranaike, Solomon 8-269-270
Bankhead, Tallulah 31-347
Bank Holiday 146-150
Bank notes,
  British 57-73-89-93-106-325
Bank of England 61
Bank of Scotland 306
Banks, Sir Joseph 171
Bannister, Roger 83-127
Bannockburn, Battle of 176
Banting, Sir Frederick 52-209-319
Banting, William 76
Barbados 335
Barbirolli, Sir John 211-337
Barham, HMS 330
Barham, Richard 169
Barker, Ronnie 269
Barnard, Dr Christiaan 313-338
Barnardo, Thomas 186-263
Barnes, Sydney 110
Barnum, Phineas T. 98-187
Barrie, J. M. 130-171
Barry, Sir Charles 133-144
Barrymore, Ethel 170-228
Barrymore, John 46-150
Barrymore, Lionel 119-320
Bart, Lionel 214
Bartholomew, Freddie 88
Bartok, Bela 85-270
Bartok, Eva 170
Baseball 171-257
Basie, Count 234
Basketball 20

Bassey, Shirley 8
Bastille 196
Basutoland 278
Battersea Bridge 203
Battledress, Army issue 111
Battle of Britain Day 259
Baudouin, King 199-251
Bay of Pigs, The 108
BBC 'pips' 36
Beagle hunt, oldest 88
Beaton, Cecil 14-18
Beatty, Earl 17-71
Beatty, Warren 90
Beaumarchais, Pierre 24-140
Beauty contests 227-263-358
Beaverbrook, Lord 146-161
Bechuanaland 274
Becket, Thomas à 364
Beecham, Sir Thomas 68-120
Beerbohm, Sir Max 141-237
Beery, Wallace 106
Beethoven, Ludwig van 86
Begin, Menachem 173
Behan, Brendan 40-80
Belgium 126-131-217-288
Bell, Alexander
  Graham 63-69-70-215
Belle Vue, Manchester 206
Bellingham, Francis 132
Belloc, Hilaire 198-209
Benaud, Richie 280
Benes, Eduard 149-247
Ben-Gurion, David 290-336
Benn, Anthony Wedgwood 94
Bennett, Arnold 87-148
Bennett, Tony 216
Benny, Jack 45-361
Bentine, Michael 26
Benz, Karl 29-95-330
Bergerac, Cyrano de 66-210
Bergman, Ingrid 242
Bering, Vitus 354
Berlin air lift 176
Berlin air raid 238
Berlin, Irving 132
Bernadotte, Count Folke 261
Bernhard, Prince 7-181
Bernhardt, Sarah 86-296
Bernstein, Leonard 238
Bessemer, Sir Henry 19-75
Best, Charles 58-209
Betjeman, Sir John 97-284
Betting shops, GB 122
Bevan, Aneurin 188-320

Bevin, Ernest 69-105
'Big Ben' 152-366
Billy the Kid 197-328
Birdseye, Clarence 66-281-344
Birkenhead 226-243
Birkenhead, Lord 194-274
Birmingham Exhibition Centre 33
Births, marriages and deaths 183
'Bismarck', battleship 148
Bismarck, Otto van 92-212
Bizet, Georges 155-299
Black, Cilla 148
'Black Friday' 268
Black Hole of Calcutta 172
Blackpool illuminations 262
Blackwall tunnel 143
Blackwell, Elizabeth 34-152
Blake, Robert 220
Blake, William 225
Blanchard, Jean Pierre 7-67
Blankers-Koen, Fanny 117
Blaydon races, last 246
Blenheim, Battle of 226
Blériot, Louis 183-207-215
Bligh, William 119-253-342
Bliss, Sir Arthur 87
Blondin, Charles 50-59-182
Blood bank, US 75
Blood, Colonel Thomas 130-237
'Bloody Sunday', Londonderry 30
'Bloody Sunday', Russia 22
Bloom, Claire 46
Bloomer, Amelia 148-365
Blücher, Gebhard von 256-351
Blue Nile, source 319
Blum, Léon 90-100
Blyton, Enid 224-333
'Bob-a-job' week 109
Boccaccio, Giovanni 356
Bodoni, Giambattista 47
Boer War 285
Bogarde, Dirk 88
Bogart, Humphrey 14-360
Boleyn, Anne 25-140-251
Bolivar, Simon 206-352
Bolivia 219
Bolshevik Revolution 312
Bonaparte, Joseph 7
Bonnie and Clyde 144
Book of Common Prayer 161
Books of stamps 76
Boone, Daniel 270-307
Booth, John Wilkes 117-131
Booth, William 101-233

301

Borden, Lizzie **153-201**
Borg, Bjorn **158-187**
Borge, Victor 3
Borgnine, Ernest 24
Borman, Frank 74
Borodino, Battle of 251
Borotra, Jean 226
Borrow, George **187-208**
Borstal Institution 290
Boston massacre 65
Boston Tea Party 351
Boswell, James **140-303**
Bosworth Field, Battle of 235
Botha, Louis **240-271**
Botham, Ian 329
Bottomley, Horatio 133
Boult, Sir Adrian **54-99**
Boulton, Matthew 231
'Bounty', mutiny 119
Boxer Rebellion 165
Boxing **158-229-230-267-343**
Boxing fatalities **81-84**
Box numbers, newspaper 188
Boycott, Geoff 295
Boyd, William 256
Boyer, Charles **241-239**
Boyle, Robert **25-365**
Boyne, Battle of the 183
Boys' Brigade 278
Boy Scouts **26-109-211-213-248**
Boy Scouts, US 39
Braddock, James J. 341
Bradley, Omar 43
Bradman, Sir Donald 240
'Bradshaw's Railway
 Companion' 299
Brahe, Tycho **298-349**
Brahms, Johannes **94-128**
Braille, Louis **4-6**
Braine, John 104
Brandenburg Gate 226
Brando, Marlon 94
Brandt, Willy 353
Brandywine Creek, Battle of 255
Brasilia 112
Braun, Wernher von **83-168**
Brazil **112-113-251**
Bread rationing **204-211**
Bream, Julian 197
Breathalyser test, first **282-366**
Brezhnev, Leonid **168-315-354**
Bridges, Robert 297
Bridgewater canal 199
Bridgewater, Duke of 63

Bright, John **87-321**
'Brighton Belle', train 365
Brighton chain pier 330
Brindley, James 274
'Britannia', Royal yacht 107
British Guiana 147
British Legion **135-316**
British Museum 15
British railways 1
Britten, Benjamin **327-339**
Broadmoor asylum 148
Bronson, Charles 318
Brontë, Anne **17-149**
Brontë, Charlotte **91-112**
Brontë, Emily **212-354**
Brooke, Rupert **114-216**
Brooking, Trevor 276
Brooklands track 188
Brooklyn bridge 145
Broome, David **61-192**
Brown, Arthur Whitten **167-205-278**
Brown, 'Capability' 37
Brown, John **130-290-337**
Browning, Elizabeth Barrett **66-182**
Browning, Robert **128-347**
Brummell, 'Beau' **90-159**
Brunel, Isambard **100-259**
Brunel, Marc Isambard **116-347**
Bryant, David 301
Brynner, Yul 193
Buchan, John **42-239**
Buchanan, James **114-153**
Buck, Pearl **66-178**
Buckingham, Duke of 236
Buckingham Palace 195
Budge, Donald 165
'Buffalo Bill' **10-57**
Bugner, Joe 73
Bulganin, Nikolai **55-163**
Bulgaria 252
Buller, Syd 220
Bunker Hill, Battle of 169
Bunsen, Robert **91-209**
Bunyan, John 244
Burbank, Luther **67-102**
Buren, Martin van **206-340**
Burgoyne, John 217
Burke, Edmund **12-191**
Burke, Robert 180
Burma 4
Burney, Fanny **6-165**
Burns, George 20
Burns, Robert **25-203**
Burr, Raymond 142

Burroughs, Edgar Rice 79-245
Burton, Richard 315
Burton, Sir Richard 79-294
Busby, Sir Matt 147
Bus service, first GB 186
Butler, R. A. 344
Butler, Samuel 170-339
Butlin, Sir Billy 164-273
Byng, John 74
Byrd, Richard 71-130-299-334
Byron, Lord 22-110

Cadbury, George 263
Cagney, James 199
Caine, Michael 74
Calais 7
Calder Hall 233-291
California 253
Callaghan, James 87
Callas, Maria 260
Calvin, John 148-192
Campbell, Donald 4-83-199
Campbell, Glen 113
Campbell, Sir Malcolm 71-366
Campbell-Bannerman,
  Sir Henry 113-251
Canada 41-183
Canadian boundary 294
Canadian Pacific Railway 312
Canaletto 111-292
Canberra, Australia 130
'Canberra', aircraft 134
Candlemas 33
Canning, George 102-221
Canoe Club 208
Canterbury Cathedral 249
Cantor, Eddie 31-284
Cape St Vincent, Battle of 45
Capitol, The 237
Capone, Al 17-25
Car, first petrol 29
Car, registration plates 1-227
Carbon paper, patent 281
Cardigan, Earl of 88-299
Carlile, Wilson 14-270
Carlos I, King 32
Carlyle, Thomas 36-339
Carmichael, Hoagy 327-363
Carmichael, Ian 170
Carnegie, Andrew 224-330
Carnera, Primo 181
Carnot, Sadi 166
Carol II, King 250
Carothers, Dr 47

Carpentier, Georges 302
Carpet-sweeper, first 263
Carroll, Lewis 14-27
Carson, Kit 144-359
Carson, Willie 321
Carte, Richard D'Oyly 94-124
Carter, Howard 62-130
Carter, Jimmy 275
Carter, Rosalyn 231
Cartier, Jacques 245-366
Cartland, Barbara 191
Cartwright, Edmund 115-304
Caruso, Enrico 56-215
Casablanca Conference 14
Casals, Pablo 296-365
Casanova, Giovanni 93-156
Casement, Roger 115-216-245
Cash, Johnny 57
Cash register, first 309
Casper, Billy 176
Castle, Barbara 280
Castlereagh, Viscount 170
Castro, Fidel 1-47-226
Catharine the Great 123-311
Catharine of Aragon 7-163-351
Cato Street conspiracy 54
Cat show, first 195
Cavell, Edith 286-339
Cavendish, Henry 55-284
Cavour, Count 158-223
Cawnpore Massacre 197
Cedar Creek, Battle of 293
Celluloid 167-364
Celsius, Anders 116-332
Cenotaph War Memorial 316
Census, first GB 181
Central Criminal Court 58
Cervantes, Miguel de 114
Ceylon (Sri Lanka) 35-143
Cézanne, Paul 19-296
Chad 224
Chadwick, Sir James 206-294
Chain, Ernst Boris 171
Chaliapin, Fyodor 44-103
Chamberlain, Sir Austen 76-290
Chamberlain, Joseph 190
Chamberlain, Neville 78-131-314
Chambers, Robert 192
Chandler, Raymond 86-205
Chaney, Lon 92-239
Chapelcross nuclear power
  station 123
Chaplin, Charlie 64-107-360
Charge of the Light Brigade 299

Charing Cross station   11
Charles I, King   30-40-87-324
Charles II, King   37-114-150
Charlie, Bonnie
  Prince   31-232-264-366
Charlton, Bobby   110-112-141-166-285
Charlton, Jack   129
Chataway, Christopher   31
Chaucer, Geoffrey   299
Checker, Chubby   277
Chekhov, Anton   17-197
Chelsea Flower Show, first   141
Cheque, first   47
Chequers   8
Chesapeake Bay, Battle of   249
Chesterton, G. K.   150-166
Chevalier, Maurice   1-256
Chiang Kai-Shek   96-305
Chicago   282
Chichester,
  Sir Francis   27-149-189-239-240-261
Chile   43-96
China   115-275-284
Chopin, Frédéric   53-291
Chou En-Lai   8
Christian I, King   111
Christie, Agatha   12-259-330
Christie's, auctioneers   340
Christmas Day   360
Christmas stamps, GB   336
Churchill, Lord Randolph   24-44
Churchill,
  Sir Winston   24-30-65-96-132-256-335
Cigarette advertising, British TV   213
Cilento, Diane   279
Circumnavigation, non-stop   113
Circumnavigation, submarine   116
Civil War, England   235
Clark, Jim   64-98
Clark, General Mark   122
Clark, Petula   320
Clay, Cassius
  (Muhammad Ali)   17-56-119-259-304
Cleese, John   301
Clemenceau, Georges   272-329
'Cleopatra's Needle'   256
Cleveland, Grover   78-176
Clifton suspension bridge   343
Clive, Robert   273-327
Clothes rationing   75-154
Clough, Brian   81
Coal industry, GB   1
Coal pit disasters   117-175-266-288-341
Cobbett, William   69-170

Cobden, Richard   93-155
Cobham, Sir Alan   127
Coca-Cola®   129
Cochise   161
Cochran, C. B.   269
Cockcroft, Sir John   148-262
Cockerell, Christopher   156
Coe, Sebastian   273
Coggan, Donald   24-283
Colbert, Claudette   257
Cole, Nat King   46-77
Coleridge, S. T.   207-295
Colledge, Cecilia   333
Collingwood, Admiral   270
Collins, Michael   235
Collins, Wilkie   8-267
Colman, Ronald   40-140
Colorado   214
Colt, Samuel   10-201
Columbus, Christopher   141-216-286
Comaneci, Nadia   317
'Come Dancing', first programme   317
'Comet', jet airliner   209
'Comic Cuts'   138
Common Market   85-157
Commonwealth Day   145
Communications satellites   97-225
Como, Perry   139
Compton, Denis   144
Comte, Auguste   19-249
'Concorde', supersonic
  airliner   9-21-62-100
Concrete, reinforced   198
Congo   301-320
Congress, US   64
Connecticut   9
Connery, Sean   238
Connolly, Maureen
  ('Little Mo')   173-261
Connors, Jimmy   246
Conrad, Joseph   216-338
Constable, John   91-163
Constantine I, King   271
Constantine II, King   66-154
Constantine, Sir Learie   265
Convicts to Australia   26
Coogan, Jackie   300
Cook, Captain   18-45-119-193-281-301
Cook, Thomas   200-327
Cooke, Alistair   325
Coolidge, Calvin   5-186
Cooper, Gary   128-134
Cooper, Henry   124
Cooper, James Fenimore   258-259

Co-operative store, first 356
Copenhagen, Battle of 93
Copernicus, Nicolaus 50-145
Corbett, James J. 49-245-251
Corinth Canal 219
Coronation Stone 104
'Coronation Street', first 344
Corps of Commissionaires 44
Cortez, Hernando 337
Corunna, Battle of 16
Cossack, HMS 47
Cotton, Henry 26
Coubertin, Pierre de 1-246
Courtneidge, Cicely 92-117
Cousteau, Jacques 163
Covent Garden market 313
Covent Garden Opera House 136-342
Coventry Cathedral 83-146-319
Coward, Sir Noel 86-351
Cowdrey, Colin 359
Cowper, William 116-331
CQD, distress signal 7
Cramm, Gottfried von 313
Cranmer, Thomas 81-184
Crawford, Joan 83-131
Crawford, Michael 19
Crazy Horse 259
Crécy, Battle of 239
Cremation, first GB 86
Crete 141
Cricket 129-136-163-168-174-208-233-
239-277-363
Cricket Tests 75-88-177-213-236-250
Crippen, Dr 31-296-328
Cripps, Sir Stafford 112-115
Cristofori, Bartolommeo 27-125
Crockett, Davy 66-230
Crome, John 357
Crompton, Samuel 178-338
Cromwell, Oliver 116-247-351
Cromwell, Richard 278
Cronin, A. J. 6-201
Crosby, Bing 123-288-292
Crosswords 307-356
Crown jewels 130
Cruft's Dog Show, first 70
Cruyff, Johann 116
Crystal Palace 335
Cuba 108-345
Cub Scouts 33
Cullinan diamond 26
Culloden, Battle of 107
Culver, Roland 244
Curacao, HMS 276

Curie, Marie 186-312-361
Curie, Pierre 110-136-361
Curry, John 253
Curtis, Tony 155
Custer, Colonel 177-340
Cyprus 194-229-310
Czechoslovakia 233-304

Daguerre, Louis 2-194-323
'Daily Courant' 71
'Daily Express' 102
'Daily Mail' 125
'Daily Mirror' 307
'Daily Telegraph' 181
Daimler, Gottlieb 66-77-242
Daladier, Edouard 170-284
Dalglish, Kenny 64
Dali, Salvador 132
Dalton, John 209-250
Damien, Father 3-106
Dankworth, Johnny 264
Danton, Georges Jacques 96-300
Darby, Abraham 68
Darling, Grace 251-294-329
Darnley, Lord 41-211
Dartford-Purfleet tunnel 323
Dartmoor prison 80-145
Darwin, Charles 43-110-362
Darwin cyclone 360
Daventry radio station 209
Davis, Bette 96
Davis Cup 221
Davis, Dwight 333
Davis, Jefferson 155-341
Davis, Joe 106
Davis Jnr, Sammy 343
Davy, Sir Humphry 150-352
Day, Doris 94
Dayan, Moshe 141-290
Day-Lewis, C. 118-143
Daylight saving 142-220
Dean, Dixie 22-61-126
Dean, James 39-274
Death duties, GB 215
Death penalty, GB 353
Debussy, Claude 85-235
Decimal coins, GB 15-114-288
Decimal currency, GB 46
Decimal postage stamps 169
Declaration of Independence 186
Declaration of war 217-247
Defoe, Daniel 117
Degas, Edgar 201-271
Delaware 342

Delibes, Léo 16-52
Delius, Frederick 29-162
De Mille, Cecil B. 21-225
Dempsey, Jack 152-176-267
Denver, John 366
Deposit, British election 37
Derby horse race 125
Deserters, British 54
'Desert Island Discs', programme 29
D'Estaing, Giscard 33-145
Destroyer, first Royal Navy 302
Dettingen, Battle of 168
'Deutschland' 171-180
Dewar, Sir James 87-264
Dewey, Melvil 345-361
Diaghilev, Sergei 79-91-232
Diaz, Bartolomeu 150
Dickens, Charles 38-161
Diefenbaker, John George 229-262
Dieppe raid 232
Diesel, Rudolf 78-274
Dietrich, Marlene 362
Dillinger, John 204
Dimbleby, Richard 146-357
Dionne quins 149
Dior, Christian 21-298
Disc jockey, first 189
'Disneyland' 200
Disney, Walt 340-350
'Disney World' 275
Disraeli, Benjamin 110-356
Dodd, Ken 313
Dog in space 308
Dolin, Anton 209
D'Oliveira, Basil 278
Dollfuss, Engelbert 207-278
Domino, Fats 57
Donat, Robert 78-161
Doonican, Val 34
Dors, Diana 297
Dorsey, Tommy 324-331
Dostoyevsky 40-316
Dotrice, Roy 126
Douglas, Kirk 344
Douglas-Home, Sir Alec 184
Doumer, Paul 128
Dowding, Lord 46-115
Downes, Terry 130
Downing Street, first PM 266
Doyle, Sir Arthur Conan 143-189
Drake, Sir Francis 27-28-95-270-348
Drake, Ted 229
Dreyfus, Alfred 193-293-357
Driving tests, GB 153

Drunken driving, first 254
Dryden, John 104-122-222
Du Barry, Countess 232
Dubcek, Alexander 332
Dukas, Paul 138-275
Duke, first created 77
Dulles, John Foster 56-145
Dumas, Alexandre (fils) 209-332
Dumas, Alexandre (père) 206-340
Dumbarton Oaks 234
Dunant, Jean Henri 48-129-304
Duncan, Isadora 148-258
Dunkirk evacuation 148-156
Dunlop, John Boyd 36-297
Durante, Jimmy 29-41
Durbin, Deanna 339
Durbridge, Francis 330
Dürer, Albrecht 97-142
Dutch East India Company 80
Dutch Guiana 330
Dvorak, Antonin 122-252
Dylan, Bob 145
Dynamite, demonstration 196
Dyson, Sir Frank 146

'Eagle', lunar module 202-203
Earhart, Amelia 142-184-206
'Early Bird' 97
Earp, Wyatt 13-79
East Anglia earthquake 113
Easter 82-116
Easter rebellion 115
Eastman, George 74-194
Eastwood, Clint 152
'Echo I', satellite 225
Eddery, Pat 78
Eddy, Mary Baker 198-338
Eddy, Nelson 66-181
Eden, Sir Anthony 14-97-164
Edgehill, Battle of 297
Edinburgh, Duke of 125-156-162
Edison, Thomas Alva 42-50-292
Edward I, King 169-189
Edward II, King 38-56-116-189-265
Edward III, King 173-318
Edward IV, King 65-100-119-180
Edward V, King 100
Edward VI, King 28-51-188-286
Edward VII, King 22-70-127-222-314
Edward VIII, King 20-149-155-175-346
Edward, Prince 70
Egypt 59-170
Eichmann, Adolf 79-102-152-350

Eiffel, Gustave 350-363
Eiffel Tower 91
Einstein, Albert 74-109
Eisenhower, Dwight 88-288
Eisenhower, Mamie 319
Ekberg, Anita 273
Election, first US 7
Election returns, first televised 54
Electric chair 219
Electricity industry 92
Elgar, Sir Edward 54-154
El Greco 99
Eliot, George 327-357
Eliot, T. S. 4-270
Elizabeth I, Queen 15-84-119-251-322
Elizabeth II, Queen 37-112-154-325
Elizabeth, Queen Mother 217
Ellis Island 366
Emerson, Ralph Waldo 118-146
Emigrant wagon, first 122-309
Emmet, Robert 264
Empire Day 145
Empire Exhibition 114
'Empress of Britain', liner 163
Engels, Friedrich 218-333
English Channel, first balloon 7
English Channel, first woman to fly 107
English Channel, first underwater swimmer 193
English Channel, first man swimmer 238
English Channel, first woman swimmer 219
English Table Tennis Association 115
Entebbe terrorists 185
Envelopes, reply-paid 109
Epiphany 6
Epping Forest 127
Epstein, Sir Jacob 234-315
Ericsson, John 68
Erie Canal 186-300
Escoffier 43-302
Ethiopia 277
European Cup, football 129-131-146-150
Eurovision 158
'Eurydice', submarine 64
Euston station 202-288
Evans, Dame Edith 39-288
Evans, Godfrey 231
Evelyn, John 58-305
Everest, Mount 94-150
Evert, Chris 356

Evesham, Battle of 217
Eyck, Jan van 191

Fagg, Arthur 170
Fahrenheit, Gabriel 135-260
Fairbanks Jnr, Douglas 344
Fairbanks, Douglas 144-347
Fairfax, Thomas 17-317
Faisal, King 85-196-252-307
Faith, Adam 175
Falk, Peter 260
Falkland Islands 93-166
Falla, Manuel de 319-328
Family allowance, GB 167
Fangio, Juan 176
Faraday, Michael 238-268
Fargo, William George 141-216
Farnborough Air Display 189
Farouk, King 42-78-119-170-208
Farrar, Dean 82-220
Farrow, Mia 40
Farthings 366
Fascist Party 83
Father's Day 171
Faulkner, William 188-269
Fawkes, Guy 31
Faye, Alice 126
FBI 208
Feather, Vic 101-210
Federal Bureau of Investigation 208
Federal Reserve 358
Fender, Percy 235-239
Ferdinand, Archduke 180
Ferrier, Kathleen 113-282
Festival of Britain 124
Fielding, Henry 113-282
Fields, Gracie 9-271
Fields, W. C. 29-360
FIFA 142
Fiji 284
Fillmore, Millard 7-68
Film censorship, GB 1
Film demonstration 82
Film, first all-talking 188
Film in CinemaScope® 268
Film in Cinerama® 274
Finch, Peter 14-272
Fingerprints, conviction 257
Finland 341
Finney, Tom 96
Fischer, Bobby 69
Fittipaldi, Emerson 347
Fitzgerald, Edward 91-166
Fitzgerald, Ella 116

Fitzsimmons, Bob 77-330
Flag-day, national 277
Flagstad, Kirsten 194-342
Flamsteed, John 232-366
Flanagan, Bud 294
Fleming, Sir Alexander 71-219
Fleming, Ian 149-225
Fletcher, Ken 167
Flinders, Matthew 76-201
Flodden Field, Battle of 253
Floodlit football, first 288
Floodlit rugby, first 296
Floods, England 75
Floral Dance 129
Florey, Lord 52-268
Florida 53-63
Flying bombs 164-252
Flying Doctor service 136
'Flying Enterprise' 10
Flynn, Errol 172-288
Foch, Ferdinand 80-276
Fokine, Michel 117-235
Fonda, Henry 137-225
Fonda, Jane 356
Fontenoy, Battle of 132
Fonteyn, Margot 139
Food rationing 185
Foot, Michael 205
Football Association 300
Football, Charity Shield 118
Football club, oldest 298
Football, FA Cup 76-102-119-120-
121-131-202
Football, internationals 18-28-49-56-
85-108-131-158-292-335
Football, league 82-104-202-234-252-
258
Football tragedies 2-69
Ford, Elizabeth 99
Ford, Gerald 196-222
Ford, Glenn 122
Ford, John 32-244
Foreman, George 10
Forester, C. S. 93-240
Formby, George 147
Forster, E. M. 1-159
Forth railway bridge 64
Forth road bridge 248-326
Foster, Stephen 13-186
Foucault, Jean 42-262
Fox, Charles James 24-257
Fox, George 13
Fox, Uffa 15
Fox, William 1-122

Fox-hunting 306
Fra Angelico 49
Fragonard, Jean 96-235
France 265
Francis, Clare 108
Franco, General 275-325-339
Franklin, Benjamin 17-108
Franklin, Sir John 163
Fraser, Dawn 248
Fraser, Malcolm 142
Frazier, Joe 12
Frederick IX, King 14
Frederick the Great 24-230
Freeman, 'Tich' 28-138
Freemason Lodge, first 176
French, Sir John 143
French fleet scuttled 332
French Foreign Legion 69
French Revolution 172-196
Freud, Sigmund 127-267
Froebel, Friedrich 112-173
Frozen foods 66
Frozen meat, first 33
Frozen meat, New Zealand 46
Fry, C. B. 116-251
Fry, Elizabeth 142-286
Fuchs, Sir Vivian 42
Fulton, Robert 55-319

Gable, Clark 32-321
Gadafy 245
Gagarin, Yuri 69-87-103
Gainsborough, Thomas 135-215
Gaitskell, Hugh 18-100
Galileo 8-46
Gallipoli 8
Gallup, George 323
Gallup poll, first GB 14
Galsworthy, John 31-227
Galton, Sir Francis 17-47
Galvani, Luigi 253-339
Galway, James 343
Gama, Vasco da 327-359
Gambia 49-115
Gandhi, Indira 19-334
Gandhi, 'Mahatma' 30-276
Gang Show, first 304
Garbo, Greta 262
Gardner, Ava 359
Gardner, Erle Stanley 71-199
Garfield, James 184-263-324
Garibaldi, Giuseppe 154-186
Garland, Judy 162-174
Garner, James 98

308

Garrick, David   20-50
Garson, Greer   273
Gas chamber, first used   39
Gas industry, GB   122
Gaskell, Elizabeth   273-317
Gatling, Richard   57-256-309
Gatwick airport   161
Gauguin, Paul   129-159
Gaulle, Charles de   314-327
Gay, John   339
Gay-Lussac, Joseph   130-341
Gaynor, Janet   280
Geller, Uri   355
Gemini 3, spacecraft   83
Gemini 4   155
Gemini 5   234
Gemini 7   339
Gemini 8   76
Gemini 10   200
General strike, GB   125-133
George I, King   162-214-294
George II, King   163-285-299-315
George III, King   29-136-156-266
George IV, King   29-178-201-225
George V, King   20-84-127-155-174-
    188
George VI, King   37-46-117-133-346-
    349
George I, King of Greece   78-88
George II, King of Greece   92
George Cross award   267
Georgia   2
German, Edward   48-316
Geronimo   48-248
Gershwin, George   193-270
Getty, Paul   158-350
Gettysburg address   324
Gettysburg, Battle of   185
Ghana   66-183
Gibbon, Edward   16-118
Gibbons, Grinling   216
Gibbs, James   218
Gibbs, Lance   273
Gibraltar   206
Gielgud, Sir John   105
Gigli, Beniamino   335
Gilbert, Sir Humphrey   253
Gilbert, Sir William   150-323
Giles, (Carl Ronald)   273
Gillette, King Camp   5-191-337
Girl Scouts, US   72
Gish, Lillian   288
Gladstone, William Ewart   140-344-
    364

Glencoe massacre   44
Glendenning, Raymond   269
Glenn, John   51-200
Glinka, Mikhail   46-153
Gobbi, Tito   298
Goddard, Paulette   155
Goebbels, Joseph   122-303
Goering, Hermann   12-289
Goethe, Johann von   82-241
Gogh, Vincent van   90-211
Gogol, Nikolai   52-91
Gold discoveries   24-230
Gold medal, first   97
Gold rush, Australia   43
Gold standard   264
Golden disc, first   41
Golden Gate bridge   148
Goldsmith, Oliver   95-315
Goldwyn, Sam   31-240
Golf   165-270-278-291
Gollancz, Sir Victor   39
Goodison Park   237
Goodman, Benny   151
Goodyear, Charles   183-364
Goossens, Leon   164
Gordon, General   26-28
Gordon, Lord George   306
Gormley, Joe   187
Gould, Jay   268
Gounod, Charles   169-292
Goya, Francisco de   90-107
Grable, Betty   184-353
Grace, Princess   258-317
Grace, W. G.   200-297
Grade, Lew   360
'Graf Spee', battleship   352
Graham, Billy   312
Grahame, Kenneth   68-188
Grainger, Percy   51-190
Grand National steeplechase   57-82-
    91-93-94
Grand Prix   178-220-272
Granger, Stewart   127
Grant, Cary   18
Grant, Ulysses   118-205
Gray, Dulcie   325
Gray, Elisha   21-69
Gray, Thomas   212-361
'Great Britain'   175-201-208
'Great Eastern'   31-169
Great Exhibition   289
Great Fire of Chicago   282
Great Fire of London   246-250
Great Reform Bill   156

Great train robbery 221
'Great Western' 99-201
Greece 128
Greeley, Horace 34-334
Greenaway, Kate 77-311
'Greenbacks' 56
Greene, Lorne 43
Greene, Richard 238
Greenstreet, Sydney 18-362
Greenwich Observatory 2-223
Gregorian calendar 55-258
Grenada 38
Grenadier Guards 151
Grenfell, Sir Wilfred 59-284
Grey, Lady Jane 43
Grey, Zane 31-297
Grieg, Edvard 167-248
Griffith, Arthur 91
Grimaldi, Joseph 152
Grimm, Jacob 4-264
Grimm, Wilhelm 55-351
Grimond, Jo 211
Grock 10-196
Grouse shooting season 225-345
Guevara, Ernesto 'Che' 166-283
Guillotine 116-169
Guinea 276
Guinness, Sir Alec 93
Gunpowder plot 310
Gustav V, King 168-303
Gustav VI, King 259-316
Gutenberg, Johann 54
Guyana 54-147
Gwyn, Nell 33-318

Haakon VII, King 216-265
Hagen, Walter 280-356
Haggard, Sir Rider 135-174
Haig, Earl 29-171
Haigh, John 219
Haile Selassie 94-126-205-240-256-307
Hailsham, Lord 283
Haiti 341
Haldane, Viscount 232
Hale, Nathan 158-266
Haley, Alex 224
Half-crown, GB 1
Halifax, Earl of 107-358
Hallé, Sir Charles 102
Halley, Edmond 14-313
Hamilton, Lady 15-117
Hammarskjöld, Dag 211-262
Hammerstein, Oscar 194

Hammond, Joan 145
Hammond, Walter 171
Hampden Park 305
Hand grenades 161
Handel, George Frederick 54-105
Handley, Tommy 9
Hangings, last GB 226
Hansom cabs 358
Hardie, Keir 228-270
Harding, Gilbert 321
Harding, Warren 215-307
Hardy, Oliver 18-220
Hardy, Thomas 11-154
Hargraves, E. H. 43
Hargreaves, James 113
'Harlem Globetrotters' 7
Harlow, Jean 63-159
Harmsworth, Lord Alfred 197-227
Harriman, Averell 320
Harris, Sir Arthur 104
Harris, Joel Chandler 185-344
Harris, Richard 275
Harris, Rolf 90
Harrison, Benjamin 73-233
Harrison, George 56
Harrison, John 84
Harrison, Rex 65
Harrison, William Henry 40-95
Hartnell, Norman 164
Harvard University 302
Harvey, Len 333
Harvey, Neil 282
Harvey, William 92-155
Hassan II, King 57
Hassett, Lindsay 241
Hastings, Battle of 288
Hastings, Warren 235-341
Hathaway, Anne 219
Havilland, Olivia de 183
Hawaii 18-234
'Haw Haw, Lord' 3
Hawkins, Jack 200-258
Hawthorne, Nathaniel 140-186
Hay, Ian 108
Haydn, Franz Joseph 91-152
Hayes, Rutherford 17-278
Hayward, Susan 74-182
Hayworth, Rita 291
Healey, Denis 243
Heart transplant, first 338
Heath, Edward 191
Heavy water, discovery 364
Heenan, Cardinal 26-312
Heifetz, Jascha 33

Heinz, Henry John 135-285
Helpmann, Robert 100
Helston, Floral Dance 129
Hemans, Felicia 137
Hemingway, Ernest 184-203
Hendren, Patsy 36-278
Henie, Sonja 99-286
Henley Regatta 86-166
Henry I, King 336
Henry II, King 65-188-354
Henry III, King 275-321
Henry IV, King 80-94-273-287
Henry V, King 80-244-260
Henry VI, King 65-142-311-341
Henry VII, King 28-112-305
Henry VIII, King 25-28-112-151-163-176-180-194
Hepburn, Audrey 125
Hepburn, Katherine 314
Hepworth, Barbara 10-141
Herbert, A. P. 268-316
Herbert, Victor 32-147
Herman, Woody 137
Hérold, Louis 28
Herriot, Edouard 86-187
Herschel, Sir John 67-132
Herschel, Sir William 73-238-320
Hertzog, J. B. 94-326
Herzl, Theodor 123-185
Hess, Dame Myra 56-330
Hess, Rudolf 117-131
Heston, Charlton 278
Heyerdahl, Thor 280
Hickok, 'Wild Bill' 148-215
Higgins, Alex 78
Highway Code 105
Hill, Graham 46-334
Hill, Sir Rowland 240-338
Hillary, Sir Edmund 202
Hilton, James 253-355
Himmler, Heinrich 144-281
'Hindenburg', airship 127-182
Hindenburg, Paul von 86-215-276
Hirohito 120-360
Hiroshima 219
Hirst, George 131-251
Hitchcock, Sir Alfred 120-226
Hitler, Adolf 30-70-111-121-216-245
Hobbs, Jack 351-356
Ho Chi Minh 247
Hockey Association 107
Hockey, first international 25
Hoddle, Glen 301
Hoffman, Dustin 221

Hogan, Ben 226
Hogarth, William 300-315
Holland, John Philip 60
Holloway, Stanley 30-275
Holly, Buddy 33-251
Holst, Gustav 146-265
Home Guard 135
'Home Service', BBC 245
Hong Kong 20-161-243-333-360
Hood, HMS 145
Hood, Samuel 179-347
Hood, Thomas 124-144
Hooke, Robert 63-200
Hoover, Herbert 223-294
Hoover, J. Edgar 1-123
Hope, Anthony 40
Hope, Bob 150
Hore-Belisha, Leslie 47
Hornung, E. W. 83
Horse race meeting, first 40
Horse racing, starting stalls 190
Houdini, Harry 97-305
Hovercraft 207-347
Howard, Catherine 44
Howard, Trevor 273
Howe, Elias 191-277
Howe, Richard 68-218
Hudson, Rock 322
Hughes, David 137
Hughes, Howard 96-359
Hughes, Thomas 82-294
Hugo, Victor 57-143
Hulbert, Jack 115
Hull, Cordell 205-276
Humber Bridge 176-199-209
Humperdinck, Engelbert 245-271
Humperdinck, Engelbert 124
Humphrey, Hubert 13-148
Hunt, Holman 93-251
Hunt, James 242
Hunt, John 174
Huskisson, William 71-259
Hussein II, King 123-224-319
Huston, John 218
Hutton, Sir Leonard 175-236
Huygens, Christian 105-160
Hyatt, John Wesley 131-167-333
Hydrogen bombs 136-305

Ibrox Park disaster 2
Ibsen, Henrik 80-144
Iceland 169
Idaho 185
Identity cards, GB 52-274

Illinois 338
'Illustrated London News' 135
IMF 61-362
Income tax 9
India 26-228
Indiana 346
'Indianapolis 500' 151
Indian Mutiny 131
Indonesia 230
Inkerman, Battle of 310
Insulin, first isolated 209
International Court of Justice 177
International Exhibition 122
International Monetary Fund 61-362
Iowa 363
Iran, Shah of 209
Irish Football Association 323
Irish Free State 341
Irish Sweep, first 327
Iron lung, first 286
Irving, Sir Henry 37-145-287
Irving, Washington 94-333
Irwin, Hale 155
Isle of Man TT race 149
Israel 135
Italy 98-251
Ivan the Terrible 16-78
Ives, Burl 166
'Izvestia' 72

Jacklin, Tony 173-189
Jackson, Andrew 75-160
Jackson, Glenda 130
Jackson, 'Stonewall' 21-131
Jacquard, Joseph 220
Jamaica 125-219
James I, King of Scotland 51
James I, King of England 84-87-171-207
James II, King of England 37-261-288
James, Henry 59-106
James, Jesse 94-249
Jameson, Leander 331
Jameson Raid 2-364
Japan 42-262
Japan, earthquake 245
Japanese surrender 227-246
Jardine, Douglas 297
Jarrow march 279
Jefferson, Thomas 104-186
Jeffries, Judge 109
Jenkins, Clive 123
Jenkins, Roy 316

Jenner, Edward 26-135-138
Jerome, Jerome K. 123-166
Jet bomber, first British 134
Jet plane, first 240
Joan of Arc 151
Jodrell Bank radio telescope 285
Joffre, Joseph 3-12
John, Augustus 4-305
'John Bull' 133
John, Elton 85
John, King 167-293-359
John of Gaunt 34
John XXIII, Pope 155-330
John Paul II, Pope 134-139-149-290
Johns, Glynis 279
Johnson, Amy 5-126-145-183
Johnson, Andrew 106-213-364
Johnson, Jack 91-162-361
Johnson, Ladybird 357
Johnson, Lyndon 22-240
Johnson, Samuel 262-348
Johnston, Robin Knox 113
Jolson, Al 147-297
Jones, Bobby 77-353
Jones, Inigo 173-197
Jones, Jennifer 62
Jones, John Paul 188-200-267
Jones, Tom 159
Jonson, Ben 163-219
Jordan 82
Joseph, Sir Keith 17
Josephine, Empress 175
Joule, James 285-359
Joyce, James 13-33
Joyce, William 3-115
Juan Carlos I, King 5-327
Jukebox, first 328
Juliana, Queen 7-121-250
Jung, Carl 158-208
Jutland, Battle of 152

Kansas 29
Kant, Immanuel 43-113
Kariba Dam 138-311
Karloff, Boris 34-328
Kaunda, Kenneth 119-298
Kaye, Danny 18
Kean, Edmund 77
Keaton, 'Buster' 32-278
Keats, John 54-305
Keble, John 89
Keegan, Kevin 45
Kekkonen, Urho 247
Keller, Helen 153-179

Kellogg-Briand Peace Pact 240
Kelly, Gene 236
Kelly, Grace 110
Kelly, Ned 316
Kelvin, Lord 178-352
Kennedy, Edward 53
Kennedy, Jacqueline 210-256
Kennedy, John F. 20-150-256-327
Kennedy, Robert 157-325
Kentucky 153
Kentucky Derby 138
Kenya 347
Kenyatta, Jomo 235-347
Kerensky, Alexander 113-163
Kern, Jerome 27-316
Kerr, Deborah 274
Key, Francis Scott 11-214
Khama, Sir Seretse 183-195-254
Khrushchev, Nikita 108-255
Kidd, 'Captain' 129-144
Kiel Canal 171
Killiecrankie, Battle of 209
Kilogram 214
King, Billie-Jean 327
King, Coretta 118
King, Mackenzie 204-352
King, Martin Luther 15-95
Kingsley, Charles 23-164
Kipling, Rudyard 18-365
Kissinger, Henry 148
Kitchener, Lord 157-176
Kitt, Eartha 26
Klemperer, Otto 135-188
KLM airline 138-281
Knievel, Evel 291
Knox, John 329
Koch, Robert 148-346
Kop at Anfield 238
Korda, Alexander 23-260
Korean War 177-209
Kosygin, Alexei 51-354
Krakatoa eruption 240
Kreisler, Fritz 29-33
Kruger, Paul 196-284
Krupp, Alfred 117-196

Labour unions 181
Ladd, Alan 29-247
Ladysmith siege 59-307
Laennec, René 48-226
Lafayette 141-250
Laine, Cleo 302
Laine, Frankie 90
Laker, Freddie 219

Laker, Jim 40
Lamarr, Hedy 314
Lamb, Charles 41-362
Lamb, William 75
Lancaster, Burt 307
Lancaster, Osbert 217
'Lancastria', troopship 169
Land, Edwin 128
Landseer, Sir Edwin 67-275
Lane, Sir Allen 189-265
Lane, Lupino 168
Langdon, David 55
Langdon, Harry 167
Langtry, Lillie 43-287
Lansbury, George 52-128
Lanza, Mario 31-281
Larwood, Harold 319
La Scala, Milan 216
Latimer, Hugh 290
Latvia 323
Laud, William 10
Lauda, Niki 53
Lauder, Sir Harry 57-217
Laughton, Charles 183-350
Launderette, first 130
Laurel, Stan 54-168
Laval, Pierre 180-289
Laver, Rod 222
Lavoisier, Antoine 129-239
Law, Andrew Bonar 260-297-304
Law, Denis 55
Lawn tennis 54-173-191-201-221
Lawrence, D. H. 62-255
Lawrence, T. E. 140-228
Lawton, Tommy 280
League of Nations 10-34
Lean, David 85
Lear, Edward 133
Lee, Christopher 148
Lee, Gypsy Rose 9-117
Lee, Robert E. 19-100-286
Lee, Viscount 313
Legal aid, GB 276
'Légion d'Honneur' 140
Lehar, Franz 121-298
Leigh, Vivien 190-310
Leighton, Margaret 57
Le Mans race 147
Lemmon, Jack 39
Lend Lease Bill 71
Lenglen, Suzanne 145-186
Lenin 21-101
Leningrad, siege of 243
Lennon, John 283-343

313

Leo XIII, Pope 38-51-62-202
Leonardo da Vinci 123
Leopold I, King 203-345
Leopold II, King 100
Leopold III, King 149-308
Lepanto, Battle of 281
Lerner, Alan Jay 244
Lesotho 278
Lesseps, Ferdinand de 324-342
Lever, William 128-263
Lewis, Sinclair 10-38
Lexington, Battle of 110
Leyland, Maurice 202
Liberace 137
Liberia 208
Libya 245-359
Lie, Trygve 198-365
Lifeboat, first purpose-built 30
'Life' magazine 364
'Light programme', BBC 211
Lilienthal, Otto 223
Lillie, Beatrice 150
Linacre, Thomas 294
Lincoln, Abraham 43-105-324
Lincoln Memorial 151
Lincolnshire horse race 73
Lind, Jenny 280-307
Lindbergh, Charles 35-61-142-239
Lindrum, Walter 242
Lindwall, Ray 277
Linley, Viscount 308
Linnaeus, Carl 10-144
'Lion' on eggs 182
Lisbon earthquake 306
Lisle, Rouget de 116
Lister, Joseph 41-96-169
Liston, Sonny 129-365
Liszt, Franz 213-296
Litter Act, GB 220
Little Big Horn 177
Little, Malcolm (X) 52
'Little Mo' 173
Littler, Emile 253
Litvinov, Maxim 199
Liverpool, Anglican Cathedral 200
Liverpool, borough 241
Liverpool, 'Echo' 301
Liverpool, Football Club 33-238-287
Liverpool, Gladstone Dock 193
Liverpool, Liver clock 174-281
Liverpool, Overhead Railway 35-365
Liverpool, port radar 212

Liverpool, RC Cathedral 135
Liverpool, last tram 258
Livesey, Roger 35-177
Livingstone, David 79-109-122-315
Lloyd, Clive 244
Lloyd, Harold 111
Lloyd, Marie 43-281
Lloyd, Selwyn 210
Lloyd George, David 8-17-86-197-342
Local Defence Volunteers 135
Local radio station, first 313
Locarno Pact 336
Locke, Bobby 325
Lockwood, Margaret 259
Lodge, Sir Oliver 235
Loewe, Frederick 162
Lollobrigida, Gina 186
London—Australia, first flight 317
London Bridge 214
'London Gazette' 321
London, Jack 12-327
London Metropolitan Police 171
London Planetarium 81
London Stock Exchange 86
London, last tram 188
London Underground Railway 10-350
Longfellow, H. W. 58-84
Lord's Cricket Ground 174
Loren, Sophia 264
Lorre, Peter 83-178
Louis, Joe 61-103-134-174
Louis XIV, King 135-245-249
Louis XVI, King 21-236
Louis XVIII, King 102-260-322
Louisiana 121
Lovell, Sir Bernard 244
Low, David 98-263
Lowell, Percival 73-317
Lowry, L. S. 54-306
Loy, Myrna 215
Loyola, Ignatius 213-359
Ludendorff, Erich 355
Lugosi, Bela 229-294
Lumière, Auguste 101
Lumumba, Premier 17
Lunar Roving Vehicle 213
Lunik I 2
Lunik II 258
Lupino, Ida 35
'Lusitania' 128-159
Luther, Martin 49-315
'Lutine' 281

314

Lutyens, Sir Edwin   1-89
Lyle, Sandy   40
Lynmouth disaster   229
Lynn, Dame Vera   80

MacArthur, Douglas   26-96
Macdonald, Flora   65
MacDonald, Ramsay   22-286-314
Macintosh, Charles   207-364
Mackenzie, Compton   17
MacLaine, Shirley   115
MacLeod, Ian   202
MacMillan, Harold   10-34-41
MacMurray, Fred   243
Madagascar   178
Madison, James   76-180
Mafeking, Relief of   138
Magellan, Ferdinand   118-250-264
Magna Carta   167
Magnusson, Magnus   286
Mahler, Gustav   139-189
Maine   75
'Maine', US battleship   46
Majority verdict, first GB   279
Makarios, Archbishop   69-216-226-349
Malan, Daniel   38-143
Malawi   188
Malaya   244
Maldive Islands   208
Malenkov, Georgi   8
Malplaquet, Battle of   255
Malta   106-265
Manchester Ship Canal   1-142
Manchester United FC   37-50
Manchuria   262
Manet, Edouard   23-121
Manhattan Island   127
Manitoba   133
Mann, Thomas   158-225
Mannerheim, Carl   27-156
Mansfield, Jayne   110-181
Mantovani   89-320
Mao Tse-Tung   253-361
Marat, Jean Paul   145-195
March, Fredric   105-244
Marciano, Rocky   244-245
Marconi, Guglielmo   116-154-202
Mare, Walter de la   116-174
Marengo, Battle of   166
Margaret, Princess   127-234
Margarine   197
Margrethe II, Queen   14-107
Maria Theresa   134-334

Marie Antoinette   290-307
'Marie Celeste'   340
Markova, Alicia   336
Marks and Spencer's, first GB   272
Marlborough, Duke of   168-176
Marlowe, Christopher   37-151
Marryat, Frederick   192-222
'Marseillaise, La'   116-197
Marsh, Rodney   316
Marshall Aid   157
Marshall, George   290-366
Marshall, Herbert   144
Marston Moor, Battle of   184
Martin, Dean   159
Martinique, volcano   129
Marvin, Lee   50
Marx, 'Chico'   82-285
Marx, 'Groucho'   233-276
Marx, 'Gummo'   112
Marx, 'Harpo'   272
Marx, Karl   74-126
Marx, 'Zeppo'   56-335
Mary, Queen Consort   147
Mary, Queen of Scots   39-137-211-343
Mary I, Queen   7-49-188-322
Maryland   119
'Mary Rose'   201
Masaryk, Jan   70-258
Masaryk, Thomas   67-258
Mascagni, Pietro   215-342
Masefield, John   133-153
Mason, James   136
Massachusetts   37
Massey, Raymond   243
Mata Hari   220-289
Matapan, Battle of   88
Maternity benefit, first GB   15
Mathis, Johnny   274
Matisse, Henri   308-366
Matterhorn   195-196
Matthau, Walter   275
Matthews, Jessie   71-232
Matthews, Stanley   32
Mature, Victor   29
Maudling, Reginald   67
Maugham, W. Somerset   25-351
'Mauretania', liner   210
Maurier, Daphne du   134
Maurier, George du   66
Mauritius   72
Maxim, Hiram   36-329
Maximilian, Emperor   101-171-188
'Mayflower'   260

315

Mayo, Charles 147-201
Mayo, Virginia 335
Mayo, William James 181-210
Mazzini, Giuseppe 70-174
Mboya, Tom 187-228
McAdam, John 265-331
McCarthy, Joe 123-319
McCartney, Paul 170
McCormack, John 166-260
McCormick, Cyrus Hall 46-134
McCrea, Joel 310
McEnroe, John 47
McKinley, William 29-250-258
McLaglen, Victor 312-346
McLaren, Bruce 154
McQueen, Steve 84
McWhirter, Norris 225
McWhirter, Ross 225-332
Meikle, Andrew 332
Meir, Golda 124-343
Melba, Dame Nellie 54-140
Melbourne, Viscount 75-329
Mellor, Stan 101-353
Melville, Herman 214-272
Mendel, Gregor 6-204
Mendelssohn, Felix 34-309
Menin Gate 206
Menuhin, Yehudi 113
Menzies, Sir Robert 355
Mercator, Gerardus 65-340
Merchant ship, nuclear 203
Meredith, Billy 75
Meredith, George 43-139
Mérimée, Prosper 267-272
Mermaid Theatre 149
Merman, Ethel 16
Mersey Ferry 182
Mersey railway tunnel 20-124
Mersey road tunnels 176-200-351-352
Mesmer, Friedrich 65-144
Messerschmitt, Wilhelm 178-259
Messina earthquake 363
Meteorological satellite 92
Methuen Treaty 362
Métro, Paris 192
Metropolitan Opera House 296
Michael, King 299-365
Michelangelo 49-66
Michelin, André 95
Michigan 26
Midsummer Day 176
Miles, Sir Bernard 271
Military Academy, US 76

Military conscription, GB 40
Millais, Sir John 160-226
Milland, Ray 3
Miller, Arthur 291
Miller, Glenn 61-351
Miller, Henry 159-361
Miller, Johnny 120
Miller, Keith 333
Millet, Jean Francois 20-278
Milligan, Spike 107
Mills, John 53
Milne, A. A. 18-31
Milton, John 313-344
Mini cabs 66
Minnelli, Liza 72
Minnesota 132
Minter, Alan 230
Mintoff, Dom 219
Mississippi 345
Missouri 223
Miss World 110
Mitchum, Robert 219
Mitterrand, Francois 300
Mix, Tom 6-286
Mohne and Eder dams 137
Molière 15-48
Mollison, Jim 110-231-304
Molotov 69
Monaco Grand Prix 105
'Mona Lisa', stolen 234
Monet, Claude 319-340
Money orders 275
Monmouth, Duke of 100-197
Monroe Doctrine 337
Monroe, James 119-186
Monroe, Marilyn 153-218
Monsarrat, Nicholas 82-221
Montana 313
Mont Blanc road tunnel 198
Mont Cenis tunnel 261
Monte Carlo Rally, first 21
Montezuma 182
Montgomery, Viscount 84-322
Moon, first direct hit 258
Moon, first photographs 2-281
Moon, first satellite 223
Moon, first 'soft' landing 34
Moore, Bobby 103-135-141-319
Moore, Henry 212
Moore, Sir John 16
Moore, Patrick 64
Moore, Roger 288
More, Kenneth 195-264
More, Sir Thomas 38-188

Morecambe, Eric 135
Morley, Robert 147
Mormon movement 97
Morris Minor car, first 286
Morrison, Herbert 3-66
Morse, Samuel 93-118-145
Moscow 260
Mosley, Sir Oswald 321-338
Moss, Stirling 261
Motel, first 347
Mother's Day 131
Motor cycle, first 242
Motoring Association, first 306
Motor shows, first 289-346
Motorway, first GB 340
Motor Vehicle registration, first 1
MOT tests 256
Mountbatten, Earl Louis 177-240
Mount Pelée, volcano 129
'Mousetrap, The' 330
Moussorgsky, Modest 81-88
Mozambique 61-177
Mozart, Wolfgang Amadeus 27-340
Muhammad Ali 17-56-119-259-304
Müller, Paul 12-286
Muni, Paul 238-266
Munich air crash 37
Murdock, William 234
Murray River, discovery 321
Murrow, Ed 116-346
Mussolini, Benito 119-207-211-305
Mutiny on the 'Bounty' 119

NAAFI 1
Nagasaki 222
Nansen, Fridtjof 134-284
Napier, John 95
Napoleon Bonaparte 57-69-102-126-
    139-147-228-258-337
Napoleon III 9-14-248
Naseby, Battle of 166
Nash, John 134
Nash, Ogden 140-232
Nasmyth, James 128-232
Nasser, Gamal 15-175-208-272-275-
    291
Nastasie, Ilie 201
Natal 360
National anthem, British 272
National anthem, US 63-258
National day of:—
    Afghanistan 148
    Algeria 306
    Argentina 191

Australia 26
Austria 300
Belgium 203
Bolivia 219
Botswana 274
Brazil 251
Burma 4
Cambodia 314
Canada 183
Chile 262
China 275
Colombia 202
Costa Rica 259
Cyprus 275
Denmark 157
Ecuador 223
England 114
Ethiopia 205
Finland 341
France 196
Gambia 49
Ghana 66
Greece 85
Hungary 95
Iceland 169
India 26
Indonesia 230
Iran 300
Iraq 196
Ireland 77
Italy 154
Japan 120
Jordan 146
Kenya 347
Kuwait 56
Laos 132
Lebanon 327
Lesotho 278
Liberia 208
Libya 245
Luxembourg 175
Madagascar 288
Malawi 188
Malaysia 244
Malta 265
Mexico 260
Mongolia 193
Morocco 63
Nepal 49
Netherlands 121
New Zealand 37
Nigeria 275
Northern Ireland 194
Norway 138

317

Pakistan 83
Panama 308
Paraguay 135
Peru 210
Philippines 164
Poland 204
Romania 236
Russia 312
Saudi Arabia 267
Scotland 335
Sierra Leone 118
South Africa 152
Spain 200
Sri Lanka 35
Sweden 316
Switzerland 214
Syria 108
Tanzania 344
Thailand 340
Togo 118
Trinidad and Tobago 244
Tunisia 153
Turkey 303
Uganda 283
Uruguay 238
Venezuela 187
Wales 61
Yugoslavia 334
Zambia 298

National Gallery 100
National Health Service 187
National insurance 197
National Park, first GB 363
National Savings certificates 50
National Savings stamps 190
Nationalisation, coal, GB 1
Nationalisation, railways, GB 1
Nationalisation, steel, GB 1
'Nautilus', submarine 21
Naval execution, last 195
Naval mutinies 106-144-182
Naval uniform 30
Neagle, Anna 294
Neale, John Mason 24-219
Nebraska 61
Nehru, Pandit 148-319
Nelson, Byron 35
Nelson, Lord Horatio 9-214-273-295
Nelson statue 308
Neptune, planet 267
Ness, Eliot 110-128
Nevada 305
New Amsterdam 252

Newcombe, John 144
Newcomen, Thomas 218
New Hampshire 173
Newhart, Bob 249
New Jersey 353
New London Bridge 214
Newman, Cardinal 52-224
Newman, Paul 26
New Mexico 6
New Orleans, Battle of 8
New Sadler's Wells Theatre 6
Newspaper, first GB 71
Newspaper, first US 265
Newton, Sir Isaac 80-360
'New town', first GB 316
New Waterloo Bridge 224
New York 208
New York subway 301
'New York Times' 262
'New York Tribune' 101
New Zealand 142-270-348
Ney, Michel 10-342
Nicholas I, Tsar 62-188
Nicholas II, Tsar 62-139-198
Nicklaus, Jack 21
Nigeria 275
Nightingale, Florence 133-226
Nijinsky, Vaslav 72-99
Nile, source 216
Nimitz, Chester 51-55
Niven, David 61
Nixon, Richard 76
Nixon, Thelma 61
Nkrumah, Kwame 55-118-262
Nobel, Alfred 196-295-345
Nore mutiny 144-182
'Normandie', liner 40-303
Normandy invasion 158
North African invasion 313
North Carolina 326
Northcliffe, Lord 197
North Dakota 307
North, Lord 104-218
North Pole, flight over 130
North Sea gas 64
North Sea oil 163
North West Mounted Police 144
Norway 159
Novak, Kim 44
Novello, Ivor 15-66
Nuclear chain reaction 337
Nuclear power station 123
Nuffield Foundation 44
Nuffield, Viscount 235-284

Nuremberg executions 290
Nuremberg tribunal 325
Nureyev, Rudolf 77
Nurmi, Paavo 165-276
Nylon 47-136-350

Oak apple day 150
Oakley, Annie 226-308
Oates, Lawrence 77
Oates, Titus 195-259
Oberon, Merle 50
Obote, Milton 25
'Observer, The' 339
O'Casey, Sean 90-262
O'Connell, Daniel 136-219
Offenbach, Jacques 172-279
O'Hara, Maureen 230
Ohio 61
Ohm, George 76-189
Oil well, first 240
Oklahoma 321
Olav V, King 184-265
Old Bailey 58
'Old Pretender' 1-162-357
Olivier, Laurence 143
Olympic Games 97
Olympic Games 2nd 184
            3rd 242
            4th 195
            5th 188
            7th 227
            8th 187
            9th 210
            10th 212
            11th 214
            14th 211
            15th 201
            16th 327
            17th 238
            18th 284
            19th 286
            20th 239
            21st 200
Olympics, first Winter 25
Ombudsman, first 92
Omdurman, Battle of 246
Onassis, Aristotle 15-75
Onassis, Jacqueline 210
O'Neal, Tatum 310
O'Neill, Eugene 290-332
Oosterhuis, Peter 124
Open prison, first GB 148
Opera House, La Scala 216
'Operation Chariot' 88

'Operation Dynamo' 148-156
'Operation Jubilee' 232
'Operation Market Garden' 261
'Operation Overlord' 158
'Operation Torch' 313
Opium War 242
Oppenheimer, Robert 49-113
Oppenheimer, Sir Ernest 143
Orangeman's Day 194
'Order of Merit' 175
Oregon 45
Orsini, Felice 14-73-345
Orwell, George 21-177
Osborne, John 347
Oscars, first 137
Osmond, Donny 344
O'Sullivan, Maureen 138
Oudenarde, Battle of 193
Oughtred, William 65-182
Ovett, Steve 283
Owen, Robert 135-322
Owens, Jesse 91-146-256
'Oxford Gazette' 321
Oyster season 218

Pacific Ocean 269
Paderewski 181-323
Paganini, Niccolo 148-301
Paine, Thomas 29-160
Paisley, Ian 97
Pakistan 83
Palace of Westminster 290
Palance, Jack 49
Palmer, Arnold 254
Palmerston, Lord 292-294
Panama 308
Panama Canal 85-186-194-228
Pankhurst, Christabel 44-266
Pankhurst, Emmeline 166-196
'Panorama', TV programme 316
Papen, Franz von 303
Parachute descent, first 296
Parcel post 214
Paris airport 68
Paris occupation 166-236
Paris underground railway 192
Park, Mungo 254
Parker, Cecil 247
Parkes, Alexander 364
Parking meters 192-198
Parliament, televised 112
Parnell, Charles Stewart 179-280
Parr, Catharine 194-251
Parry, Sir Hubert 58

Parson, Sir Charles   42-165
Parton, Dolly   19
Partridge season   32-245
Pascal, Blaise   171-232
Passenger railroad, US   145
Passport photographs   32
Pasternak, Boris   41-151
Pasteur, Louis   272-362
Pathé, Charles   361
Patterson, Floyd   4-172-335
Patti, Adelina   271
Patton, George   316-356
Paul I, Tsar   71
Paul VI, Pope   6-173-182-219-270
Pavlova, Anna   23-31
Paxton, Sir Joseph   160-216
PAYE   97
Peace of Vereeniging   152
Peak District   363
Pearl Harbor   342-358
Pearson, Sir Arthur   55-344
Pearson, Lester   114-362
Peary, Robert   51-97-127
Peck, Gregory   96
Pedro, Dom   320-336
Peel, John   318
Peel, Sir Robert   36-184
Pelé   297-324
Penalty kick, first   258
'Penguin' paperbacks   212
Penlee lifeboat   354
Penn, William   212-288
Pennine Way   114
Pennsylvania   347
Penny post   10
Pentecost   15
Pepys, Samuel   1-54-147-152-156-336
Perceval, Spencer   132
Peron, Isabel   84
Peron, Juan   55-172-183-282
Perrault, Charles   12-137
Perry, Fred   139
Pershing, John   197-257
Peru   210
Pescarolo, Henri   269
Pestalozzi, Johann   12-48
Pétain, Philippe   115-205
Peter III, Tsar   52
Peter the Great   28-151
Peterloo massacre   229
Petrol rationing   110
Pheasant season   32-275
Philippines   186
Phillips, Captain Mark   266

Phillpotts, Eden   309
Phoenix Park murders   127
Picasso, Pablo   99-299
Piccard, Auguste   28-84
Pickford, Mary   99-150
Pierce, Franklin   282-328
Piggott, Lester   310
Pilgrim Fathers   260-356
Pilot's licence, first   68
Piltdown skull   326-353
Pinkerton, Alan   183-238
Pitman, Isaac   4-12-320
Pitt, William (elder)   132-320
Pitt, William (younger)   9-23-149-
342
Pius IX, Pope   38-51
Pius XII, Pope   62-283
Pizarro, Francisco   178
Plassey, Battle of   175
Plate, Battle of River   348
Player, Gary   306
Pleasence, Donald   279
Plimsoll, Samuel   41-155
PLUTO   225
Pluto, planet   73
Pneumatic tyres   345
Poe, Edgar Allan   19-281
Point-to-point, first   62
Poison gas   113
Poitier, Sidney   51
Poitiers, Battle of   263
Polaris submarines   161-260
Police Training College   131
Policewoman, first   256
Polk, James Knox   167-307
Pompadour, Madame de   106-364
Pompidou, Georges   93-187
Ponchielli, Amilcare   16-245
Pony Club   306
Pony Express   94-298
Pope, Alexander   142-151
Porter, Cole   161-289
Portland cement, patent   295
Portland Vase   38
Post, Wiley   204-228-327
Postal orders   1
Postal system, two-tier   260
Postcard, first issue   275
Post codes, Germany   214
Post codes, GB   277
Postmarks   110
Post Office, books of stamps   76
Post Office, savings bank   260
Post Office, speaking clock   206

Post Office Tower 282
Post Office, US 72
Potatoes, first import 210
Potsdam Conference 199
Potter, Beatrix 210-357
Potter, Stephen 32
Powell, Enoch 168
Power, Tyrone 126-320
Premium Bonds 153-306
Presley, Elvis 8-229
Press Association 181
Prestonpans, Battle of 265
Prévin, André 97
Price, Vincent 148
Priestley, J. B. 257
Priestley, Joseph 37-73
Primrose Day 110
Prince of Wales, HMS 345
Princeton, Battle of 3
Prior, James 285
Prohibition 16-340
Prokofiev, Sergei 65-114
Promenade Concerts 280
Public execution, last 147
Puccini, Giacomo 334-357
Puerto Rico 292
Pugin, Augustus 258
Pullman carriages 153
Pullman, George 63-293
'Punch' magazine 199
Purcell, Henry 326
Pushkin, Alexander 41-147
Pyramids, Battle of 203

Qaddhafi 245
'QE 2' 85-123-264
Quads, Miles 333
Quant, Mary 42
Quayle, Anthony 251
Quebec 185
Quebec Bridge 338
'Queen Elizabeth', liner 9-271-320
'Queen Elizabeth 2', liner 85-123-264
'Queen Mary', liner 270-276
Quiberon Bay, Battle of 325
Quimby, Harriet 107
Quinn, Anthony 112
Quins 149-318
Quisling, Vidkun 200-254-298

R34 188-195
R100 351
R101 279-288

Rachmaninov, Sergei 88-93
Radar 57
Radetsky, Joseph 5-307
Radio, first commercial GB 328
Radio, first daily news 358
Radio licences 306
'Radio 1', BBC 274
Radio programme, first 319
'Radio Times' 274
Radium, discovery 361
Raffles, Sir Stamford 187
Raft, George 271
Raglan, Lord 180-274
Raikes, Robert 96-258
Railway bookstall 306
Railway station, first 7
Railway timetable, national 299
Railway trials 280
Railways, nationalisation 1
Rainier, Prince 110-130-152
Rains, Claude 151-315
Raleigh, Sir Walter 303
Ramillies, Battle of 144
Ramsay, Sir William 205-276
Ramsey, Sir Alf 22
Ramsey, Dr Michael 24-179
Rank, J. Arthur 358
Raphael 88-97
Rathbone, Basil 165
Rattigan, Terence 162-335
Ravel, Maurice 67-363
Rayleigh, Lord 182-317
Reade, Charles 102-160
Reagan, Ronald 20-37-90
Record charts 202-319
Records, LP 261
'Red Baron' 112-123
Red Cross, International 48-303
Red Cross Society 217
Redgrave, Michael 80
Red River Colony 133
Reed, Sir Carol 116-365
Reeves, Jim 213-233
Regazzoni, Clay 249
Regent's Park 118-154
Reichstag, fire 58
Rembrandt 197-278
Rennie, John 159-278
Renoir, Pierre Auguste 56-338
Republican Party, US 59-187
Republic of Ireland 109
'Repulse', battleship 345
Reuter, Paul Julius 56-203
Revere, Paul 1-109-131

Reynolds, Burt 42
Reynolds, Debbie 92
Reynolds, Sir Joshua 54-198
Rhine crossing 67
Rhode Island 150
Rhodes, Cecil 86-187
Rhodes, Wilfred 303
Rhodesia 62
Rice, Tim 315
Richard I, King 97-188-247-252
Richard II, King 6-174-198-273
Richard III, King 188-235-276
Richard, Cliff 288
Richards, Gordon 91-126-158-192-
279-290
Richardson, Sir Ralph 354
Richardson, Samuel 186
Richelieu, Cardinal 253-339
Richthofen, Manfred von 112-123
Riebeck, Jan van 112
Rimsky-Korsakov 78-173
Ritter, Tex 2-12
Robert the Bruce 159-193
Roberts, Lord 274-319
Robertson-Justice, James 167
Robeson, Paul 23-100
Robespierre, Maximilien 127-210
Robey, Sir George 334
Robinson, Edward G. 26-347
Robinson, Heath 152-257
Robinson, Sugar Ray 124
Robson, Dame Flora 88
Rockefeller, John D. 144-190
Rockefeller, Nelson 26-190
Rodgers, Richard 180-365
Rodin, Auguste 317-322
Rodney, Lord 145
Rogers, Ginger 198
Rogers, Roy 310
'Rogues Gallery' 307
Rolls, Charles Stewart 194
Romberg, Sigmund 211-314
Rome liberation 156
Rommel, Erwin 307-320
Romney, George 320
Röntgen, Wilhelm von 41-87-313
Rooke, Sir George 206
Rooney, Mickey 267
Roosevelt, Eleanor 285-312
Roosevelt, Franklin D. 20-30-46-
103-312
Roosevelt, Theodore 6-258-301
Rosebery, Lord 128-142
Rossetti, Dante Gabriel 100-133

Rossini, Gioacchino 60-318
Rotary Club 54
Rouget de Lisle 178
Roundell, aircraft identification 346
Round-the-world flight, first 62
Round-the-world flight, first solo
204
Rous, Sir Stanley 116
Rousseau, Henri 142-246
Rousseau, Jean Jacques 180-184
Royal Academy of Arts 345
Royal Air Force 36-92-185-346
Royal Albert Hall 89-141
Royal Ascot, first 220
Royal Automobile Club 223
Royal Canadian Mounted Police
32-144
Royal College of Surgeons 173
Royal Command performance 183
Royal Exchange 23
Royal Flying Corps 135
Royal George, HMS 242
Royal Mail coach, first 215
Royal Military Academy 93-104
Royal Naval Air Service 175
Royal Naval Lifeboat Institution 64
Royal Oak, HMS 288
Royal Opera House 136
Royal Society 113
Royal Tank Corps 210
Royce, Sir Frederick 87-113
Rubens, Peter Paul 151-181
Rubinstein, Anton 325-333
Rubinstein, Artur 28-355
Rugby 276
Rugby Football Union 26
Rugby internationals 87
Rugby League 242-251-349
Runcie, Robert 276
Runcorn Bridge 203
Rusk, Dean 40
Ruskin, John 20-39
Russell, Bertrand 33-139
Russell, Jane 173
Russo-Japanese War 39-249
Russo-Turkish War 63
Ruth, 'Babe' 37-229
Rutherford, Lord 243-293
Rutherford, Margaret 132-143

Saccharin 58
Sadat, Anwar 280-291-360
Sadler's Wells Theatre 6
Sadowa, Battle of 185

Safety pin **101**
Saint-Saëns, Camille **283-351**
St Andrew's Day **335**
St Bartholomew's Day massacre **237**
St Crispin's Day **299**
St George's Day **114**
St Gotthard tunnel **60**
St Helena **142**
St John's Ambulance **176**
St Lawrence Seaway **116**
St Nazaire raid **88**
St Paul's Cathedral **173-337-340**
St Peter's Church, Rome **323**
St Pierre, Martinique **129**
St Swithin's Day **197**
St Teresa **278**
Salamanca, Battle of **204**
Salazar, Antonio **119-209**
Salerno landing **253**
Salisbury Cathedral **264**
Salk, Jonas **302**
Salvation Army **184**
'Salyut' space station **110**
Sand Creek massacre **334**
Sand, George **160-183**
Sandwich Islands **18**
San Francisco earthquake **109-110**
Sankey, Ira **241**
San Salvador **286**
Saperstein, Abraham **7**
Saratoga, Battle of **291**
Sargent, Sir Malcolm **120-277**
'Satchmo' **186-188**
Satellite, accidents **27-114**
Satellite, first American **31**
Satellite, first British **126**
Satellite, first Canadian **273**
Satellite, first Japanese **42**
Savalas, Telly **20**
'Savannah', steamship **172**
Saville, Jimmy **305**
Sax, Adolphe **40-311**
Sayers, Dorothy L. **165-353**
Scanlon, Hugh **300**
Scapa Flow **173**
'Scharnhorst', battleship **361**
Scheckter, Jody **29**
Schmelling, Max **164-272**
School leaving age **92**
Schubert, Franz **31-324**
Schuman, Robert **181-248**
Schumann, Robert **160-211**
Schweitzer, Albert **14-248**
Scott, Captain **18-89-158-167**

Scott, Peter **258**
Scott, Randolph **23**
Scott, Sir Walter **228-265**
Scottish Football Association **73**
'Scouting for Boys' **16**
Searle, Ronald **63**
Seat belts **31**
Secombe, Harry **252**
Sedgemoor, Battle of **188**
Sedgman, Frank **303**
Segovia, Andres **49**
Segrave, Sir Henry **165**
Seixas, Victor **243**
Selfridge's store **75**
Sellers, Peter **206-252**
Sennet, Mack **17-310**
Serpentine, Christmas Day dip **360**
Severn Road Bridge **252**
Sewell, Anna **90-116**
Sex Discrimination Act **362**
Sextuplets **11**
Seychelles **180**
Seymour, Jane **151**
Shackleton, Sir Ernest **5-46**
Shaftesbury, Lord **119**
Shakespeare, William **114-332**
Shankly, Bill **273**
Sharif, Omar **101**
Sharp, Jack **28**
Sharpeville shootings **81**
Shaw, Artie **144**
Shaw, George Bernard **208-307**
Shearer, Moira **17**
Sheene, Barry **255**
Shelley, Mary **32-243**
Shelley, P. B. **190-217**
Shepard, Alan **126**
Sheppard, Jack **321**
Sheraton, Thomas **296**
Sheridan, R. B. **189-304**
Sherman, General **39-45**
Shinwell, Emanuel **292**
Shipton, Eric **88-214**
Shoemaker, Willie **148-232**
Shostakovich, Dmitri **222-269**
Show jumping **192**
Shrapnel **121**
Shute, Nevil **12-17**
Sibelius, Jean **264-343**
Sicily invasion **192**
Sickness benefit, GB **15**
Sierra Leone **118**
Sikorski, Wladyslaw **141-186**
Sikorsky, Igor **146-300**

Sillitoe, Alan 64
Silvers, Phil 132
Sim, Alastair 232-283
Simenon, Georges 44
Simmons, Jean 31
Simplon Rail tunnels 140-290
Simpson, Bobby 34
Sinatra, Frank 347
Sinatra, Nancy 160
Singapore 45-46
Singer, Isaac 205-301
Sinn Fein 333
'Sirius', steamship 113
Sitting Bull 350
Skopje earthquake 208
Skylab 39-135-193
Slavery, abolished 353
Sloane, Sir Hans 11
Slocum, Joshua 115-185
Smeaton, John 160-302
Smetana, Bedrich 62-133
Smirke, Sir Robert 109
Smith, Adam 157-199
Smith, Cyril 180
Smith, Harvey 364
Smith, Ian 99-104-316
Smith, John 97
Smith, Joseph 179-358
Smith, W. H. 176-280-306
Smith, Sir William 301
Smithfield Meat Market 329
Smithson, James 179
Smithsonian Institution 223
Smollett, Tobias 261
Smuts, Jan Christian 145-255
Snead, Sam 148
Snowden, Philip 136-200
Snowdon, Earl of 67
Soane, Sir John 20-254
Soap rationing, GB 40-253
Sobers, Garry 210-244
Solzhenitsyn, Alexander 346
SOS, distress signal 162-277
Soul, David 241
Sousa, John Philip 66-311
Soult, Nicolas 89-331
South Africa 101
South Carolina 144
South Dakota 307
Southey, Robert 81-225
South Pole 334-349
Sovereigns, coins 187
Soviet State Airline 40
Soyuz I, accident 114

Soyuz II 182
Spaceman, first American 126
Space shuttle 103-105
Space station 'Salyut' 110
Space walk, first 78
Spanish Armada 141-211
Spanish Civil War 89-200
'Spectator' 61
Speed limits, GB 72-187-357
Speed records 297-320
Speedway, GB 129
Speke aerodrome 183
Speke, John 216-259
Spence, Sir Basil 226
Spencer, Lady Diana 183
Sperry, Elmer 168-286
'Sphairistike' 54
Spitz, Mark 41
Spock, Dr 123
Spode, Josiah 198
Spooner, William 204-242
Sputnik II 308
Sri Lanka 35-143
Stage knighthood, first 145
Stalin, Joseph 65-356
Stamps, British 127-275
Stamps, US 183
Stanley, Sir Henry 28-131-315
Stanwyck, Barbara 198
'Stars and Stripes' 166
'Star-Spangled Banner' 63-258
Starr, Ringo 189
Statue of Liberty 302
Statute of Westminster 346
Steamboat, first 230
Steam locomotive 185
Steamship, Atlantic 172
Steel, David 91
Steel industry, GB 1-210
Steele, Tommy 352
Steiger, Rod 105
Steinbeck, John 58-355
Stendhal 23-83
Stephenson, George 161-225
Stephenson, Robert 286-290
Sterling currency 264
Sterne, Laurence 78-329
Stevenson, Adlai 36-196
Stevenson, Robert Louis 318-338
Stewart, Jackie 163
Stewart, James 141
Stock car racing 107
Stoker, Bram 111
Stokowski, Leopold 109-257

Stone of Scone   104-360
Stopes, Marie   276
Stowe, Harriet Beecher   166-183
Stradivari, Antonio   353
Strauss, Johann (elder)   74-269
Strauss, Johann (younger)   155-299
Strauss, Richard   163-252
Stravinsky, Igor   97-169
Street collection, first   282
Street railway, first   223
Streisand, Barbra   115
Strijdom, Johannes   237
Stuart, James—'Old Pretender'
   1-162-357
Stubbs, George   192-237
Sturgeon, William   143-339
Submarine, first British   276
Submarine, diesel   137
Submarines, nuclear   21-295
Submarines, Polaris   161-260
Sudan   1
Suez Canal   116-157-165-208-322
'Suffragette' Derby   156
Sugar rationing   270
Sullivan, Sir Arthur   134-327
Sullivan, Jim   337
Sullivan, John L.   33-190-289
Sunday post, last delivery   164
'Sunday Times'   35
Sun Yat-Sen   72-317
Supermarket, first GB   12
Supersonic airliner, first   366
Supersonic flight, first   288
Suppé, Franz von   109-142
Surinam   330
Surtees, John   42
Surtsey Island   319
Sutcliffe, Herbert   329
Sutherland, Graham   237
Sutherland, Joan   312
Swan, Sir Joseph   148-305
Swansea, City status   350
Swaziland   250
Sweden   129-247
Sweet rationing   35
Swift, Jonathan   293-335
Swinton, Sir Ernest   295
Sydney Harbour Bridge   79

Taft, William Howard   68-259
Talavera, Battle of   210
Talbot, William Fox   42-261
Tanganyika   344
Tanks, military   29-259

Tanzania   117
Tarleton, Nel   12-14
Tasman, Abel   329-348
Tate Gallery   203
Tate, Sir Henry   71-340
Taylor, A. J. P.   85
Taylor, Elizabeth   58
Taylor, Robert   160-218
Taylor, Zachary   191-329
Tay Railway Bridge   172-363
Tchaikovsky   128-311
Teach, Edward   327
Tear gas   3
Telegraph service, London/Paris
   318
Telephone directory, first GB   15
Telephone service, Britain/India
   122
Telephone service, Paris/Brussels
   55
Telephone service, STD   340
Telephone service, 999   183
Telescope, first demonstration   276
Televised, first boxing   235
Televised, first football   254
Televised, first tennis   173
Television, BBC2 opened   112
Television, colour   183-185-319
Television, commercial GB   266
Television, Eurovision   158
Television, first announcer   239
Television, first broadcast GB   307
Television, first demonstration   27
Television, gardening programme
   326
Television licences   153
Telford, Thomas   222-246
Telstar satellite   192
Temple, Shirley   114
Tennessee   153
Tennyson, Alfred Lord   219-280-324
Tereshkova, Valentina   66-168
Territorial Army   300
Territorial waters   158
Terry, Ellen   58-203
Test-tube baby   207
Tewkesbury, Battle of   125
Texas   364
Thackeray, W. M.   200-359
Thames Tunnel   85
Thatcher, Margaret   125-287
Theatre, oldest GB   151
'The Listener'   16
'The Tatler'   103

'The Times' 53-92
Thetis, HMS 73-153
Thiers, Adolphe 247
Third-class rail travel 155
Thomas, Dylan 301-314
Thomson, Jeff 229
Thomson, Peter 236
Thomson, Sir J. J. 243-353
Thorndike, Dame Sybil 161-298
Thorpe, Jeremy 120
'Thresher', US submarine 101
Thrower, Percy 30
Thurber, James 307-343
Tidal power station 331
Tierney, Gene 325
'Time' magazine 63
Timoshenko 49-91
Tintoretto 152-273
Tippett, Sir Michael 2
Tiros I 92
'Tirpitz', battleship 317
'Titanic', liner 106-152
Titian 240
Tito, (Josip Broz) 14-125-146
Todd, Richard 163
Tojo, Hideki 358
Tolkien, J. R. R. 3-246
Tolstoy, Leo 241-312
Tombaugh, Clyde 73
Tonga 156
Toplady, Augustus 227-309
'Torrey Canyon', tanker 78-90
Torricelli, Evangelista 289-299
Toscanini, Arturo 16-85
Toulouse-Lautrec 253-329
Tower Bridge 182
Towton, Battle of 89
Tracy, Spencer 96-162
Trades Union Congress, first 154
Traffic lights 218-310
Traffic wardens 87-259
Train disasters 59-143-191-347
Train, first public GB 271
Tramcars, first electric 64
Trams, first 243-331
Transatlantic, cable 218
Transatlantic, rowing 201-209-247
Transatlantic, steamship 113
Transatlantic, telephone 7
Transatlantic, wireless signal 347
Travolta, John 49
Treaty of Amiens 85
Treaty of Ghent 359
Treaty of Nanking 242

Treaty of Paris 90
Treaty of Portsmouth 249
Treaty of Prague 236
Treaty of San Stefano 63
Treaty of Utrecht 102
Treaty of Vereeniging 152
Treaty of Versailles 180
Treaty of Waitangi 37
Treaty of Westphalia 298
Trevino, Lee 336
Trevithick, Richard 104-113
Trinidad and Tobago 244
Tristan da Cunha 227-284
'Triton', submarine 116
Trolleybus, first GB 172
Trolleybuses, London 129
Trollope, Anthony 115-341
Trooping of the Colour 156
Trotsky, Leo 31-233-300-362
'Truculent', submarine 12
Trudeau, Pierre 292
Trueman, Fred 37
Truman, Elizabeth 44-292
Truman, Harry S. 129-361
Tucker, Sophie 13-41
Tull, Jethro 52
Tunisia 80-207
Tunney, Gene 146-267-312
Turkish Republic 303
Turner, Joseph 114-354
Turner, Lana 39
Turpin, Dick 98
Tussaud, Madame 107
Tutankhamun, tomb of 331
Tutin, Dorothy 99
Twain, Mark 112-335
'Twiggy' 263
(Two) 2LO, radio station 132
Two-tier postal system 260
Tyburn, first execution 126
Tyler, John 18-89
Tyler, Wat 167
Tyndale, William 280
Tyne Bridge 284

Uganda 252-283
Umberto I, King 74-211
Umberto II, King 78
Unemployment benefit, first GB 15
UNESCO 309
Union Jack 103
Union of Scotland & England 122
Union of South Africa 152
United Nations 178-234-298

'United States', liner 189
Universal Postal Union 283
University Boat Race 84-94-162
Uranus, planet 73
Uruguay 238
USA declared war 97
USA, first British ambassador 187
US Air Force Academy 92
US Library 115
US Marine Corps 315
US Mint 93
US Navy 87
Ustinov, Peter 107
Utah 4
U Thant 22-330-356

Vaccination 135
Valentino, Rudolph 127-236
Valera. Eamon de 177-242-288
Value added tax 92
Vanbrugh. Sir John 86
Vance, Cyrus 87
Vancouver, George 131-174
Van Dyck, Sir Anthony 82-344
Vanguard, HMS 294-335
Vatican City 42-159
Vaughan, Frankie 34
Vaughan Williams, Ralph 239-286
Vauxhall Bridge 147
Velasquez, Diego 158-219
Verdi, Giuseppe 27-284
Verity, Hedley 139-194-213
Vermeer, Jan 305-350
Vermont 64
Verne, Jules 39-84
Verrazano Bridge 326
Verwoerd, Hendrik 250-252
Vespucci, Amerigo 53-69
Veteran car rally 317
Vichy Government 184
Victor Emmanuel I, King 9-77
Victor Emmanuel II, King 74
Victor Emmanuel III, King 130-363
Victoria, Queen 22-41-62-140-145-
    151-172-180
'Victoria and Albert', yacht 116
Victoria Cross 29-173-178
Victory, HMS 205
Vidocq, Eugène 206
Viking 1 233
Villa, Pancho 157-172
Villeneuve 113-366
Vimiero, Battle of 234
Vinci, Leonardo da 123

Virginia 177
Virgin Islands, purchase 25
Vitoria, Battle of 173
Volta, Alessandro 49-65
Voltaire 151
Voroshilov, Marshal 35-338
Vorster, Johannes 257-348
Vostok 1 103
Votes cast. equal 287
Votes, women GB 37-108-349
Votes, women New Zealand 263
Votes, women US 239
Vulcanisèd rubber 326
Vyshinsky, Andrei 327-333

WAAC 88
Wade, Virginia 192
Wagner, Richard 44-143
Walbrook, Anton 324
Walcott, Jersey Joe 31
Waldheim, Kurt 356
Waldteufel, Emile 344
Wales, Prince of 38-183-208-319
Wales, Princess of 183
Wallace, Edgar 41-339
Wallace, George 136-238
Wallace, William 236
Wallach, Eli 342
Wallis, Barnes 270
Wall Street crash 303
Walpole, Sir Hugh 73
Walpole, Sir Robert 78-94-239-266
Walton, Izaak 222-350
Walton, Sir William 68-89
Wanamaker, Sam 166
Warbeck, Perkin 328
Warfield. Bessie Wallis 171
Warner, Jack 298
Warship, first iron-clad 364
Warship, first plastic 18
Washansky, Louis 338
Washbrook, Cyril 341
Washington 316
Washington, George 53-121-349
Washington Memorial 283
Waterloo, Battle of 170
Waterloo Bridge 170-224
Water polo 133
Watson, Tom 248
Watt, James 19-232
Watteau, Antoine 200-284
Watts, Isaac 330
Waugh, Evelyn 101-302
Wayne, John 147-163

Weather charts 92
Weather forecasts, TV 211
Webb, Matthew 206-238
Webber, Andrew Lloyd 82
Weber, Carl von 157-323
Webster, Noah 149-290
'Webster's Dictionary' 105
Wedgwood, Josiah 3-194
Weekes, Everton 57
Weiskopf, Tom 314
Weissmuller, Johnny 154
Welch, Raquel 249
Welles, Orson 127
Wellington, Duke of 26-120-258-323
Wells, 'Bombardier' Billy 163-244
Wells, H. G. 226-265
Wesley, Charles 89-353
Wesley, John 62-169
West, Mae 230-327
West, Virginia 172
Westinghouse, George 72-280
Westminster, Palace of 290
West Point 76
Wheatley, Dennis 8
Wheatstone, Sir Charles 37-293
Wheeler, Sir Mortimer 204
Whipsnade Zoo 144
Whistler, James McNeill 192-199
Whitaker, Joseph 125-136
'Whitaker's Almanack' 345
White House, The 237-287
White, Wilfred Hyde 133
Whitehead, Robert 3-319
Whitney, Eli 8-343
Whittaker, Roger 82
Whittle, Frank 136-153
Whitworth, Sir Joseph 22
WHO 98
Whymper, Edward 118-195
Wides, cricket 261
Widmark, Richard 361
Wilberforce, William 211-237
Wilde, Jimmy 45-70-136
Wilde, Oscar 290-335
Wilder, Thornton 108-342
Wilding, Michael 190-205
Wildlife Preservation Society 346
Wilhelmina, Queen 244-248-333
Wilkes, John 291-361
Wilkie, Wendell 49-282
Wilkins, Sir Hubert 77
Willard, Jesse 350-364
William I, Kaiser 18
William II, Kaiser 27-156-314

William I, King (William the Conqueror) 253-360
William II, King 215-270
William III, King 68-102-309
William IV, King 44-172-234-252
William, Prince 173
Williams, Andy 338
Williams, Emlyn 331
Williams, George 285
Williams, Tennessee 56-86
Williamson, Henry 226-336
Willis, Lord Ted 13
Wills-Moody, Helen 280
Wilson, Sir Harold 71
Wilson, Woodrow 34-363
Wimbledon 191-201
Winchell, Walter 51-98
Windsor, Duchess of 171
Windsor, Duke of (Edward VIII) 20-149-155-175-346
Windsor, Royal House of 199
Wingate, Orde 84
Wisconsin 150
Wisden, John 96-249
Wisdom, Norman 35
Wise, Ernie 332
Wodehouse, P. G. 45-289
Wolfe, James 2-257
Wolfit, Sir Donald 48-111
Wolsey, Cardinal 334
Woman Mayor, first GB 314
Women's Institute 50-255
Wood, Sir Henry 63-232-280
Woodcock, George 294
Woolf, Virginia 25-88
Woolley, Frank 148
Woolworth, F. W. 104-221
Woolworth Stores 53-310
Wordsworth, William 97-98-114
World Cup football 173-195-198-212
World War II 129-227-246-247
Worrell, Sir Frank 73
Wounded Knee, Battle of 364
Wren, Sir Christopher 56-294
Wright, Billy 37
Wright, Orville 30-232-352
Wright, Wilbur 107-143-151
WRNS 8
WVS 137
Wyman, Jane 4
Wynyard, Diana 16

X, Malcolm 52

Xavier, Francis 98-357

Yale, Linus 127
Yalta, Conference 35-42
Yeats, W. B. 28-165
Yellowstone Park 61
Yorktown, surrender 293
Young, Brigham 153-242
Young Conservatives 188
Yugoslavia 334

Zaire 301
Zambia 298

Zamenof, Dr 105-350
Zanuck, Darryl F. 249-357
Zanzibar 345
Zatopek, Emil 263
Zebra crossings 305
Zeppelin airships 171-182-248-258-
  289-364
Zeppelin, Graf von 68-190
Ziegfeld, Florenz 81-204
Zip fastener 120
Zog, King of Albania 2
Zola, Emile 93-273